McDougal Littell
LITERATURE

InterActive
READER & WRITER
for Critical Analysis

Grade 12

McDougal Littell
EVANSTON, ILLINOIS • BOSTON • DALLAS

COVER

RainyEmbankment (1929), Fox Photos. © Hulton Archive/Getty Images; *background* © Getty Images.

ISBN 13: 978-0-618-92078-5   ISBN 10: 0-618-92078-1

Printed in the United States of America.

2 3 4 5 6 7 8 9–DOM–12 11 10 09 08

SENIOR PROGRAM CONSULTANTS

Janet Allen
Internationally-known Reading and Literacy Specialist

Arthur N. Applebee
Leading Professor, School of Education, University of Albany, State University of New York; Director of the Center on English Learning and Achievement

Jim Burke
Lecturer, Author, English Teacher, Burlingame, California

Douglas Carnine
Professor of Education, University of Oregon

Yvette Jackson
Executive Director, National Urban Alliance for Effective Education

Robert Jiménez
Professor of Language, Literacy, and Culture, Vanderbilt University

Judith A. Langer
Distinguished Professor, University of Albany, State University of New York; Director of the Center on English Learning and Achievement; Director of the Albany Institute for Research in Education

Robert J. Marzano
Senior Scholar, Mid-Continent Research for Education and Learning (McREL), Denver, Colorado

Donna M. Ogle
Professor of Reading and Language, National-Louis University, Chicago, Illinois; Past President, International Reading Association

Carol Booth Olson
Senior Lecturer, Department of Education, University of California , Irvine

Carol Ann Tomlinson
Professor of Educational Research, Foundations, and Policy, University of Virginia; Co-Director of the University's Institutes on Academic Diversity

ENGLISH LEARNER SPECIALISTS

Mary Lou McCloskey
Past President, TESOL; Director of Teacher Development and Curriculum Design for Educo, Atlanta, Georgia

Lydia Stack
Past President, TESOL; International ESL Consultant

CURRICULUM SPECIALIST

William L. McBride
Nationally-known Speaker, Educator, and Author

TABLE OF CONTENTS

The InterActive Reader & Writer is a literature book to mark on, write in, and make your own. As you will see, this book helps you become an active reader. It also helps you become a better writer.

An Easy-to-Carry Literature Text

This book won't weigh you down. It fits as comfortably in your hand as it can in your backpack. Yet it is packed with great things to read and do:

- Important works of literature by leading authors
- A rich selection of nonfiction texts—Web pages, magazine articles, and more
- A variety of genres—such as epics, poems, essays, and short stories
- Activities that will help you think more deeply about yourself and the world beyond

Becoming a Critical Reader

Most people get more out of a work of literature the second time they read it. To help you get the most out of the literature in *The InterActive Reader & Writer*, you'll read each core literary work two times.

- You'll read it once on your own, marking the text as you choose.
- You'll read it a second time, using the notes in the margins to help you think critically about the text.

BEFORE READING ACTIVITIES

Big Question The first activity in each unit gets you thinking about a real-life question that the literature addresses.

Learn the Terms A brief skill lesson helps you understand the most important features of the literature and teaches terms you will need in order to talk and write about the selection. Additional skills terms increase your ability to think critically about literature.

DURING READING ACTIVITIES

A wide variety of side column notes challenges you to dig deeply into each selection.

VOCABULARY SUPPORT

Words to Know Important words are underlined and boldfaced in blue. Their definitions appear nearby in the side column.

Specialized Vocabulary Vocabulary notes in nonfiction selections explain special words used in certain careers or fields of study.

TEST PREPARATION

No one likes tests, but everyone likes doing well on them. *The Interactive Reader & Writer* will help you become a better test-taker.

TestSmart TestSmart questions appear right next to the text you are reading. These give you an opportunity to practice answering multiple-choice questions about literature— without worrying about being scored!

Test Tips You'll be given helpful strategies to use when answering test questions.

Assessment Practice Multiple-choice test items help you focus on how well you've read the texts provided. They also help you prepare for real tests.

Written Responses Many tests ask you to write one or more paragraphs about a reading passage. This book gives you the opportunity to write about each selection you read. A **Test-Taker's Toolkit** shows you how to develop each written response, step-by-step.

NONFICTION READING

Each main literature selection in *The InterActive Reader & Writer* is paired with a nonfiction selection that relates in some way to the literature. You will learn many different strategies for getting the most out of the nonfiction you read. These strategies will help you on tests, in other classes, and in the world outside of school. For example, you will learn how to:

- Analyze main ideas
- Evaluate news articles
- Determine author's message
- Identify facts and opinions

LINKS TO

McDougal Littell Literature

If you are using **McDougal Littell Literature,** you will find the **InterActive Reader & Writer** to be the perfect companion. **The InterActive Reader & Writer** helps you read certain core selections from **McDougal Littell Literature** more carefully and more carefully and in greater depth.

Read on to learn more!

The InterActive Reader & Writer with for Critical Analysis has an easy-to-follow organization, as shown by these sample pages from the essay "A Modest Proposal" by Jonathan Swift.

1 **Anchor Selection**
Each lesson is made up of a cluster of readings. The main literature selection is called the **anchor selection.** You will read this first.

2 **Related Nonfiction**
The title in smaller type is the **Related Nonfiction** piece. As you preview each lesson, read the title and think about how this piece might relate to the anchor selection.

UNIT 3
THE RESTORATION AND THE 18TH CENTURY

LESSON 3A

A Modest Proposal
BY JONATHAN SWIFT **1**

RELATED NONFICTION
Guilty of Poverty, Youth: "Street Kids" in Honduras **2**

JUST-STARVE-US. WORKHOUSE

Tell Ah! Tell us can aught be worse?
Than hungry Maw & empty Purse!!
MERCY SHOW & PITY US,
GREAT OVERSEER.

98

How can we fight **3** INJUSTICE?

There's an old proverb that states, "The pen is mightier than the sword." Jonathan Swift wielded his pen like a rapier, using it to slash away at injustice. Though some may claim that the power of the pen is greatly diminished these days, people still fight injustice with words—in speeches, in newspapers and magazines, and on the Internet.

CHART IT With a small group, brainstorm some contemporary examples of injustice. Write three of them down in the chart. For each example, identify some tactics that people can use to fight the injustice.

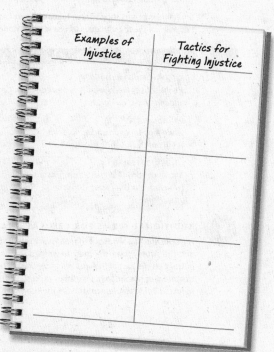

Examples of Injustice	Tactics for Fighting Injustice

4

ASSESSMENT GOALS

By the end of this lesson, you will be able to . . .

- analyze satire
- apply critical thinking skills to analyze text
- evaluate news articles
- analyze a writing prompt and plan a problem-solution essay

A MODEST PROPOSAL   **99**

3 **Big Question**
Each lesson begins with an activity that gets you thinking about a real-life question that the literature addresses. Sometimes you'll work in a group to complete this activity. After reading, you'll return to this question. Don't be surprised if you have a different perspective.

4 **Assessment Goals**
This box sums up the lesson's main learning goals. The first goal names the **literature skill.** The second goal is your overall **critical thinking objective.** The third goal names the skill you'll be learning with the **nonfiction** selections. The last goal names the **writing activity** you'll complete at the end of the lesson.

Learn the Terms:
Academic Vocabulary
This page introduces important terms and explains what to look for in the literature you read.

 You will come back to these academic terms several times during the unit. For example, in this lesson you will come across the term *irony* in the side notes of the main selection.

3 **Additional Terms for Critical Analysis**
Additional terms for critical analysis will challenge you to think and write about the literature even more deeply.

---

1 LEARN THE TERMS: ACADEMIC VOCABULARY

Satire

SATIRE is a literary technique in which behaviors or institutions are ridiculed for the purpose of improving society. What sets satire apart from other forms of social and political protest is humor. For example, Swift used his savage wit to attack prominent British politicians and to protest unjust policies in Ireland.

The following chart shows three types of IRONY that Swift used in his satires. Look for examples of these techniques as you read "A Modest Proposal."

2

TECHNIQUE	EXAMPLE
SITUATIONAL IRONY a contrast between what is expected and what actually occurs	After safely completing a dangerous mountain climb, a climber slips in the shower and hurts herself.
VERBAL IRONY when a writer or character says one thing but means the opposite	A football player fumbles the ball and loses the game. When he reaches the sideline, his coach tells him, "Nice play!"
UNDERSTATEMENT a form of irony that creates emphasis by saying less than what is true or appropriate	Reporting from a town that was hit by a hurricane, a reporter describes the place as "a bit messy."

3 ADDITIONAL TERMS FOR CRITICAL ANALYSIS

The selection you are about to read is an example of JUVENALIAN SATIRE. This kind of satire bitterly condemns human wrongdoing and foolishness, and reflects moral outrage on the part of the speaker. In contrast, HORATIAN SATIRE is a more tolerant treatment of human folly. Instead of expressing anger, Horatian satire reflects the speaker's ironic amusement toward the subject.

A Modest Proposal

FOR PREVENTING THE CHILDREN OF POOR PEOPLE IN IRELAND
FROM BEING A BURDEN TO THEIR PARENTS OR COUNTRY,
AND FOR MAKING THEM BENEFICIAL TO THE PUBLIC

JONATHAN SWIFT

(6)

BACKGROUND By 1700, Ireland was completely dominated by England. The Catholic majority could not vote, hold public office, buy land, or receive an education—policies that reduced most Irish people to poverty. When crops failed, many faced starvation. Jonathan Swift, outraged by England's treatment of Ireland, wrote a satirical attack on this injustice in "A Modest Proposal."

It is a melancholy object to those who walk through this great town[1] or travel in the country, when they see the streets, the roads, and cabin doors, crowded with beggars of the female sex, followed by three, four, or six children, all in rags and importuning every passenger for an alms.[2] These mothers, instead of being able to work for their honest livelihood, are forced to employ all their time in strolling to beg <u>sustenance</u> for their helpless infants, who, as they grow up, either turn thieves for want[3] of work, or leave their dear native country to fight for the Pretender[4] in Spain, or sell themselves to the Barbadoes.[5] ▶

10   I think it is agreed by all parties that this prodigious number of children in the arms, or on the backs, or at the heels of their mothers, and

---

1. **this great town:** Dublin, Ireland.
2. **importuning** (ĭm'pôr-tōōn'ĭng) . . . **alms** (ämz): begging from every passerby for a charitable handout.
3. **want:** lack; need.
4. **Pretender:** James Edward Stuart, who claimed the English throne, from which his now deceased father, James II, had been removed in 1688. Because James II and his son were Roman Catholic, the common people of Ireland were loyal to them.
5. **sell . . . Barbadoes:** To escape poverty, some Irish migrated to the West Indies, obtaining money for their passage by agreeing to work as slaves on plantations there for a set period.

---

(4)

SECOND READ:
CRITICAL ANALYSIS

MARK & ANALYZE

Read this selection once on your own, marking the text in any way that is helpful to you.

Then read the narrative a second time, using the questions in the margins to help you analyze the literature. When you see this pencil ✎, you'll be asked to mark up the text.

sustenance (sŭs'tə-nəns)
n. a means of support or nourishment

ANALYZE

Underline the generalizations the speaker makes about poor children in lines 1–9. ✎

How do these statements help set up the proposal to come?

_____

_____

_____

_____

A MODEST PROPOSAL   **101**

---

(4) **SECOND READ:**
CRITICAL ANALYSIS

You'll read each selection once on your own, marking the text as you wish. Then you'll read it a second time, using the questions in the margins to provide a deeper understanding of the selection.

(5) ✎

The pencil symbol appears whenever you are being asked to circle, underline, or mark the text in other ways.

(6) *BACKGROUND*

This paragraph gives important information about the selection you are about to read. Always read this section before starting the main text.

frequently of their fathers, is in the present deplorable state of the kingdom a very great additional grievance; and therefore whoever could find out a fair, cheap, and easy method of making these children sound, useful members of the commonwealth would deserve so well of the public as to have his statue set up for a preserver of the nation.

But my intention is very far from being confined to provide only for the children of professed beggars; it is of a much greater extent, and shall take in the whole number of infants at a certain age who are born of
20 parents in effect as little able to support them as those who demand our charity in the streets.

As to my own part, having turned my thoughts for many years upon this important subject, and maturely weighed the several schemes of other projectors,[6] I have always found them grossly mistaken in their computation. It is true, a child just dropped from its dam[7] may be supported by her milk for a solar year, with little other nourishment; at most not above the value of two shillings, which the mother may certainly get, or the value in scraps, by her lawful occupation of begging; and it is exactly at one year old that I propose to provide for them in such a manner
30 as instead of being a charge upon their parents or the parish, or wanting food and raiment for the rest of their lives, they shall on the contrary contribute to the feeding, and partly to the clothing, of many thousands. ◀

There is likewise another great advantage in my scheme, that it will prevent those voluntary abortions, and that horrid practice of women murdering their bastard children, alas, too frequent among us, sacrificing the poor innocent babes, I doubt,[8] more to avoid the expense than the shame, which would move tears and pity in the most savage and inhuman breast.

The number of souls in this kingdom being usually reckoned one
40 million and a half, of these I calculate there may be about two hundred thousand couple whose wives are breeders; from which number I subtract thirty thousand couples who are able to maintain their own children, although I apprehend there cannot be so many under the present distresses of the kingdom; but this being granted, there will remain an hundred and seventy thousand breeders. I again subtract fifty thousand for those women who miscarry, or whose children die by accident or disease within the year. There only remain an hundred and twenty thousand children of poor parents annually born. The question therefore is, how this number ◀

6. **projectors:** persons who propose public projects or plans.
7. **dam** (dăm): female parent. The term is used mostly for farm animals.
8. **doubt:** suspect.

Side column:

1 ▷

When you come to this symbol, follow the arrow to the side column. Answer the question. Then read on.

INTERPRET

Reread lines 25–26, in which the author refers to a new mother as a "dam." What effect does this choice of words have?

_____

_____

_____

_____

ANALYZE

Reread the boxed text. Why does the speaker use mathematical language when discussing the poor?

_____

_____

_____

_____

shall be reared and provided for, which, as I have already said, under the
present situation of affairs, is utterly impossible by all the methods hitherto
proposed. For we can neither employ them in handicraft or agriculture;
we neither build houses (I mean in the country) nor cultivate land. They
can very seldom pick up a livelihood by stealing till they arrive at six years
old, except where they are of towardly parts;[9] although I confess they learn
the <u>rudiments</u> much earlier, during which time they can however be
looked upon only as probationers, as I have been informed by a principal
gentleman in the county of Cavan, who protested to me that he never
knew above one or two instances under the age of six, even in a part of the
kingdom so renowned for the quickest proficiency in that art.

I am assured by our merchants that a boy or girl before twelve years old
is no salable commodity; and even when they come to this age they will
not yield above three pounds, or three pounds and half a crown at most on
the Exchange; which cannot turn to account[10] either to the parents or the
kingdom, the charge of nutriment and rags having been at least four times
that value.

I shall now therefore humbly propose my own thoughts, which I hope
will not be liable to the least objection.

I have been assured by a very knowing American of my acquaintance
in London, that a young healthy child well nursed is at a year old a most
delicious, nourishing, and wholesome food, whether stewed, roasted,
baked, or boiled; and I make no doubt that it will equally serve in a
fricassee or a ragout.[11]

I do therefore humbly offer it to public consideration that of the
hundred and twenty thousand children, already computed, twenty
thousand may be <u>reserved for breed,</u>[12] whereof only one fourth part to
be males, which is more than we allow to sheep, black cattle, or swine;
and my reason is that <u>these children are seldom the fruits of marriage,</u> a
circumstance not much regarded by our savages, therefore one male will
be sufficient to serve four females. That the remaining hundred thousand
may at a year old be offered in sale to the <u>persons of quality and fortune</u>
through the kingdom, always advising the mother to let them suck
plentifully in the last month, so as to render them plump and fat for a
good table. A child will make two dishes at an entertainment for friends;
and when the family dines alone, the fore or hind quarter will make a

---

9. **are of towardly** (tôrd′lē) **parts:** have a promising talent.
10. **turn to account:** earn a profit; benefit; prove useful.
11. **fricassee** (frĭk′ə-sē′) . . . **ragout** (ră-gōō′): types of meat stews.
12. **reserved for breed:** kept for breeding (instead of being slaughtered).

② **rudiment** (rōō′də-mənt) *n.* a
basic principle or element

CONTRAST

Reread the boxed text.
Compare the way the speaker
describes the poor with the
way he describes the rich.

_____

_____

_____

_____

Underline details that support
your answer.

③

② **Vocabulary**
Important vocabulary
words are underlined and
boldfaced blue. A definition
and a respelling appear in
the side column.

③ Here you are being asked
to mark up the text. Notice
how one student responded
to the note in the side
column.

④ **Footnotes**
Some selections in this
book include footnotes for
special words and phrases.
When you see a number in
the text, look down at the
bottom of the page for a
definition.

The selection continues . . .

TestSmart

TestSmart questions will give you practice answering multiple-choice questions typically found on tests.

Each **TestSmart** question has a **TIP** that gives you useful strategies for figuring out answers to test questions.

Notice how this **TIP** relates to one of the literary terms presented in the lesson.

encumbrance (ĕn-kŭm′brəns) *n.* a burden

famine (făm′ĭn) *n.* a period in which there is a severe shortage of food

TESTSMART ①

The speaker's optimism about the problem of poor people is ironic because

Ⓐ new medicines allowed Irish people to live longer

Ⓑ Ireland's population was holding steady

Ⓒ he actually emphasizes the horrible neglect of the poor

Ⓓ poverty encourages people to work harder

TIP When a test question asks you why a passage is **ironic**, keep in mind that irony is a contrast between expectation or appearance and reality. To answer the question, think about which answer choice describes such a conflict. Eliminate any choices that do not reflect the reality conveyed by the paragraph.

Some persons of a desponding spirit are in great concern about that vast number of poor people who are aged, diseased, or maimed, and I have been desired to employ my thoughts what course may be taken to ease the nation of so grievous an <u>encumbrance</u>. But I am not in the least pain upon that matter, because it is very well known that they are every day dying and rotting by cold and <u>famine</u>, and filth and vermin, as fast as can be reasonably expected. And as to the younger laborers, they are now in almost as hopeful a condition. They cannot get work, and consequently
160 pine away for want of nourishment to a degree that if at any time they are accidentally hired to common labor, they have not strength to perform it; and thus the country and themselves are happily delivered from the evils to come. ◄

I have too long digressed, and therefore shall return to my subject. I think the advantages by the proposal which I have made are obvious and many, as well as of the highest importance.

For first, as I have already observed, it would greatly lessen the number of Papists, with whom we are yearly overrun, being the principal breeders of the nation as well as our most dangerous enemies; and who stay at
170 home on purpose to deliver the kingdom to the Pretender, hoping to take their advantage by the absence of so many good Protestants, who have chosen rather to leave their country than stay at home and pay tithes against their conscience to an Episcopal curate.[22]

Secondly, the poorer tenants will have something valuable of their own, which by law may be made liable to distress,[23] and help to pay their landlord's rent, their corn and cattle being already seized and money a thing unknown.

Thirdly, whereas the maintenance of an hundred thousand children, from two years old and upwards, cannot be computed at less than ten
180 shillings a piece per annum, the nation's stock will be thereby increased fifty thousand pounds per annum, besides the profit of a new dish introduced to the tables of all gentlemen of fortune in the kingdom who have any refinement in taste. And the money will circulate among ourselves, the goods being entirely of our own growth and manufacture.

Fourthly, the constant breeders, besides the gain of eight shillings sterling per annum by the sale of their children, will be rid of the charge of maintaining them after the first year.

---

22. **Protestants . . . curate** (kyŏŏr′ĭt): Swift is criticizing absentee Anglo-Irish landowners who lived—and spent their income from their property—in England.
23. **distress:** seizure of a person's property for the payment of debts.

Fifthly, this food would likewise bring great custom to taverns, where the vintners will certainly be so prudent as to procure the best receipts[24] for
190 dressing it to perfection, and consequently have their houses frequented by all the fine gentlemen, who justly value themselves upon their knowledge in good eating; and a skillful cook, who understands how to oblige his guests, will contrive to make it as expensive as they please.

Sixthly, this would be a great inducement to marriage, which all wise nations have either encouraged by rewards or enforced by laws and penalties. It would increase the care and tenderness of mothers toward their children, when they were sure of a settlement for life to the poor babes, provided in some sort by the public, to their annual profit instead of expense. We should see an honest emulation among the married women, which of them
200 could bring the fattest child to the market. Men would become as fond of their wives during the time of their pregnancy as they are now of their mares in foal, their cows in calf, or sows when they are ready to farrow; nor offer to beat or kick them (as is too frequent a practice) for fear of a miscarriage. ▶

Many other advantages might be enumerated. For instance, the addition of some thousand carcasses in our exportation of barreled beef, the <u>propagation</u> of swine's flesh, and improvement in the art of making good bacon, so much wanted among us by the great destruction of pigs, too frequent at our tables, which are no way comparable in taste or
210 magnificence to a well-grown, fat, yearling child, which roasted whole will make a considerable figure at a lord mayor's feast or any other public entertainment. But this and many others I omit, being studious of brevity. ▶

Supposing that one thousand families in this city would be constant customers for infants' flesh, besides others who might have it at merry meetings, particularly weddings and christenings, I compute that Dublin would take off annually about twenty thousand carcasses, and the rest of the kingdom (where probably they will be sold somewhat cheaper) the remaining eighty thousand.

I can think of no one objection that will possibly be raised against
220 this proposal, unless it should be urged that the number of people will be thereby much lessened in the kingdom. This I freely own, and it was indeed one principal design in offering it to the world. I desire the reader will observe, that I calculate my remedy for this one individual kingdom of Ireland and for no other that ever was, is, or I think ever can be upon

---

24. **receipts:** recipes.

② EVALUATE
How convincing do you find the speaker's argument in lines 194–204 that his proposal would improve family life? Explain.

_____

_____

_____

_____

propagation (prŏp'ə-gā'shən) _n._ the act of reproducing, multiplying, or increasing

③ TESTSMART

VOCABULARY
The most likely meaning of the word _brevity_ in line 212 is

Ⓐ courageous approach to problems

Ⓑ concise use of language

Ⓒ ironic discourse

Ⓓ the act of making merry

TIP Use **context clues** to figure out the meaning of an unfamiliar word. Reread lines 205–212, and underline any words or phrases that provide clues to the meaning of the word _brevity._ ✎

② Challenging Questions
Challenging questions such as this one ask you to use high-level critical thinking skills in order to achieve a deeper understanding of the selection.

③ TestSmart Vocabulary
Some **TestSmart** questions will ask about words found in the selection. The **TIP** that follows will help strengthen your word-attack skills in testing situations.

① This is an example of a side note that makes use of one of the **Learn the Terms** concepts. Feel free to look back at that page if necessary.

ANALYZE **①**

Reread lines 243–245 and footnote 28. What is **ironic** about Swift's dismissal of the "expedients" in the previous paragraph?

_____

_____

_____

earth. Therefore let no man talk to me of other expedients: of taxing our absentees at five shillings a pound: of using neither clothes nor household furniture except what is of our own growth and manufacture: of utterly rejecting the materials and instruments that promote foreign luxury: of curing the expensiveness of pride, vanity, idleness, and gaming in our
230   women: of introducing a vein of parsimony,[25] prudence, and temperance: of learning to love our country, in the want of which we differ even from Laplanders and the inhabitants of Topinamboo:[26] of quitting our animosities and factions, nor acting any longer like the Jews, who were murdering one another at the very moment their city was taken:[27] of being a little cautious not to sell our country and conscience for nothing: of teaching landlords to have at least one degree of mercy toward their tenants: lastly, of putting a spirit of honesty, industry, and skill into our shopkeepers; who, if a resolution could now be taken to buy only our native goods, would immediately unite to cheat and exact upon us in the
240   price, the measure, and the goodness, nor could ever yet be brought to make one fair proposal of just dealing, though often and earnestly invited to it.

   Therefore I repeat, let no man talk to me of these and the like expedients,[28] till he hath at least some glimpse of hope that there will ever be some hearty and sincere attempt to put them in practice. ◀

   But as to myself, having been wearied out for many years with offering vain, idle, visionary thoughts, and at length utterly despairing of success, I fortunately fell upon this proposal, which, as it is wholly new, so it hath something solid and real, of no expense and little trouble, full in our own
250   power, and whereby we can incur no danger in disobliging England. For this kind of commodity will not bear exportation, the flesh being of too tender a consistence to admit a long continuance in salt, although perhaps I could name a country which would be glad to eat up our whole nation without it.

   After all, I am not so violently bent upon my own opinion as to reject any offer proposed by wise men, which shall be found equally innocent, cheap, easy, and effectual. But before something of that kind shall be

---

25. **parsimony** (pär′sə-mō′nē): frugality; thrift.
26. **Topinamboo** (tŏp′ĭ-năm′bōō): an area in Brazil supposedly inhabited by wild savages.
27. **Jews . . . taken:** In A.D. 70, during a Jewish revolt against Roman rule, the inhabitants of Jerusalem, by fighting among themselves, made it easier for the Romans to capture the city.
28. **let no man . . . expedients:** In his writings, Swift had suggested "other expedients" without success.

advanced in contradiction to my scheme, and offering a better, I desire the
author or authors will be pleased maturely to consider two points. First, as
260 things now stand, how they will be able to find food and raiment for an
hundred thousand useless mouths and backs. And secondly, there being
a round million of creatures in human figure throughout this kingdom,
whose sole subsistence put into a common stock[29] would leave them in
debt two millions of pounds sterling, adding those who are beggars by
profession to the bulk of farmers, cottagers, and laborers, with their wives
and children who are beggars in effect; I desire those politicians who
dislike my overture, and may perhaps be so bold to attempt an answer,
that they will first ask the parents of these mortals whether they would not
at this day think it a great happiness to have been sold for food at a year
270 old in the manner I prescribe, and thereby have avoided such a perpetual
scene of misfortunes as they have since gone through by the oppression
of landlords, the impossibility of paying rent without money or trade, the
want of common sustenance, with neither house nor clothes to cover them
from the inclemencies of the weather, and the most inevitable prospect of
entailing the like or greater miseries upon their breed forever. ▶

I profess, in the sincerity of my heart, that I have not the least personal
interest in endeavoring to promote this necessary work, having no other
motive than the public good of my country, by advancing our trade,
providing for infants, relieving the poor, and giving some pleasure to the
280 rich. I have no children by which I can propose to get a single penny; the
youngest being nine years old, and my wife past childbearing.

TESTSMART

Which of the following
words *best* characterizes the
suggestion that poor adults
would have been better off
if they had been sold for
food as babies?

(A) prudent

(B) immoral

(C) forceful

(D) unusual

TIP Notice that the
question asks which is the
best answer. This tells you
that more than one answer
may be possible. Reread
lines 266–275, and **decide
which choice best fits the
message** of Swift's satire.

2 **Big Question** ?

Think about the
contemporary examples
of injustice that you listed
on page 99. How effective
would a **satire** similar to
"A Modest Proposal" be in
fighting these injustices?
Explain your answer.

_____

_____

_____

2  **Big Question** ?

At the end of each main
literature selection, you'll
be asked to think again
about the **Big Question** you
discussed before reading.

---

29. **common stock:** ordinary stock in a company or business venture.

1. Assessment Practice I: Reading Comprehension

After reading each main literature selection, you'll have an opportunity to practice your test-taking skills and strategies by answering questions about the selection. The direction line will tell you how to mark the answers.

2. Literary Skills

Certain test items, such as 1 through 4, will ask questions that are related to the literary skills. You can review these skills by rereading **Learn the Terms,** page 100.

3. Test Strategies

Some test items will give you a chance to use the **TestSmart TIPs** you learned earlier in the lesson. Here, notice how the **TIP** on page 109 can help answer test item 6.

4. Vocabulary

The last two test items focus on vocabulary. Remember to use the line numbers to help locate and reread the sentences in which the words appear.

Assessment Practice I ①

Reading Comprehension

DIRECTIONS *Answer these questions about "A Modest Proposal" by filling in the correct ovals.*

1. Suggesting that infants should be served at christenings (lines 213–218) is ironic because christenings

  Ⓐ are held by the rich

  Ⓑ celebrate a baby's birth

  Ⓒ are not held in Ireland

  Ⓓ commemorate privilege

2. Which word *best* describes the satire in lines 174–177?

  Ⓐ verbal irony

  Ⓑ situational irony

  Ⓒ understatement

  Ⓓ Juvenalian satire

3. Which of the following is an example of verbal irony?

  Ⓐ the title of the essay

  Ⓑ the speaker's description of mothers begging for food

  Ⓒ the estimate of 200,000 "breeders" in Ireland

  Ⓓ the argument that the proposal will encourage marriage

4. What technique does Swift use to create satire in lines 133–137, where the speaker suggests that some people might consider slaughtering and eating girls 12 to 14 years old "a little bordering upon cruelty"?

  Ⓐ situational irony

  Ⓑ verbal irony

  Ⓒ understatement

  Ⓓ hyperbole

5. Why does the speaker lack faith in the alternative solutions listed near the end of the essay?

  Ⓐ Similar proposals have been ignored in the past.

  Ⓑ These solutions have been tried and they didn't work.

  Ⓒ He is jealous of the people who have proposed these solutions.

  Ⓓ He thinks his own proposal is the most humane.

6. Which word *best* describes the effect that Swift wanted to have on his readers?

  Ⓐ exciting

  Ⓑ persuasive

  Ⓒ convincing

  Ⓓ horrifying

7. The word *prodigious* in line 10 means

  Ⓐ impoverished

  Ⓑ athletic

  Ⓒ enormous

  Ⓓ insignificant

8. What does the word *procure* mean in line 189?

  Ⓐ heal

  Ⓑ obtain

  Ⓒ prohibit

  Ⓓ cook

110 UNIT 3A: THE RESTORATION AND THE 18TH CENTURY

For help, use the *Test-Taker's Toolkit* below.

Responding in Writing

9. Short Response Does the real message of "A Modest Proposal" come across clearly, or could Swift's use of irony confuse readers into mistaking the satire for a sincere proposal? Write a brief evaluation of the essay, referring to at least two examples of irony to support your opinion.

_____

_____

_____

_____

_____

TEST-TAKER'S TOOLKIT

- ⊗ **ACADEMIC VOCABULARY** Remember that **situational irony** is a contrast between what is expected and what actually occurs; **verbal irony** occurs when a writer says one thing but means the opposite; and **understatement** is saying less than what is true or appropriate.

- ⊗ **GRAPHIC ORGANIZER** Use the chart below to help you plan your response.

Example of Irony	How It Relates to Swift's Message

---

5 Responding in Writing
After each main literature selection, you'll write a short response. This activity might ask you to use some of the literary terms you have studied.

6 Test-Taker's Toolkit
The **Test-Taker's Toolkit** helps you plan your response. Completing the graphic organizer will give you the ideas you'll use in your writing.

① Related Nonfiction

Once you've completed the literature section, you'll get ready to read the **Related Nonfiction.**

② What's the Connection?

This activity gets you thinking and talking about the nonfiction selection you are about to read. It also explains how it connects to the literature selection.

③ Learn the Skill

Before you read the **Related Nonfiction,** you will learn a useful skill or strategy. You will encounter the boldfaced terms later as you are reading and as you complete the practice test.

---

① Related Nonfiction

Guilty of Poverty, Youth: "Street Kids" in Honduras
NEWSPAPER ARTICLE

Use with "A Modest Proposal," p. 98

What's the Connection? ②

In "A Modest Proposal," satirist Jonathan Swift presents a scathing commentary on the mistreatment and neglect of the poor in 18th-century Ireland. The news article you are about to read describes the plight of poor children in modern-day Honduras.

HELPING HANDS Poverty is a difficult problem to tackle in any society, even one far wealthier than Honduras. With a partner, brainstorm ways to help people who are living on the street. Consider measures that can be taken by governments, charitable organizations, and concerned individuals. For each idea, note possible objections to the measure.

Antipoverty Ideas	Possible Objections

③

LEARN THE SKILL: EVALUATE NEWS ARTICLES

How do you know if a **news article** can be trusted? Use the following criteria to help you evaluate news articles.

Criteria	Look for . . .
The article is **objective.**	a balanced point of view, not a biased one
The information is **accurate.**	verifiable facts
The article is **thorough.**	background that tells who, what, when, where, why; representations of all sides of the story

For more on evaluating news articles, see the Evaluate Evidence entry in the Nonfiction Skills Handbook beginning on page R2.

112 UNIT 3A: THE RESTORATION AND THE 18TH CENTURY

Guilty of Poverty, Youth: "Street Kids" in Honduras

by Malcolm Garcia

CLOSE READ

④ SET A PURPOSE

to learn about

poor children in

Honduras

⑤ **EVALUATE NEWS ARTICLES**

Is the headline of the article **objective,** or does it convey the author's opinion about his topic? Explain.

_____

_____

_____

_____

_____

TEGUCIGALPA, HONDURAS— When Honduran police snatched 11-year-old Roberto Alvarez off the street this summer, he was just about to buy candy with money he earned polishing shoes.

"I don't know where my family is," he said from a bare dormitory room at Hogares de Proteccion ₁₀ Kennedy, a rundown facility of cement block buildings and a garbage-strewn playground that houses about 130 street children. A black metal bunk bed without mattresses stood in one corner slashed with light coming through a barred window. "I don't like it here," Roberto said.

Faced with chronic poverty and ₂₀ a soaring crime rate, the Honduran government last spring began a sweep of street children such as Roberto, removing them to government-sponsored centers.

The centers, authorities say, offer the children a future by providing them with counseling and referrals to agencies. As of September, more than 1,000 children had been ₃₀ picked up and sheltered for varying lengths of stays in one of four centers in the country. Each center

④ **Set a Purpose**
You will begin the nonfiction selection by setting a purpose for reading. One student's purpose for reading appears on the lines provided. Yours may be different.

⑤ **Evaluate News Articles**
These notes ask you to apply the skill or strategy you learned before reading.

1 **Challenging Questions**
Here is another challenging question that requires you to form an answer based on critical analysis. Be sure to support your answer.

EXAMINE PERSPECTIVES **1**

Do Jose Manuel Capellin and Eduardo Villanueva view the policy of rounding up street children from a similar perspective? Explain why or why not.

_____

_____

_____

_____

EVALUATE NEWS ARTICLES

Underline information in the boxed text that is factual. Circle information that is not factual. ✎

Explain why the circled information cannot be verified.

_____

_____

_____

has room for 150 children, and all are full, according to Lesbia Lagos, director of Hogares de Proteccion Kennedy.

Children—some as young as 6—are taken to the centers by teams of police and social workers
40 if they are seen begging, prostituting themselves or just walking the streets alone at night. Lagos said children who have families are returned home only if their parents have an income and the children attend school. Otherwise they are referred to nongovernmental organizations that work with children.

But many of these agencies
50 won't accept the referrals, and the children stay much longer, possibly years, until they turn 18 and are considered adults.

"We won't take them if they've been taken by force because the child will just go back to the streets and hide," said Jose Manuel Capellin, national director of Casa Alianza, a nonprofit organization
60 that assists poor and homeless children in Honduras and other parts of Central America.

"It is an impossible situation," said attorney Eduardo Villanueva, who represents children in the courts. "It is criminalizing poverty." ◀

The roundups reflect the tremendous social problems in one of
70 the poorest and youngest democracies in the Western Hemisphere.

In Honduras, half the population of 6.5 million is under 18. The average monthly income is about $65, and the unemployment rate hovers at 28 percent. There are no reliable estimates as to the numbers of street children in Honduras. They are believed by government
80 officials and advocates alike to be in the thousands. ◀

The sweeps come at a time when police are arresting hundreds of teenagers and young adults in a crackdown on gangs. Membership in gangs is now considered an "illicit association," which carries a sentence of up to seven years in jail. The law is a response to an
90 increase of violent crime over the past decade by young gangs that have carved up major cities into their turf.

Human rights advocates argue that these initiatives violate civil rights, break up families and do little to improve the lives of impoverished children. Many families live in makeshift homes of aluminum
100 siding or in cramped, single-room apartments above the clogged din of downtown.

"The people now feel they are living in a police state," said lawyer Gustavo Zelaya. "Is the solution always to have severe punishment?"

Business owners, however, support the crackdown. "Street chil-
110 dren used to be all over downtown,"

HONDURAS FACTS

Government type: republic

Capital: Tegucigalpa

Economic rank: 2nd poorest country in Central America

Per Capita Gross Domestic Product: $3,100 ▶

Population below poverty line: 53%

Unemployment rate: 28%

Agricultural products: bananas, coffee, citrus, beef, timber, shrimp

Industries: sugar, coffee, textiles, clothing, wood products

Source: CIA: The World Factbook

2

SPECIALIZED
Vocabulary

A nation's gross domestic product (GDP) is the total market value of all the finished goods and services the country has produced in a given period of time. The term *per capita* means "per person." How would you define *per capita gross domestic product?*

_____

_____

_____

3

TESTSMART

Which two people interviewed for the article present opposing viewpoints on the issue?

Ⓐ Gustavo Zelaya and Gina Burgos

Ⓑ Gina Burgos and Lesbia Lagos

Ⓒ Jose Manuel Capellin and Gustavo Zelaya

Ⓓ Roberto Alvarez and Eduardo Villanueva

TIP A test question may ask you to compare viewpoints of people who are quoted in an article. To answer such a question, reread all of their quotes and **draw conclusions** about the feelings and beliefs that they bring to the subject they are commenting on.

said Gina Burgos, 48, general manager of the posh, castle-shaped Medieval Bar and Restaurant. "You couldn't go anywhere without them following you, coming into businesses asking for money, grabbing you. It's better now but a little strange. Where have they gone? They just disappeared from 120 downtown."

Some apparently have not gone far. The government estimates that about 1,000 street children struggle to survive in barrios not far from downtown Tegucigalpa. They scavenge in the open-air markets, competing with feral dogs for scraps of food discarded by vendors.

130 Countless other children spend hours on the streets working to help support their families. They earn about $1 to $2 a day. However, they also fall under the government's definition of street children.

"Some of these children are helping their mothers and fathers, I know this," Lagos said. "But 140 to work only, without education, they will become like their mothers and fathers. Nothing." ▶

---

2 **Specialized Vocabulary**
When a nonfiction selection contains a term that is unique to a certain area of study, a note is provided that will help you figure out the term's meaning.

3 💡 **TestSmart**

Notice how this **TestSmart** side note gives you a strategy for answering test items that relate to the featured skill, evaluating news articles.

1 **Assessment Practice II:**
Reading Comprehension
In this second practice test, you'll answer test items about both selections you have read in the lesson.

2 **Nonfiction Skill**
Some test items ask about the nonfiction skill or strategy you learned. If there are page or line references in the question, use them to locate and reread the text you are being asked about before you choose an answer.

3 **Connecting Texts**
Test items such as 5 and 6 ask you to connect information from the anchor selection and the Related Nonfiction. You can look back at the selections if you need to.

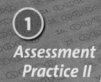

1
Assessment Practice II

Reading Comprehension

DIRECTIONS *Answer these questions about the two selections in this lesson by filling in the correct ovals.*

1. Gustavo Zelaya's statement in lines 103–107 supports the perspective that the street sweeps
   - (A) criminalize poverty
   - (B) are necessary
   - (C) help impoverished children
   - (D) improve downtown areas

2. Which person interviewed for the news article would be *least* likely to agree that street sweeps criminalize poverty?
   - (A) Roberto Alvarez
   - (B) Eduardo Villanueva
   - (C) Lesbia Lagos
   - (D) Gustavo Zelaya

3. Which statistic provided in the article helps explain why Hondurans are so poor?
   - (A) unemployment rate: 28%
   - (B) location: Central America
   - (C) industries: sugar, coffee, textiles
   - (D) population: 6.5 million

4. The graphic on page 115 adds to the article's credibility by providing
   - (A) a map of Honduras
   - (B) verifiable facts
   - (C) a balanced view
   - (D) background on street children

5. Modern-day Honduras and 18th-century Ireland are alike because in both places, poverty is
   - (A) sanitized
   - (B) ignored
   - (C) ridiculed
   - (D) widespread

3

6. Which societal element does *not* exist in both 18th-century Ireland and modern-day Honduras?
   - (A) generations of poverty
   - (B) a problem with theft
   - (C) anti-Catholic laws
   - (D) a business class

7. The word *hovers* in line 76 of the news article means
   - (A) floats above
   - (B) remains near
   - (C) watches closely
   - (D) threatens ominously

8. The most likely meaning of *barrios* in line 124 of the news article is
   - (A) garbage pits
   - (B) government agencies
   - (C) suburban sprawl
   - (D) urban slums

Timed Writing Practice ④

PROMPT

Swift wasn't serious about the plan he outlined in "A Modest Proposal," but he took the problem of Irish poverty very seriously. Write a problem-solution essay in which you propose one step that should be taken to help the poor. Narrow the focus of your essay to (address a specific example) of poverty. You can focus on the conditions described in one of the selections you have read, or you can choose another example of poverty that you are familiar with. Provide at least three reasons for your solution, and one or two details to support each reason.

TEST-TAKER'S TOOLKIT ⑥

1. ANALYZE THE PROMPT

A. Underline the type of writing you are being asked to do.

B. Circle any key words that describe what should be included in your writing. One example has been circled for you.

2. PLAN YOUR RESPONSE

A. Make notes Decide which example of poverty you will focus on, and brainstorm a list of possible solutions. Choose the solution you will propose in your essay. In the chart here, list three reasons why your solution will help the poor, and list details to support your reasons.

B. Organize your information In the introductory paragraph, describe the specific problem of poverty that you will address in the essay, and clearly state a solution. Then you can write a paragraph for each reason you noted in your chart. Use your details to support each reason. End the essay with a conclusion in which you sum up your ideas.

Reason 1	Detail(s)
Reason 2	Detail(s)
Reason 3	Detail(s)

3. WRITE AND REVIEW

A. Capture your readers' attention by including a vivid description or a striking question in your introduction.

B. Be sure to leave time to check your spelling and grammar.

RELATED NONFICTION **117**

---

④ **Timed Writing Practice**
This writing activity is an opportunity to practice responding to a prompt on a writing test—without the stress of test-taking!

⑤ **Budget Your Time**
This feature helps you plan how much time to spend on each step. The blue text shows how one student budgeted her time.

⑥ **Test-Taker's Toolkit**
The Test-Taker's Toolkit shows you how to break the writing process into three easy steps. Fill in the graphic organizer provided. This will help you gather the information you'll need to write your full response. (You may want to copy the graphic organizer onto a larger sheet of paper.)

Thinking Critically

The skills and strategies found in this book will help you tackle critical thinking questions you encounter in school—and on tests in particular. Critical thinking questions are often challenging because the answers are usually not directly stated in the text. But you will find that tackling these types of questions is worth the extra brain power it takes to answer them. That's because they help you get more out of the selections you read. Here is a list of the critical thinking skills and strategies you will encounter most often in this book:

Make Inferences
Make logical guesses based on details in the text and your own experiences.

- Keep track of important details in your reading.
- Ask: How can what I already know help me "read between the lines"?

Draw Conclusions
Decide what's happening based on evidence, experience, and reasoning.

- Start by making inferences as you read.
- Then combine your inferences to reach a logical conclusion.

Analyze
Break things down to gain a better understanding.

- Consider the experiences and feelings that make a character act a certain way.
- In nonfiction, look for details to help you learn how something works or is defined.

Interpret
Find deeper meaning in what you read.

- Consider the outcome of events and what they might mean.
- Think about what the author is trying to tell the reader.

Evaluate
Examine something to decide its value or worth.

- You can decide to evaluate the actions of a particular character, for example.
- You can also decide on the value of what you are reading.

Make Judgments
Form an opinion based on information given.

- Gather evidence from the text.
- Be ready to support your opinion.

continued on next page

Compare/Contrast

Identify similarities and differences in two or more subjects.

- Make a list of the qualities of each subject. In what ways are the lists the same? Different?
- Decide if the subjects are more alike or more different.

Synthesize

Combine information together to gain a better understanding.

- Think of what you already know about the subject.
- Add this to the facts, details, and ideas presented in your reading.

Make Generalizations

Form a broad statement about a subject.

- Gather evidence.
- Then decide what ideas are suggested by this evidence.

Classify

Decide how pieces of information might fit into categories.

- Look for common characteristics in the information provided.
- Cite evidence from your reading to show why you classified as you did.

Examine Perspectives

Think about the values and beliefs presented.

- Look for a writer's statements of opinion.
- Decide how perspective affects the information you get.

UNIT 1

THE ANGLO-SAXON AND MEDIEVAL PERIODS

LESSON 1A

from *Beowulf*
BY THE BEOWULF POET

RELATED NONFICTION
A Monster Fit for Any Medium

Where do MONSTERS *lurk?*

Unlike the monsters in *Beowulf*, those in our world are not always easy to identify. Evil can hide in the most unexpected places: behind a smiling face, between the lines of a law, in otherwise noble-sounding words. Even when evil is clearly exposed, people may disagree on how to confront it.

LIST IT With a small group of classmates, list examples of real-life or fictional monsters. Discuss what the monsters on your list have in common, and then come up with a definition of the word. Share your list and definition with other groups.

Examples of Monsters
1. Jack the Ripper

2. Adolf Hitler

Definition

ASSESSMENT GOALS

By the end of this lesson, you will be able to. . .

• analyze the characteristics of an epic

• apply critical thinking skills to analyze text

• analyze main ideas in a work of nonfiction

• analyze a writing prompt and plan an analytical essay

Characteristics of an Epic

An **EPIC** is a long narrative poem that depicts the adventures of a great hero. *Beowulf* is the only surviving epic written in Old English—the language of the Anglo-Saxon people, who lived in England in the early Middle Ages. Although it was composed in England, *Beowulf* describes legendary events involving Scandinavian ancestors of the Anglo-Saxons. The poem was originally intended to be chanted aloud in public.

Beowulf reflects the culture and values of the Anglo-Saxons, but it has characteristics that are common to most epic poetry. Review the characteristics in the graphic below to help you analyze the poem.

EPIC

Hero
The hero, who is of noble birth or high position, performs deeds requiring incredible courage and strength.

Character Traits
The hero embodies character traits that reflect important ideals of society.

Diction and Tone
The poem uses formal diction (the writer's choice of words and sentence structure) and a serious tone (the expression of the writer's attitude toward a subject).

Universal Themes
The poem reflects universal themes (themes common to most cultures and periods) and timeless values.

ADDITIONAL TERMS FOR CRITICAL ANALYSIS

The following terms describe important techniques used by the Beowulf poet:

- A **CAESURA** (sĭ-zhŏŏr′ə) is a pause that divides a line of verse in which each part has two accented syllables. A caesura helps maintain the rhythm of the lines.

- A **KENNING** is a metaphorical compound word or phrase in Old English poetry that takes the place of a simple noun, such as a name. For example, in *Beowulf* "sin-stained demon" is a kenning used in place of the monster Grendel's name.

BEOWULF

BACKGROUND *Beowulf* is set in Scandinavia around the 500s among two groups: the Danes of what is now Denmark and the Geats (gēts) of what is now Sweden. The Geat warrior Beowulf crosses the sea to defeat Grendel, a monster who is terrorizing the Danes. He later returns to his homeland to succeed his uncle as king of the Geats.

Hrothgar (hrôth′gär′) *is king of the Danes. He has built a wonderful mead hall called Herot* (hĕr′ət), *where his subjects congregate and make merry. As this selection opens, a fierce and powerful monster named Grendel is about to invade the mead hall.*

GRENDEL

A powerful monster, living down
In the darkness, growled in pain, impatient ▶
As day after day the music rang
Loud in that hall, the harp's rejoicing
5 Call and the poet's clear songs, sung
Of the ancient beginnings of us all, recalling
The Almighty making the earth, shaping
These beautiful plains marked off by oceans,
Then proudly setting the sun and moon
10 To glow across the land and light it;
The corners of the earth were made lovely with trees
And leaves, made quick with life, with each
Of the nations who now move on its face. And then
As now warriors sang of their pleasure:

Circle examples of alliteration in lines 1–2. ✏ What mood does the alliteration help to convey?

_____

_____

15　So Hrothgar's men lived happy in his hall
　　Till the monster stirred, that demon, that fiend,
　　Grendel, who haunted the moors,[1] the wild
　　Marshes, and made his home in a hell
　　Not hell but earth. He was spawned[2] in that slime,
20　Conceived by a pair of those monsters born
　　Of Cain,[3] murderous creatures banished
　　By God, punished forever for the crime
　　Of Abel's death. The Almighty drove
　　Those demons out, and their exile was bitter,
25　Shut away from men; they split
　　Into a thousand forms of evil—spirits
　　And fiends, goblins, monsters, giants,
　　A brood forever opposing the Lord's
　　Will, and again and again defeated. ◀

30　　　Then, when darkness had dropped, Grendel
　　Went up to Herot, wondering what the warriors
　　Would do in that hall when their drinking was done.
　　He found them sprawled in sleep, suspecting
　　Nothing, their dreams undisturbed. The monster's
35　Thoughts were as quick as his greed or his claws:
　　He slipped through the door and there in the silence
　　Snatched up thirty men, smashed them
　　Unknowing in their beds and ran out with their bodies,
　　The blood dripping behind him, back
40　To his **lair**, delighted with his night's slaughter.
　　　At daybreak, with the sun's first light, they saw
　　How well he had worked, and in that gray morning
　　Broke their long feast with tears and laments
　　For the dead. Hrothgar, their lord, sat joyless
45　In Herot, a mighty prince mourning
　　The fate of his lost friends and companions,
　　Knowing by its tracks that some demon had torn
　　His followers apart. He wept, fearing
　　The beginning might not be the end. And that night ◀

INTERPRET

Reread the boxed text and think about the supernatural creatures that are "again and again defeated." What **universal theme** might these lines suggest?

_____

_____

_____

lair (lâr) *n.* the den or resting place of a wild animal

EVALUATE

Underline the fear Hrothgar has for the future. ✎

Is this fear well-founded? Explain.

_____

_____

_____

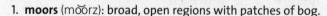

1. **moors** (mŏŏrz): broad, open regions with patches of bog.
2. **spawned:** given birth to.
3. **Cain:** the eldest son of Adam and Eve. According to the Bible (Genesis 4), he murdered his younger brother Abel.

50   Grendel came again, so set
     On murder that no crime could ever be enough,
     No savage assault quench his lust
     For evil. Then each warrior tried
     To escape him, searched for rest in different
55   Beds, as far from Herot as they could find,
     Seeing how Grendel hunted when they slept.
     Distance was safety; the only survivors
     Were those who fled him. Hate had triumphed.
       So Grendel ruled, fought with the righteous,
60   One against many, and won; so Herot
     Stood empty, and stayed deserted for years,
     Twelve winters of grief for Hrothgar, king
     Of the Danes, sorrow heaped at his door
     By hell-forged hands. His misery leaped ▶
65   The seas, was told and sung in all
     Men's ears: how Grendel's hatred began,
     How the monster relished his savage war
     On the Danes, keeping the bloody feud
     Alive, seeking no peace, offering
70   No truce, accepting no settlement, no price
     In gold or land, and paying the living
     For one crime only with another. No one
     Waited for reparation[4] from his plundering claws:
     That shadow of death hunted in the darkness,
75   Stalked Hrothgar's warriors, old
     And young, lying in waiting, hidden
     In mist, invisibly following them from the edge
     Of the marsh, always there, unseen.
       So mankind's enemy continued his crimes,
80   Killing as often as he could, coming
     Alone, bloodthirsty and horrible. Though he lived
     In Herot, when the night hid him, he never
     Dared to touch king Hrothgar's glorious
     Throne, protected by God—God,[5] ▶
85   Whose love Grendel could not know. But Hrothgar's

MAKE INFERENCES

What does the **kenning** "hell-forged hands" suggest about Grendel?

_____

_____

_____

CLASSIFY

Reread the boxed text. Write *g* next to lines that are associations with *good*. Write *e* next to those that are associations with *evil*. ✏

---

4. **reparation:** something done to make amends for loss or suffering. In Germanic society, someone who killed another person was generally expected to make a payment to the victim's family as a way of restoring peace.

5. The reference to God shows the influence of Christianity on the Beowulf Poet.

Heart was bent. The best and most noble
Of his council debated remedies, sat
In secret sessions, talking of terror
And wondering what the bravest of warriors could do.
90 And sometimes they sacrificed to the old stone gods,
Made heathen[6] vows, hoping for Hell's
Support, the Devil's guidance in driving
Their **affliction** off. That was their way,
And the heathen's only hope, Hell
95 Always in their hearts, knowing neither God
Nor His passing as He walks through our world, the Lord
Of Heaven and earth; their ears could not hear
His praise nor know His glory. Let them
Beware, those who are thrust into danger,
100 Clutched at by trouble, yet can carry no solace
In their hearts, cannot hope to be better! Hail
To those who will rise to God, drop off
Their dead bodies and seek our Father's peace! ◀

BEOWULF
      So the living sorrow of Healfdane's son[7]
105 Simmered, bitter and fresh, and no wisdom
Or strength could break it: that agony hung
On king and people alike, harsh
And unending, violent and cruel, and evil.
      In his far-off home Beowulf, Higlac's
110 Follower[8] and the strongest of the Geats—greater
And stronger than anyone anywhere in this world—
Heard how Grendel filled nights with horror
And quickly commanded a boat fitted out,
Proclaiming that he'd go to that famous king,
115 Would sail across the sea to Hrothgar,
Now when help was needed. None ◀

---

6. **heathen** (hē′thən): pagan; non-Christian. Though the Beowulf Poet was a
   Christian, he recognized that the characters in the poem lived before the
   Germanic tribes were converted to Christianity, when they still worshiped
   "the old stone gods."
7. **Healfdane's son:** Hrothgar.
8. **Higlac's follower:** a warrior loyal to Higlac (hĭg′lăk′), king of the Geats (and
   Beowulf's uncle).

affliction (ə-flĭk′shən) n. a
force that oppresses or causes
suffering

INTERPRET
What does the Beowulf poet
seem to be saying about
the heathens' chances for a
resolution to their problem
with Grendel?

_____

_____

_____

_____

Underline phrases that
support your answer. ✎

MAKE INFERENCES
Reread lines 109–116. What
traits of an **epic hero** does
Beowulf possess? Name two.

1. _____

2. _____

Of the wise ones regretted his going, much
As he was loved by the Geats: the omens were good,
And they urged the adventure on. So Beowulf
120 Chose the mightiest men he could find,
The bravest and best of the Geats, fourteen
In all, and led them down to their boat;
He knew the sea, would point the prow
Straight to that distant Danish shore. . . .

*Beowulf and his men sail over the sea to the land of the Danes to offer help
to Hrothgar. They are escorted by a Danish guard to Herot, where Wulfgar,
one of Hrothgar's soldiers, tells the king of their arrival. Hrothgar knows of
Beowulf and is ready to welcome the young prince and his men.*

125   Then Wulfgar went to the door and addressed
The waiting seafarers with soldier's words:
    "My lord, the great king of the Danes, commands me
To tell you that he knows of your noble birth
And that having come to him from over the open
130 Sea you have come bravely and are welcome.
Now go to him as you are, in your armor and helmets,
But leave your battle-shields here, and your spears,
Let them lie waiting for the promises your words
May make."
            Beowulf arose, with his men
135 Around him, ordering a few to remain
With their weapons, leading the others quickly
Along under Herot's steep roof into Hrothgar's
Presence. Standing on that prince's own hearth,
Helmeted, the silvery metal of his mail shirt[9]
140 Gleaming with a smith's high art,[10] he greeted
The Danes' great lord: ▶
            "Hail, Hrothgar!
Higlac is my cousin[11] and my king; the days
Of my youth have been filled with glory. Now Grendel's
Name has echoed in our land: sailors

TESTSMART

Which phrase *best* sums up
the Beowulf poet's tone in
lines 134–141?

(A) respectful admiration

(B) doubtful consideration

(C) reluctant respect

(D) concealed contempt

TIP A test question
may ask about **tone,** the
author's attitude toward
the character or subject.
To answer a question
about tone, reread the
text and **think about the
connotations of the words**
the author has used. In this
case, the words used to
describe Beowulf's actions
("ordering" and "leading")
and appearance ("Gleaming
with a smith's high art")
can help you figure out the
poet's attitude toward him.

---

9. **mail shirt:** flexible body armor made of metal links or overlapping metal scales.

10. **smith's high art:** the skilled craft of a blacksmith (a person who fashions objects
    from iron).

11. **cousin:** here, a general term for a relative. Beowulf is actually Higlac's nephew.

145 Have brought us stories of Herot, the best
Of all mead-halls, deserted and useless when the moon
Hangs in skies the sun had lit,
Light and life fleeing together.

My people have said, the wisest, most knowing
150 And best of them, that my duty was to go to the Danes'
Great king. They have seen my strength for themselves,
Have watched me rise from the darkness of war,
Dripping with my enemies' blood. I drove
Five great giants into chains, chased
155 All of that race from the earth. I swam
In the blackness of night, hunting monsters
Out of the ocean, and killing them one
By one; death was my errand and the fate
They had earned. Now Grendel and I are called
160 Together, and I've come. Grant me, then, ◀
Lord and protector of this noble place,
A single request! I have come so far,
Oh shelterer of warriors and your people's loved friend,
That this one favor you should not refuse me—
165 That I, alone and with the help of my men,
May **purge** all evil from this hall. I have heard,
Too, that the monster's scorn of men
Is so great that he needs no weapons and fears none.
Nor will I. My lord Higlac
170 Might think less of me if I let my sword
Go where my feet were afraid to, if I hid
Behind some broad linden shield:[12] my hands
Alone shall fight for me, struggle for life
Against the monster.[13] God must decide ◀
175 Who will be given to death's cold grip.
Grendel's plan, I think, will be
What it has been before, to invade this hall
And **gorge** his belly with our bodies. If he can,
If he can. And I think, if my time will have come,
180 There'll be nothing to mourn over, no corpse to prepare
For its grave: Grendel will carry our bloody
Flesh to the moors, crunch on our bones

MAKE GENERALIZATIONS

Underline each accomplishment Beowulf mentions in the boxed text. Why do you think people from Beowulf's time valued this kind of superhuman strength and courage?

_____

_____

purge (pûrj) *v.* to cleanse or rid of something undesirable

MAKE JUDGMENTS

Beowulf insists that "my hands / Alone shall fight for me." In your opinion, is this promise courageous or foolish? Why?

_____

_____

gorge (gôrj) *v.* to stuff with food; glut

12. **linden shield:** a shield made from the wood of a linden tree.
13. Beowulf insists on fighting Grendel without weapons.

And smear torn scraps of our skin on the walls

Of his den. No, I expect no Danes

185 Will fret about sewing our shrouds,[14] if he wins.

And if death does take me, send the hammered

Mail of my armor to Higlac, return

The inheritance I had from Hrethel,[15] and he

From Wayland.[16] Fate will unwind as it must!" ▶

190   Hrothgar replied, protector of the Danes:

      "Beowulf, you've come to us in friendship, and because

Of the reception your father found at our court.

Edgetho[17] had begun a bitter feud,

Killing Hathlaf, a Wulfing[18] warrior:

195 Your father's countrymen were afraid of war,

If he returned to his home, and they turned him away.

Then he traveled across the curving waves

To the land of the Danes. I was new to the throne,

Then, a young man ruling this wide

200 Kingdom and its golden city: Hergar,

My older brother, a far better man

Than I, had died and dying made me,

Second among Healfdane's sons, first

In this nation. I bought the end of Edgetho's

205 Quarrel, sent ancient treasures through the ocean's

Furrows to the Wulfings; your father swore

He'd keep that peace. My tongue grows heavy,

And my heart, when I try to tell you what Grendel

Has brought us, the damage he's done, here

210 In this hall. You see for yourself how much smaller

Our ranks have become, and can guess what we've lost

To his terror. Surely the Lord Almighty

Could stop his madness, smother his lust! ▶

How many times have my men, glowing

215 With courage drawn from too many cups

Of ale, sworn to stay after dark

---

14. **shrouds:** cloths in which dead bodies are wrapped.

15. **Hrethel** (hrĕth′əl): a former king of the Geats—Higlac's father and Beowulf's
grandfather.

16. **Wayland:** a famous blacksmith and magician.

17. **Edgetho** (ĕj′thō): Beowulf's father.

18. **Wulfing:** a member of another Germanic tribe.

COMPARE

Reread the command in the boxed text. At what other time (later in the story) does Beowulf dictate what should happen upon his death?

_____

_____

Compare these two commands.

_____

_____

_____

_____

ANALYZE

What values does Hrothgar convey during his long speech to Beowulf?

_____

_____

_____

Underline the statements that support your answer. ✎

And stem that horror with a sweep of their swords.
And then, in the morning, this mead-hall glittering
With new light would be drenched with blood, the benches
220 Stained red, the floors, all wet from that fiend's
Savage assault—and my soldiers would be fewer
Still, death taking more and more.
But to table, Beowulf, a banquet in your honor:
Let us toast your victories, and talk of the future."
225   Then Hrothgar's men gave places to the Geats,
Yielded benches to the brave visitors
And led them to the feast. The keeper of the mead
Came carrying out the carved flasks,
And poured that bright sweetness. A poet
230 Sang, from time to time, in a clear
Pure voice. Danes and visiting Geats
Celebrated as one, drank and rejoiced. . . :

THE BATTLE WITH GRENDEL

*After the banquet, Hrothgar and his followers leave Herot, and Beowulf and
his warriors remain to spend the night. Beowulf reiterates his intent to fight
Grendel without a sword and, while his followers sleep, lies waiting, eager for
Grendel to appear.*

    Out from the marsh, from the foot of misty
Hills and bogs, bearing God's hatred,
235 Grendel came, hoping to kill
Anyone he could trap on this trip to high Herot. ◀
He moved quickly through the cloudy night,
Up from his swampland, sliding silently
Toward that gold-shining hall. He had visited Hrothgar's
240 Home before, knew the way—
But never, before nor after that night,
Found Herot defended so firmly, his reception
So harsh. He journeyed, forever joyless,
Straight to the door, then snapped it open,
245 Tore its iron fasteners with a touch
And rushed angrily over the threshold.[19]
He strode quickly across the inlaid
Floor, snarling and fierce: his eyes

ANALYZE

Read the boxed text and
underline each **caesura,** or
midline pause. 🖊

In what way does the rhythm
created by these pauses
reinforce the action described
here?

_____

_____

_____

---

19. **threshold:** the strip of wood or stone at the bottom of a doorway.

Gleamed in the darkness, burned with a gruesome
250 Light. Then he stopped, seeing the hall
Crowded with sleeping warriors, stuffed
With rows of young soldiers resting together.
And his heart laughed, he relished the sight,
Intended to tear the life from those bodies
255 By morning; the monster's mind was hot
With the thought of food and the feasting his belly
Would soon know. But fate, that night, intended
Grendel to gnaw the broken bones
Of his last human supper. Human
260 Eyes were watching his evil steps,
Waiting to see his swift hard claws.
Grendel snatched at the first Geat
He came to, ripped him apart, cut
His body to bits with powerful jaws,
265 Drank the blood from his veins and bolted
Him down, hands and feet; death
And Grendel's great teeth came together,
Snapping life shut. Then he stepped to another
Still body, clutched at Beowulf with his claws,
270 Grasped at a strong-hearted wakeful sleeper
—And was instantly seized himself, claws
Bent back as Beowulf leaned up on one arm.
    That shepherd of evil, guardian of crime,
Knew at once that nowhere on earth
275 Had he met a man whose hands were harder;
His mind was flooded with fear—but nothing
Could take his **talons** and himself from that tight
Hard grip. Grendel's one thought was to run ▶
From Beowulf, flee back to his marsh and hide there:
280 This was a different Herot than the hall he had emptied.
But Higlac's follower remembered his final
Boast and, standing erect, stopped
The monster's flight, fastened those claws
In his fists till they cracked, clutched Grendel
285 Closer. The **infamous** killer fought
For his freedom, wanting no flesh but retreat,
Desiring nothing but escape; his claws
Had been caught, he was trapped. That trip to Herot
Was a miserable journey for the writhing monster!

talon (tăl′ən) *n.* a claw

TESTSMART

Which phrase from lines 273–278 is an example of a kenning?

Ⓐ that shepherd of evil

Ⓑ flooded with fear

Ⓒ take his talons

Ⓓ that tight / Hard grip

TIP Remember that a **kenning** is a metaphorical compound word or phrase that takes the place of a simple noun, such as a name. To determine which phrase is a kenning in this question, ask yourself which one could be a **substitute** for *Grendel*.

infamous (ĭn′fə-məs) *adj.* having a very bad reputation

290   The high hall rang, its roof boards swayed,
And Danes shook with terror. Down
The aisles the battle swept, angry
And wild. Herot trembled, wonderfully
Built to withstand the blows, the struggling
295 Great bodies beating at its beautiful walls;
Shaped and fastened with iron, inside
And out, artfully worked, the building
Stood firm. Its benches rattled, fell
To the floor, gold-covered boards grating
300 As Grendel and Beowulf battled across them.
Hrothgar's wise men had fashioned Herot
To stand forever; only fire,
They had planned, could shatter what such skill had put
Together, swallow in hot flames such splendor
305 Of ivory and iron and wood. Suddenly ◀
The sounds changed, the Danes started
In new terror, cowering in their beds as the terrible
Screams of the Almighty's enemy sang
In the darkness, the horrible shrieks of pain
310 And defeat, the tears torn out of Grendel's
Taut throat, hell's captive caught in the arms
Of him who of all the men on earth
Was the strongest.

                    That mighty protector of men
Meant to hold the monster till its life
315 Leaped out, knowing the fiend was no use
To anyone in Denmark. All of Beowulf's
Band had jumped from their beds, ancestral
Swords raised and ready, determined
To protect their prince if they could. Their courage
320 Was great but all wasted: they could hack at Grendel
From every side, trying to open
A path for his evil soul, but their points
Could not hurt him, the sharpest and hardest iron
Could not scratch at his skin, for that sin-stained demon
325 Had bewitched all men's weapons, laid spells
That blunted every mortal man's blade.
And yet his time had come, his days
Were over, his death near; down

CONTRAST

Underline words and phrases in lines 293–305 that help you visualize Herot.

Then briefly contrast Herot with Grendel's home.

_____

_____

_____

_____

To hell he would go, swept groaning and helpless
330 To the waiting hands of still worse fiends.
Now he discovered—once the afflictor
Of men, tormentor of their days—what it meant
To feud with Almighty God: Grendel
Saw that his strength was deserting him, his claws
335 Bound fast, Higlac's brave follower tearing at
His hands. The monster's hatred rose higher,
But his power had gone. He twisted in pain,
And the bleeding sinews[20] deep in his shoulder
Snapped, muscle and bone split
340 And broke. The battle was over, Beowulf
Had been granted new glory: Grendel escaped,
But wounded as he was could flee to his den,
His miserable hole at the bottom of the marsh,
Only to die, to wait for the end
345 Of all his days. And after that bloody ▶
Combat the Danes laughed with delight.
He who had come to them from across the sea,
Bold and strong-minded, had driven affliction
Off, purged Herot clean. He was happy,
350 Now, with that night's fierce work; the Danes
Had been served as he'd boasted he'd serve them; Beowulf,
A prince of the Geats, had killed Grendel,
Ended the grief, the sorrow, the suffering
Forced on Hrothgar's helpless people
355 By a bloodthirsty fiend. No Dane doubted
The victory, for the proof, hanging high
From the rafters where Beowulf had hung it, was the monster's
Arm, claw and shoulder and all. ▶

And then, in the morning, crowds surrounded
360 Herot, warriors coming to that hall
From faraway lands, princes and leaders
Of men hurrying to behold the monster's
Great staggering tracks. They gaped with no sense
Of sorrow, felt no regret for his suffering,
365 Went tracing his bloody footprints, his beaten
And lonely flight, to the edge of the lake

---

20. **sinews** (sĭn′yo͞oz): the tendons that connect muscles to bones.

VISUALIZE

Reread the boxed text. Underline examples of imagery the poet uses to help you visualize the defeat of Grendel. ✎

ANALYZE

What **character traits** does Beowulf reveal during and after his battle with Grendel?

During the battle: _____

_____

_____

_____

After the battle: _____

_____

_____

_____

Where he'd dragged his corpselike way, doomed
And already weary of his vanishing life.
The water was bloody, steaming and boiling
370 In horrible pounding waves, heat
Sucked from his magic veins; but the swirling
Surf had covered his death, hidden
Deep in murky darkness his miserable
End, as hell opened to receive him.

375   Then old and young rejoiced, turned back
From that happy pilgrimage, mounted their hard-hooved
Horses, high-spirited stallions, and rode them
Slowly toward Herot again, retelling
Beowulf's bravery as they jogged along.
380 And over and over they swore that nowhere
On earth or under the spreading sky
Or between the seas, neither south nor north,
Was there a warrior worthier to rule over men.
(But no one meant Beowulf's praise to belittle
385 Hrothgar, their kind and gracious king!)
        And sometimes, when the path ran straight and clear,
They would let their horses race, red
And brown and pale yellow backs streaming
Down the road. And sometimes a proud old soldier
390 Who had heard songs of the ancient heroes
And could sing them all through, story after story,
Would weave a net of words for Beowulf's
Victory, tying the knot of his verses
Smoothly, swiftly, into place with a poet's
395 Quick skill, singing his new song aloud
While he shaped it, and the old songs as well. . . .

ANALYZE

Reread the boxed text. In what ways does the description of the old soldier's storytelling reflect the characteristics of **epic** poetry?

_____

_____

_____

_____

GRENDEL'S MOTHER

Although one monster has died, another still lives. From her lair in a cold and murky lake, where she has been brooding over her loss, Grendel's mother emerges, bent on revenge.

  So she reached Herot,
Where the Danes slept as though already dead;
Her visit ended their good fortune, reversed
400 The bright vane[21] of their luck. No female, no matter
How fierce, could have come with a man's strength,
Fought with the power and courage men fight with,
Smashing their shining swords, their bloody,
Hammer-forged blades onto boar-headed helmets,[22]
405 Slashing and stabbing with the sharpest of points.
The soldiers raised their shields and drew
Those gleaming swords, swung them above
The piled-up benches, leaving their mail shirts
And their helmets where they'd lain when the terror took hold of them.
410 To save her life she moved still faster,
Took a single victim and fled from the hall,
Running to the moors, discovered, but her supper
Assured, sheltered in her dripping claws.
She'd taken Hrothgar's closest friend,
415 The man he most loved of all men on earth;
She'd killed a glorious soldier, cut
A noble life short. No Geat could have stopped her:
Beowulf and his band had been given better
Beds; sleep had come to them in a different
420 Hall. Then all Herot burst into shouts:
She had carried off Grendel's claw. Sorrow
Had returned to Denmark. They'd traded deaths,
Danes and monsters, and no one had won,
Both had lost! . . . ▶

MAKE JUDGMENTS

Underline vivid words and phrases that help you visualize the rampage of Grendel's mother. ✎

Do you think she should be judged as harshly for her actions as Grendel was for his? Explain.

_____

_____

_____

_____

---

21. **vane:** a device that turns to show the direction the wind is blowing—here associated metaphorically with luck, which is as changeable as the wind.

22. **boar-headed helmets:** Germanic warriors often wore helmets bearing the images of wild pigs or other fierce creatures in the hope that the images would increase their ferocity and protect them against their enemies.

Devastated by the loss of his friend, Hrothgar sends for Beowulf and recounts
what Grendel's mother has done. Then Hrothgar describes the dark lake where
Grendel's mother has dwelt with her son.

425 "They live in secret places, windy
Cliffs, wolf-dens where water pours
From the rocks, then runs underground, where mist
Steams like black clouds, and the groves of trees
Growing out over their lake are all covered
430 With frozen spray, and wind down snakelike
Roots that reach as far as the water
And help keep it dark. At night that lake
Burns like a torch. No one knows its bottom,
No wisdom reaches such depths. A deer,
435 Hunted through the woods by packs of hounds,
A stag with great horns, though driven through the forest
From faraway places, prefers to die
On those shores, refuses to save its life
In that water. It isn't far, nor is it
440 A pleasant spot! When the wind stirs
And storms, waves splash toward the sky,
As dark as the air, as black as the rain
That the heavens weep. Our only help, ◀

Again, lies with you. Grendel's mother
445 Is hidden in her terrible home, in a place
You've not seen. Seek it, if you dare! Save us,
Once more, and again twisted gold,
Heaped-up ancient treasure, will reward you
For the battle you win!"[23] . . .

THE BATTLE WITH GRENDEL'S MOTHER
*Beowulf accepts Hrothgar's challenge, and the king and his men accompany the
hero to the dreadful lair of Grendel's mother. Fearlessly, Beowulf prepares to
battle the terrible creature.*

450   He leaped into the lake, would not wait for anyone's
Answer; the heaving water covered him
Over. For hours he sank through the waves;

MAKE INFERENCES

Circle words in the boxed text
that create a vivid impression
of the lake where Grendel's
mother lives. 🖊

Why might the Beowulf poet
have chosen to include such a
long description of the lake?

_____

_____

_____

_____

23. Germanic warriors placed great importance on amassing treasure as a way of
acquiring fame and temporarily defeating fate.

At last he saw the mud of the bottom.
And all at once the greedy she-wolf
455 Who'd ruled those waters for half a hundred
Years discovered him, saw that a creature
From above had come to explore the bottom
Of her wet world. She welcomed him in her claws,
Clutched at him savagely but could not harm him,
460 Tried to work her fingers through the tight
Ring-woven mail on his breast, but tore
And scratched in vain. Then she carried him, armor
And sword and all, to her home; he struggled
To free his weapon, and failed. The fight
465 Brought other monsters swimming to see
Her catch, a host of sea beasts who beat at
His mail shirt, stabbing with tusks and teeth
As they followed along. Then he realized, suddenly,
That she'd brought him into someone's battle-hall,
470 And there the water's heat could not hurt him,
Nor anything in the lake attack him through
The building's high-arching roof. A brilliant
Light burned all around him, the lake
Itself like a fiery flame. ▶
                    Then he saw
475 The mighty water witch, and swung his sword,
His ring-marked blade,[24] straight at her head;
The iron sang its fierce song,
Sang Beowulf's strength. But her guest
Discovered that no sword could slice her evil
480 Skin, that Hrunting[25] could not hurt her, was useless
Now when he needed it. They wrestled, she ripped
And tore and clawed at him, bit holes in his helmet,
And that too failed him; for the first time in years
Of being worn to war it would earn no glory;
485 It was the last time anyone would wear it. But Beowulf
Longed only for fame, leaped back
Into battle. He tossed his sword aside,

ANALYZE

Reread the boxed text. Look for details of the battle and its setting that are characteristic of an **epic**. Then write a detail beneath each characteristic below.

Grand-scale setting:

_____

Powerful, supernatural enemies:

_____

The hero's superhuman feat:

_____

---

24. **his ring-marked blade:** For the battle with Grendel's mother, Beowulf has been given an heirloom sword with an intricately etched blade.

25. **Hrunting** (hrŭn'tĭng): the name of Beowulf's sword. (Germanic warriors' swords were possessions of such value that they were often given names.)

Angry; the steel-edged blade lay where
He'd dropped it. If weapons were useless he'd use
490 His hands, the strength in his fingers. So fame
Comes to the men who mean to win it
And care about nothing else! He raised
His arms and seized her by the shoulder; anger
Doubled his strength, he threw her to the floor.
495 She fell, Grendel's fierce mother, and the Geats'
Proud prince was ready to leap on her. But she rose
At once and repaid him with her clutching claws,
Wildly tearing at him. He was weary, that best
And strongest of soldiers; his feet stumbled
500 And in an instant she had him down, held helpless.
Squatting with her weight on his stomach, she drew
A dagger, brown with dried blood, and prepared
To avenge her only son. But he was stretched
On his back, and her stabbing blade was blunted
505 By the woven mail shirt he wore on his chest.
The hammered links held; the point
Could not touch him. He'd have traveled to the bottom of the earth,
Edgetho's son, and died there, if that shining
Woven metal had not helped—and Holy
510 God, who sent him victory, gave judgment
For truth and right, Ruler of the Heavens,
Once Beowulf was back on his feet and fighting.

Then he saw, hanging on the wall, a heavy
Sword, hammered by giants, strong
515 And blessed with their magic, the best of all weapons
But so massive that no ordinary man could lift
Its carved and decorated length. He drew it
From its scabbard, broke the chain on its hilt,
And then, savage, now, angry
520 And desperate, lifted it high over his head
And struck with all the strength he had left,
Caught her in the neck and cut it through,
Broke bones and all. Her body fell
To the floor, lifeless, the sword was wet
525 With her blood, and Beowulf rejoiced at the sight. ◀

CONTRAST

In what ways does Beowulf's battle with Grendel's mother differ from his earlier battle with her son?

_____

_____

_____

_____

The brilliant light shone, suddenly,
As though burning in that hall, and as bright as Heaven's
Own candle, lit in the sky. He looked
At her home, then following along the wall
530 Went walking, his hands tight on the sword,
His heart still angry. He was hunting another
Dead monster, and took his weapon with him
For final revenge against Grendel's vicious
Attacks, his nighttime raids, over
535 And over, coming to Herot when Hrothgar's
Men slept, killing them in their beds,
Eating some on the spot, fifteen
Or more, and running to his <u>loathsome</u> moor
With another such sickening meal waiting
540 In his pouch. But Beowulf repaid him for those visits,
Found him lying dead in his corner,
Armless, exactly as that fierce fighter
Had sent him out from Herot, then struck off
His head with a single swift blow. The body
545 Jerked for the last time, then lay still.

The wise old warriors who surrounded Hrothgar,
Like him staring into the monsters' lake,
Saw the waves surging and blood
Spurting through. They spoke about Beowulf,
550 All the graybeards,[26] whispered together
And said that hope was gone, that the hero
Had lost fame and his life at once, and would never
Return to the living, come back as triumphant
As he had left; almost all agreed that Grendel's
555 Mighty mother, the she-wolf, had killed him.
The sun slid over past noon, went further
Down. The Danes gave up, left
The lake and went home, Hrothgar with them.
The Geats stayed, sat sadly, watching,
560 Imagining they saw their lord but not believing
They would ever see him again. ▶
                                    —Then the sword
Melted, blood-soaked, dripping down
Like water, disappearing like ice when the world's

loathsome (lōth'səm) *adj.*
disgusting

MAKE INFERENCES

Why do you think Hrothgar's men lose faith in Beowulf and leave the lake, while Beowulf's men remain?

_____

_____

_____

_____

---

26. **graybeards:** old men.

What does the word *fetters* mean in line 565?

(A) furry animals

(B) chains

(C) stars

(D) gold coins

TIP When a test question asks about an unfamiliar word, reread the sentence in which the word appears and replace it with each of the choices. **Use context clues from the sentence** to decide which answer makes the most sense.

DRAW CONCLUSIONS

Why do you think the Geats want the Danes to see Grendel's head?

_____

_____

_____

Eternal Lord loosens invisible

565 Fetters and unwinds icicles and frost ◀

As only He can, He who rules

Time and seasons, He who is truly

God. The monsters' hall was full of

Rich treasures, but all that Beowulf took

570 Was Grendel's head and the hilt of the giants'

Jeweled sword; the rest of that ring-marked

Blade had dissolved in Grendel's steaming

Blood, boiling even after his death.

And then the battle's only survivor

575 Swam up and away from those silent corpses;

The water was calm and clean, the whole

Huge lake peaceful once the demons who'd lived in it

Were dead.

     Then that noble protector of all seamen[27]

Swam to land, rejoicing in the heavy

580 Burdens he was bringing with him. He

And all his glorious band of Geats

Thanked God that their leader had come back unharmed;

They left the lake together. The Geats

Carried Beowulf's helmet, and his mail shirt.

585 Behind them the water slowly thickened

As the monsters' blood came seeping up.

They walked quickly, happily, across

Roads all of them remembered, left

The lake and the cliffs alongside it, brave men

590 Staggering under the weight of Grendel's skull,

Too heavy for fewer than four of them to handle—

Two on each side of the spear jammed through it—

Yet proud of their ugly load and determined

That the Danes, seated in Herot, should see it. ◀

595 Soon, fourteen Geats arrived

At the hall, bold and warlike, and with Beowulf,

Their lord and leader, they walked on the mead-hall

Green. Then the Geats' brave prince entered

Herot, covered with glory for the daring

600 Battles he had fought; he sought Hrothgar

---

27. **that noble protector of all seamen:** Beowulf, who will be buried in a tower that will serve as a navigational aid to sailors.

To salute him and show Grendel's head.
He carried that terrible trophy by the hair,
Brought it straight to where the Danes sat,
Drinking, the queen[28] among them. It was a weird
605 And wonderful sight, and the warriors stared. . . . ▶

BEOWULF'S LAST BATTLE

With Grendel's mother destroyed, peace is restored to the land of the Danes,
and Beowulf, laden with Hrothgar's gifts, returns to the land of his own
people, the Geats. After his uncle and cousin die, Beowulf becomes king of
the Geats and rules in peace and prosperity for 50 years. One day, however, a
fire-breathing dragon that has been guarding a treasure for hundreds of years
is disturbed by a thief, who enters the treasure tower and steals a cup. The
dragon begins terrorizing the Geats, and Beowulf, now an old man, takes on
the challenge of fighting it.

　　And Beowulf uttered his final boast:
　　"I've never known fear, as a youth I fought
In endless battles. I am old, now,
But I will fight again, seek fame still,
610 If the dragon hiding in his tower dares
To face me."
　　　　　　Then he said farewell to his followers,
Each in his turn, for the last time:
　　"I'd use no sword, no weapon, if this beast
Could be killed without it, crushed to death
615 Like Grendel, gripped in my hands and torn
Limb from limb. But his breath will be burning
Hot, poison will pour from his tongue.
I feel no shame, with shield and sword
And armor, against this monster: when he comes to me
620 I mean to stand, not run from his shooting
Flames, stand till fate decides
Which of us wins. My heart is firm,
My hands calm: I need no hot
Words. Wait for me close by, my friends.
625 We shall see, soon, who will survive
This bloody battle, stand when the fighting ▶

---

28. **queen:** Welthow, wife of Hrothgar.

MAKE JUDGMENTS

What do you think Beowulf's followers should have done when he described his plans to fight the dragon alone?

_____

_____

_____

_____

Is done. No one else could do
What I mean to, here, no man but me
Could hope to defeat this monster. No one
630 Could try. And this dragon's treasure, his gold
And everything hidden in that tower, will be mine
Or war will sweep me to a bitter death!"

Then Beowulf rose, still brave, still strong,
And with his shield at his side, and a mail shirt on his breast,
635 Strode calmly, confidently, toward the tower, under
The rocky cliffs: no coward could have walked there!
And then he who'd endured dozens of desperate
Battles, who'd stood boldly while swords and shields
Clashed, the best of kings, saw
640 Huge stone arches and felt the heat
Of the dragon's breath, flooding down
Through the hidden entrance, too hot for anyone
To stand, a streaming current of fire
And smoke that blocked all passage. And the Geats'
645 Lord and leader, angry, lowered
His sword and roared out a battle cry,
A call so loud and clear that it reached through
The hoary²⁹ rock, hung in the dragon's
Ear. The beast rose, angry,
650 Knowing a man had come—and then nothing
But war could have followed. Its breath came first,
A steaming cloud pouring from the stone,
Then the earth itself shook. Beowulf
Swung his shield into place, held it
655 In front of him, facing the entrance. The dragon
Coiled and uncoiled, its heart urging it
Into battle. Beowulf's ancient sword
Was waiting, unsheathed, his sharp and gleaming
Blade. The beast came closer; both of them
660 Were ready, each set on slaughter. The Geats'
Great prince stood firm, unmoving, prepared
Behind his high shield, waiting in his shining
Armor. The monster came quickly toward him,
Pouring out fire and smoke, hurrying
665 To its fate. Flames beat at the iron

---

29. **hoary** (hôr′ē): gray with age.

MAKE JUDGMENTS

What are your own thoughts about Beowulf's actions at this point in the narrative? Is he behaving the way a wise king should?

_____

_____

_____

ANALYZE

Reread the boxed text. Underline examples of imagery the poet uses to set the stage for Beowulf's last climactic battle.

Then write three adjectives that describe each character.

The dragon:

1. _____

2. _____

3. _____

Beowulf:

1. _____

2. _____

3. _____

Shield, and for a time it held, protected
Beowulf as he'd planned; then it began to melt,
And for the first time in his life that famous prince
Fought with fate against him, with glory
670 Denied him. He knew it, but he raised his sword
And struck at the dragon's scaly hide.
The ancient blade broke, bit into
The monster's skin, drew blood, but cracked
And failed him before it went deep enough, helped him
675 Less than he needed. The dragon leaped
With pain, thrashed and beat at him, spouting
Murderous flames, spreading them everywhere.
And the Geats' ring-giver[30] did not boast of glorious
Victories in other wars: his weapon
680 Had failed him, deserted him, now when he needed it
Most, that excellent sword. Edgetho's
Famous son stared at death,
Unwilling to leave this world, to exchange it
For a dwelling in some distant place—a journey
685 Into darkness that all men must make, as death
Ends their few brief hours on earth. ▶

Quickly, the dragon came at him, encouraged
As Beowulf fell back; its breath flared,
And he suffered, wrapped around in swirling
690 Flames—a king, before, but now
A beaten warrior. None of his comrades
Came to him, helped him, his brave and noble
Followers; they ran for their lives, fled
Deep in a wood. And only one of them
695 Remained, stood there, miserable, remembering,
As a good man must, what kinship should mean.
His name was Wiglaf, he was Wexstan's son
And a good soldier; his family had been Swedish,
Once. Watching Beowulf, he could see
700 How his king was suffering, burning. Remembering
Everything his lord and cousin had given him,
Armor and gold and the great estates

---

30. **ring-giver:** king; lord. When a man swore allegiance to a Germanic lord in return for his protection, the lord typically bestowed a ring on his follower to symbolize the bond.

Wexstan's family enjoyed, Wiglaf's
Mind was made up; he raised his yellow
705 Shield and drew his sword. . . .
       And Wiglaf, his heart heavy, uttered
The kind of words his comrades deserved:
       "I remember how we sat in the mead-hall, drinking
And boasting of how brave we'd be when Beowulf
710 Needed us, he who gave us these swords
And armor: all of us swore to repay him,
When the time came, kindness for kindness
—With our lives, if he needed them. He allowed us to join him,
Chose us from all his great army, thinking
715 Our boasting words had some weight, believing
Our promises, trusting our swords. He took us
For soldiers, for men. He meant to kill
This monster himself, our mighty king,
Fight this battle alone and unaided,
720 As in the days when his strength and daring dazzled
Men's eyes. But those days are over and gone
And now our lord must lean on younger
Arms. And we must go to him, while angry
Flames burn at his flesh, help
725 Our glorious king! By almighty God,
I'd rather burn myself than see
Flames swirling around my lord.
And who are we to carry home
Our shields before we've slain his enemy
730 And ours, to run back to our homes with Beowulf
So hard-pressed here? I swear that nothing
He ever did deserved an end
Like this, dying miserably and alone,
Butchered by this savage beast: we swore
735 That these swords and armor were each for us all!" . . . ◀

TestSmart

Which of the following values does Wiglaf *not* appeal to in his speech to the Geat warriors?

(A) pride

(B) ambition

(C) loyalty

(D) sympathy

TIP If a test question asks about what is *not* in the text, you can use the **process of elimination** to find the correct answer. To answer this question, reread the speech to see which values Wiglaf appeals to. If you find an answer choice reflected in the text, you can eliminate it, or take it off the list of possible correct answers. For example, when Wiglaf reminds the warriors that they boasted of how brave they would be if Beowulf ever needed them, he is appealing to their pride, so you know that A is not the correct answer.

THE DEATH OF BEOWULF

Wiglaf joins Beowulf, who again attacks the dragon single-handed; but the remnant of his sword shatters, and the monster wounds him in the neck. Wiglaf then strikes the dragon, and he and Beowulf together finally succeed in killing the beast. Their triumph is short-lived, however, because Beowulf's wound proves to be mortal.

     Beowulf spoke, in spite of the swollen,
<u>Livid</u> wound, knowing he'd unwound
His string of days on earth, seen
As much as God would grant him; all worldly
740 Pleasure was gone, as life would go,
Soon:
       "I'd leave my armor to my son,
Now, if God had given me an heir,
A child born of my body, his life
Created from mine. I've worn this crown
745 For fifty winters: no neighboring people
Have tried to threaten the Geats, sent soldiers
Against us or talked of terror. My days
Have gone by as fate willed, waiting
For its word to be spoken, ruling as well
750 As I knew how, swearing no unholy oaths,
Seeking no lying wars. I can leave
This life happy; I can die, here,
Knowing the Lord of all life has never
Watched me wash my sword in blood
755 Born of my own family. Belovèd
Wiglaf, go, quickly, find
The dragon's treasure: we've taken its life,
But its gold is ours, too. Hurry,
Bring me ancient silver, precious
760 Jewels, shining armor and gems,
Before I die. Death will be softer,
Leaving life and this people I've ruled
So long, if I look at this last of all prizes." ▶

     Then Wexstan's son went in, as quickly
765 As he could, did as the dying Beowulf
Asked, entered the inner darkness
Of the tower, went with his mail shirt and his sword.

---

livid (lĭv'ĭd) *adj.* discolored from being bruised

DRAW CONCLUSIONS

Reread the boxed text. What does this reference to material rewards (as well as other references to riches elsewhere in the poem) tell you about the Anglo-Saxon's view of treasures?

_____

_____

_____

_____

Flushed with victory he groped his way,
A brave young warrior, and suddenly saw
770 Piles of gleaming gold, precious
Gems, scattered on the floor, cups
And bracelets, rusty old helmets, beautifully
Made but rotting with no hands to rub
And polish them. They lay where the dragon left them;
775 It had flown in the darkness, once, before fighting
Its final battle. (So gold can easily
Triumph, defeat the strongest of men,
No matter how deep it is hidden!) And he saw,
Hanging high above, a golden
780 Banner, woven by the best of weavers
And beautiful. And over everything he saw
A strange light, shining everywhere,
On walls and floor and treasure. Nothing
Moved, no other monsters appeared;
785 He took what he wanted, all the treasures
That pleased his eye, heavy plates
And golden cups and the glorious banner,
Loaded his arms with all they could hold.
Beowulf's dagger, his iron blade,
790 Had finished the fire-spitting terror
That once protected tower and treasures
Alike; the gray-bearded lord of the Geats
Had ended those flying, burning raids
Forever. ◀

Then Wiglaf went back, anxious
795 To return while Beowulf was alive, to bring him
Treasure they'd won together. He ran,
Hoping his wounded king, weak
And dying, had not left the world too soon.
Then he brought their treasure to Beowulf, and found
800 His famous king bloody, gasping
For breath. But Wiglaf sprinkled water
Over his lord, until the words
Deep in his breast broke through and were heard.
Beholding the treasure he spoke, haltingly:
805   "For this, this gold, these jewels, I thank
Our Father in Heaven, Ruler of the Earth—
For all of this, that His grace has given me,

INTERPRET

In the boxed text, underline the **kenning** that refers to Beowulf and another one that refers to the dragon. What do these descriptions emphasize about each character?

The dragon:

_____

_____

_____

Beowulf:

_____

_____

_____

_____

Allowed me to bring to my people while breath
Still came to my lips. I sold my life
810 For this treasure, and I sold it well. Take ▶
What I leave, Wiglaf, lead my people,
Help them; my time is gone. Have
The brave Geats build me a tomb,
When the funeral flames have burned me, and build it
815 Here, at the water's edge, high
On this spit³¹ of land, so sailors can see
This tower, and remember my name, and call it
Beowulf's tower, and boats in the darkness
And mist, crossing the sea, will know it."
820   Then that brave king gave the golden
Necklace from around his throat to Wiglaf,
Gave him his gold-covered helmet, and his rings,
And his mail shirt, and ordered him to use them well:
    "You're the last of all our far-flung family.
825 Fate has swept our race away,
Taken warriors in their strength and led them
To the death that was waiting. And now I follow them."
    The old man's mouth was silent, spoke
No more, had said as much as it could;
830 He would sleep in the fire, soon. His soul
Left his flesh, flew to glory. . . . ▶
    And when the battle was over Beowulf's followers
Came out of the wood, cowards and traitors,
Knowing the dragon was dead. Afraid,
835 While it spit its fires, to fight in their lord's
Defense, to throw their javelins³² and spears,
They came like shamefaced jackals,³³ their shields
In their hands, to the place where the prince lay dead,
And waited for Wiglaf to speak. He was sitting
840 Near Beowulf's body, wearily sprinkling
Water in the dead man's face, trying
To stir him. He could not. No one could have kept
Life in their lord's body, or turned

---

31. **spit:** a narrow point of land extending into a body of water.

32. **javelins** (jăv′lĭnz): light spears used as weapons.

33. **jackals** (jăk′əlz): doglike animals that sometimes feed on the flesh of dead beasts.

Do you agree with Beowulf when he says that he sold his life well? Why or why not?

_____

_____

_____

MAKE GENERALIZATIONS

Underline the lines in which Beowulf describes the legacy he wishes others to construct in his memory. ✎

Why is it important for leaders to leave legacies behind?

_____

_____

_____

_____

Aside the Lord's will: world
845 And men and all move as He orders,
And always have, and always will.

Then Wiglaf turned and angrily told them
What men without courage must hear.
Wexstan's brave son stared at the traitors,
850 His heart sorrowful, and said what he had to:

"I say what anyone who speaks the truth
Must say. . . .

Too few of his warriors remembered
To come, when our lord faced death, alone.
855 And now the giving of swords, of golden
Rings and rich estates, is over,
Ended for you and everyone who shares
Your blood: when the brave Geats hear
How you bolted[34] and ran none of your race
860 Will have anything left but their lives. And death
Would be better for them all, and for you, than the kind
Of life you can lead, branded with disgrace!". . . ◀

Then the warriors rose,
Walked slowly down from the cliff, stared
865 At those wonderful sights, stood weeping as they saw
Beowulf dead on the sand, their bold
Ring-giver resting in his last bed;
He'd reached the end of his days, their mighty
War-king, the great lord of the Geats,
870 Gone to a glorious death. . . .

MOURNING BEOWULF

Then the Geats built the tower, as Beowulf
Had asked, strong and tall, so sailors
Could find it from far and wide; working
For ten long days they made his monument,
875 Sealed his ashes in walls as straight
And high as wise and willing hands
Could raise them. And the riches he and Wiglaf
Had won from the dragon, rings, necklaces,
Ancient, hammered armor—all
880 The treasures they'd taken were left there, too,

34. **bolted:** ran away; fled.

Silver and jewels buried in the sandy
Ground, back in the earth, again
And forever hidden and useless to men.
And then twelve of the bravest Geats
885 Rode their horses around the tower,
Telling their sorrow, telling stories
Of their dead king and his greatness, his glory,
Praising him for heroic deeds, for a life
As noble as his name. So should all men
890 Raise up words for their lords, warm
With love, when their shield and protector leaves
His body behind, sends his soul
On high. And so Beowulf's followers
Rode, mourning their belovèd leader,
895 Crying that no better king had ever
Lived, no prince so mild,[35] no man
So open to his people, so deserving of praise.

EVALUATE

Reread the boxed text. How would you describe the **tone** of these lines?

_____

_____

_____

Big Question

Which of the monsters in this **epic** did you find the most frightening? Explain why.

_____

_____

_____

_____

35. **mild:** gentle or kindly.

Reading Comprehension

DIRECTIONS *Answer these questions about* Beowulf *by filling in the correct ovals.*

1. Which character trait is demonstrated by Beowulf's decision to fight Grendel with his bare hands?

   (A) cleverness

   (B) bravery

   (C) caution

   (D) cruelty

2. Reread lines 425–443. Which word *best* describes the mood conveyed in this description of the lake?

   (A) menacing

   (B) solemn

   (C) humid

   (D) tranquil

3. Which line from lines 453–456 contains a caesura?

   (A) At last he saw the mud of the bottom.

   (B) And all at once the greedy she-wolf

   (C) Who'd ruled those waters for half a hundred

   (D) Years discovered him, saw that a creature

4. Which phrase from lines 475–484 is an example of a kenning?

   (A) The mighty water witch

   (B) The iron sang its fierce song

   (C) slice her evil / Skin

   (D) holes in his helmet

5. After killing the fire-breathing dragon, why does Beowulf ask Wiglaf to bring him the dragon's treasure?

   (A) He plans to give the treasure to his children.

   (B) He is afraid that the Geats will steal the treasure.

   (C) He wants to test Wiglaf's bravery.

   (D) He will get comfort from seeing his last prize.

6. Which of the following characteristics does *Beowulf* have in common with most epic poems?

   (A) a hero who slays dragons

   (B) a cold, northern setting

   (C) a serious tone

   (D) a lack of female characters

7. What does the word *fret* mean in line 185?

   (A) wear away

   (B) create a hole

   (C) worry

   (D) decorate

8. From the description in lines 513–523, you can tell that the word *scabbard* in line 518 refers to a

   (A) sea creature

   (B) handle

   (C) wound

   (D) case

Responding in Writing

9. Short Response Write a character sketch of Beowulf in the form of a speech to be delivered at his funeral. Focus on three traits that make Beowulf an epic hero.

_____

_____

_____

_____

_____

_____

TEST-TAKER'S TOOLKIT

- **ACADEMIC VOCABULARY** When you're asked to write a **character sketch,** you should briefly describe the character's important traits. You may need to infer these traits from details in the story, such as the character's words, thoughts, and actions, as well as the comments of other characters.

- **GRAPHIC ORGANIZER** Use the chart below to help you plan your response. Look back at the epic to help you remember details about Beowulf.

Trait 1	Supporting Details
Trait 2	Supporting Details
Trait 3	Supporting Details

A Monster Fit for Any Medium
NEWSPAPER ARTICLE

Use with Beowulf, *p. 2*

What's the Connection?

The epic poem *Beowulf* portrays a larger-than-life hero who battles monsters. The newspaper article "A Monster Fit for Any Medium" describes some modern interpretations of the *Beowulf* story and explores the role of monsters in imagination and culture.

INTERVIEW A CHARACTER Epics draw a sharp line between good and evil. What if that line became blurred? What if we came to see that even monsters like Grendel have a human side? Imagine that Grendel has the opportunity to respond to each question below. Write what you think his "human side" would say.

Question	What Grendel Might Say
How do you feel about having to suffer for Cain's misdeeds?	
No one believes you have a human side. How does that make you feel?	
What's it like to be the ultimate outcast?	

LEARN THE SKILL: ANALYZE MAIN IDEAS

In a newspaper article, most paragraphs have a **main idea,** or central point. Facts, descriptions, or examples related to a main idea are called **supporting details.** Here's how to identify a main idea:

- Main ideas are often expressed directly in a topic sentence.
- A main idea may just be implied or suggested by details. You can figure out the main idea by asking yourself how the details in a paragraph fit together.

For more on analyzing main ideas, see the Nonfiction Skills Handbook beginning on page R2.

A Monster Fit for Any Medium

by Willa J. Conrad

Eric Owens as the title character in the world-premiere production of *Grendel* at Los Angeles Opera

SET A PURPOSE

Monsters are no strangers to the modern arts. Consider the long history of horror movies, which always have in common a non-human or transformed human who, turned evil by some past misdeed or sin, now preys on the virtuous living. ▶

There's the vampire craze in immensely popular books (Anne
10 Rice) and television (*Buffy the Vampire Slayer*) and Wagner's perennial dwarfs, giants and dragons in the "Ring" cycle. Darth Vader, George Lucas' big screen

ANALYZE MAIN IDEAS

Summarize the main idea of the first paragraph.

idea of good talent gone terribly bad, would certainly qualify.

The ancient English epic poem *Beowulf*, in which a Swedish knight of that name defeats Grendel, the semi-human descendant of the biblical Cain (who killed his brother Abel, thus dooming his own offspring for eternity), might be called a progenitor of the hybrid monstrous form. ◀

Beowulf found its way to manuscript only around the year 1000, making it the first surviving epic in Old English. Scholars believe that its weaving of historical fact and fantasized characters was part of a centuries-old oral tradition—a true medieval classic. At least since the early 20th century, *Beowulf*, in its many translations, has been a regular in high school and college literature courses.

Yet it's not the epic quality of the tale, or even its relative familiarity to modern audiences that motivated composer Elliot Goldenthal to write his first opera using the story. It was John Gardner's 1971 novel, *Grendel*, which flips the story around to the monster's point of view.

Goldenthal's *Grendel: Transcendence of the Great Big Bad*, with libretto by the composer's longtime partner, Julie Taymor, and J. D. McClatchy, has its New York premiere performances this week at the Lincoln Center Festival after a world premiere last month in Los Angeles. . . . ◀

Taymor and McClatchy have explored this dark side of human nature in their libretto, which liberally mixes modern and Old English, strong, iconic imagery and earthy humor. The opera opens with Grendel grumbling at a ram mounting a tree stump above his lair. Later, his ancient adviser, a worldly dragon (mezzo-soprano Denyce Graves) sings "It's . . . hard, you understand, confining myself to concepts familiar to the Dark Ages."

This being a Taymor-directed production, the opera also includes puppetry, wildly imaginative costumes, dancers, and film. The title character is sung by bass-baritone Eric Owens, whom many critics have said gave a career-making performance in Los Angeles last month. Former Alvin Ailey dancer Desmond Richardson dances the silent role of Beowulf. Owens sings in modern English, but other characters and the chorus sing in excerpts from the Old English text.

"Throughout the opera, Grendel isn't just one thing," Owens, 35, says. Indeed, Taymor and McClatchy's Grendel is a multi-faceted character aware of his humanity but unable to channel the rage he feels at being outcast and defined as pure evil by his enemies, the Danes. He also has a disturbing habit of eating children, an instinct so basic he barely realizes he is acting on it

---

INTERPRET

What does the author mean when she says that Grendel is "a progenitor of the hybrid monstrous form"?

_____

_____

_____

_____

SPECIALIZED Vocabulary

Many specialized terms are associated with opera. The word *libretto* (line 49) refers to the text of an opera. General context clues can help you determine that *mezzo-soprano* (lines 65–66) and *bass baritone* (line 74) refer to a singer's musical range.

until too late. Much of the action takes place inside Grendel's mind, which it falls to Owens to portray in numerous solo arias. ▶

"That's what happens in the novel as well, this idea of nihilism and Grendel rattling around alone in his head," Owens says. "It's more stream of consciousness than linear narrative, and, in a way, it's easier for me on stage to just follow what's in my head."

This flipping about of the emphasis and viewpoint of the original text is not unusual, says Harvard professor Daniel Donoghue, who edited and annotated the popular, controversial 2000 translation of *Beowulf* by the Irish poet Seamus Heaney.

"I guess it is an inevitability that to retell the story of Beowulf, except in a faithful translation, you always bring to it the literary and cultural values currently practiced," Donoghue says. "There are over 80 translations of *Beowulf*. It's sort of a truism to say each is a new interpretation."

Grendel the opera is not even the only current theatrical re-telling of the story. From July 18–22, Lincoln Center Festival will also present medieval harpist Benjamin Bagby's *Beowulf*, in which Bagby sings and speaks the Old English text with projected modern translations while accompanying himself on harp. That may be closer to how medieval audiences would have heard the story presented.

Beowulf & Grendel, a short run of a new film by Canadian director Sturla Gunnarsson set in Iceland and starring Scottish actor Gerard Butler and Swedish film star Stellan Skarsgard, opened at the Quad Cinema in New York last week. Gunnarsson has said he intends to "strip away the mask of the hero myth, leaving a raw and tangled tale that rings true today." ▶

Donoghue said he is aware of an animated *Beowulf* in development that is to feature Hollywood stars as voices in key roles.

Why all this interest in a thousand-year-old-story?

"Since the second half of the 20th century, there's been a lot of poets and writers making an effort to move away from finding ultimate meaning in the transcendental," Donoghue says. "Instead, they search for meaning and value in the here and now, the human condition. The thing that makes Grendel appealing is he's a descendant of Cain, which means he is at least partly human. In a way, he is a negative, reverse image of what the noble, virtuous human should be. The original poet gets people to think about the transition from being a monster to being human. This blurring of the line between what is monstrous and human has appealed to readers throughout the ages."

ANALYZE MAIN IDEAS

Reread lines 85–100. What details support the idea that Grendel is a multi-faceted character?

_____

_____

_____

_____

TestSmart

Sturla Gunnarsson's treatment of the Beowulf story supports which of the following ideas in the article?

(A) *Beowulf* is partly set in Sweden.

(B) Epic heroes used to wear masks.

(C) When you retell a story, you bring to it current cultural values.

(D) People have lost interest in the Beowulf story.

TIP If you are asked to relate a **supporting detail** to a **main idea,** consider which of the ideas are **likely to be expressed in the article.** Usually you'll be able to find the idea in the same paragraph as the detail or in a nearby preceding paragraph.

Reading Comprehension

DIRECTIONS *Answer these questions about the two selections in this lesson by filling in the correct ovals.*

1. The author of "A Monster Fit for Any Medium" mentions Anne Rice's books to support the idea that

   (A) monster stories change over time

   (B) monsters are depicted in a variety of media

   (C) vampires prey on living people

   (D) vampire stories date back centuries

2. Which main idea is *not* suggested in "A Monster Fit for Any Medium"?

   (A) There is a sharp line between good and evil.

   (B) The line between good and evil is blurry.

   (C) Humans may have a monstrous side.

   (D) Monsters may have a human side.

3. The description of Darth Vader (lines 13–16) supports the idea that people are fascinated by

   (A) George Lucas's *Star Wars* films

   (B) concepts familiar to the Dark Ages

   (C) non-human monsters such as dragons

   (D) humans transformed into evil monsters

4. One main difference between the original *Beowulf* characters and their modern counterparts is that the modern characters tend to be

   (A) all good or all bad

   (B) multidimensional

   (C) progenitors of the hybrid monster

   (D) human or semi-human

5. Taymor and McClatchy's Grendel is different from the original monster because he is

   (A) Cain's descendant

   (B) a man eater

   (C) aware of his humanity

   (D) an outcast

6. Taymor and McClatchy's Grendel is similar to the original Grendel because both

   (A) are outcasts

   (B) are multifaceted

   (C) live under water

   (D) feel emotion

7. The most likely meaning of *virtuous* in line 7 of "A Monster Fit for Any Medium" is

   (A) questionable

   (B) proud

   (C) remarkable

   (D) moral

8. The word *transcendental* in lines 159–160 of "A Monster Fit for Any Medium" refers to

   (A) supernatural elements of life

   (B) earthly existence

   (C) the "here and now"

   (D) a reverse image of virtue

Timed Writing Practice

BUDGET YOUR TIME

You have 45 minutes to respond. Decide how much time to spend on each step.

Analyze _____

Plan _____

Write _____

Review _____

45

PROMPT

Both of the selections you have read describe (monsters). Why are stories about monsters so popular? What do they reveal about the world and about human nature? Write an analytical essay in which you discuss two or three monster stories and examine their meanings. You may write about monsters depicted in literature, movies, and other media.

TEST-TAKER'S TOOLKIT

1. ANALYZE THE PROMPT

A. Identify the type of writing you are asked to do.

_____

B. Circle key words that indicate the topic of your writing.

_____

C. Restate the prompt in your own words on the lines to the right.

_____

_____

2. PLAN YOUR RESPONSE

A. **Make notes** Brainstorm a list of monster stories you might want to write about. Choose two or three for which you can provide the most details. Then create a chart that will help you compile and organize your details.

B. **Organize your information** An analytical essay should begin with an introduction of the topic and a statement of your main idea. Then you can write one or two paragraphs about each of the monster stories you will discuss in your essay. Be sure to end with a conclusion that summarizes your key points.

Stories About Monsters	What They Reveal
1. Beowulf	1.

3. WRITE AND REVIEW

A. A strong opener can help your essay get a good score. Try beginning with a quotation or a shocking detail from a monster story to grab your readers' attention.

B. Be sure to leave time to check your spelling and grammar.

UNIT 1

THE ANGLO-SAXON AND MEDIEVAL PERIODS

LESSON 1B

from *Sir Gawain and the Green Knight*

BY THE GAWAIN POET

RELATED NONFICTION

The Birth of Chivalry

Is HONOR worth dying for?

For the knights of the Middle Ages, honor came with heavy obligations. According to the code of chivalry, a knight was supposed to be brave, modest, courteous, loyal, and honest. His role was to protect the weak and battle evildoers, including anyone who threatened his king or his church. If necessary, he had to sacrifice his life to uphold these ideals.

DISCUSS What ideals are important for your own sense of honor? Record your thoughts in a word web. Then, with a partner, discuss the sacrifices you would be willing to make to defend your honor.

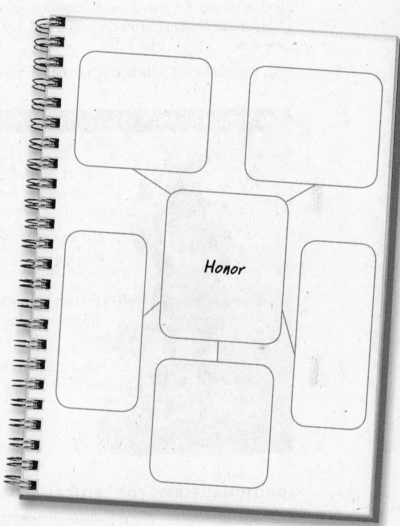

Honor

ASSESSMENT GOALS

By the end of this lesson, you will be able to. . .

- analyze a medieval romance
- apply critical thinking skills to analyze text
- analyze author's purpose in a nonfiction text
- analyze a writing prompt and plan a short story

Medieval Romance

A **MEDIEVAL ROMANCE** is a verse or prose narrative that usually involves adventurous heroes, idealized love, exotic places, and supernatural events. Romances first appeared in France during the 12th century, and they soon spread to England. Many of the best-known romances celebrate the legendary King Arthur and his knights, who often risk their lives for the love of a noble lady or to uphold the code of behavior known as chivalry. *Sir Gawain and the Green Knight* is considered one of the finest Arthurian romances.

Study the graphic below to help you recognize the characteristics of medieval romance.

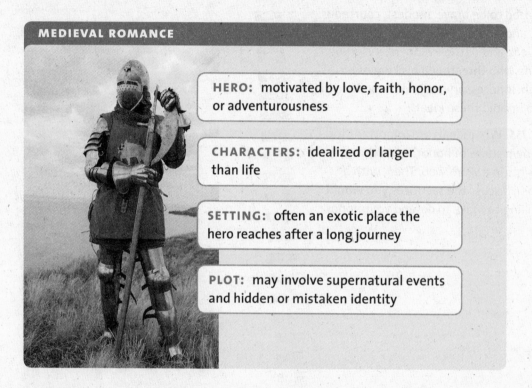

MEDIEVAL ROMANCE

HERO: motivated by love, faith, honor, or adventurousness

CHARACTERS: idealized or larger than life

SETTING: often an exotic place the hero reaches after a long journey

PLOT: may involve supernatural events and hidden or mistaken identity

ADDITIONAL TERMS FOR CRITICAL ANALYSIS

The following terms will help you analyze the events in *Sir Gawain and the Green Knight*.

• An **EXTERNAL CONFLICT** is a struggle between a character and an outside force, such as an enemy.

• An **INTERNAL CONFLICT** is a struggle that takes place within the mind of a character, such as worrying about a difficult decision.

Sometimes a single event contains both types of conflict. For example, a knight in battle may externally struggle against his opponent while struggling internally to remain brave in the face of danger.

Sir Gawain
AND THE
Green Knight

MARK & ANALYZE

Read this selection once on your own, marking the text in any way that is helpful to you.

Then read the narrative a second time, using the questions in the margins to help you analyze the literature. When you see this pencil ✏, you'll be asked to mark up the text.

BACKGROUND Like many of the Arthurian romances, *Sir Gawain and the Green Knight* starts off in Camelot, where King Arthur rules over the knights of the Round Table. Gawain is the king's nephew and one of the greatest knights in his court.

As the poem begins, Arthur and his knights are gathered to celebrate Christmas and the new year with feasting and revelry. In the midst of their festivities, an enormous man—who is entirely green—bounds through the door. ▶

Splendid that knight errant stood in a splay[1] of green,
And green, too, was the mane of his mighty destrier;[2]
Fair fanning tresses enveloped the fighting man's shoulders,
And over his breast hung a beard as big as a bush;
5 The beard and the huge mane burgeoning[3] forth from his head
Were clipped off clean in a straight line over his elbows,
And the upper half of each arm was hidden underneath
As if covered by a king's chaperon,[4] closed round the neck.
The mane of the marvelous horse was much the same,
10 Well crisped and combed and carefully pranked with knots,[5]

ANALYZE

As you read *Sir Gawain and the Green Knight* a second time, circle examples of recurring symbols such as the color green. In the margins, make notes about what these symbols might mean. ✏

---

1. **knight errant** (ĕr'ənt): a knight who wanders about, searching for adventure in order to prove his chivalry; **splay:** display.
2. **destrier** (dĕs'trē-ər): war horse.
3. **burgeoning** (bûr'jə-nĭng): growing.
4. **chaperon** (shăp'ə-rōn'): hood.
5. **pranked with knots:** decorated with bows.

CONNECT

What important object later in the story is also interwoven with golden threads?

_____

_____

Threads of gold interwoven with the glorious green,
Now a thread of hair, now another thread of gold;
The tail of the horse and the forelock[6] were tricked the same way,
And both were bound up with a band of brilliant green
15 Adorned with glittering jewels the length of the dock,[7]
Then caught up tight with a thong in a criss-cross knot
Where many a bell tinkled brightly, all burnished gold.
So monstrous a mount, so mighty a man in the saddle
Was never once encountered on all this earth
                              till then;
20   His eyes, like lightning, flashed,
        And it seemed to many a man,
        That any man who clashed
        With him would not long stand.

But the huge man came unarmed, without helmet or hauberk,[8]
25 No breastplate or gorget or iron cleats[9] on his arms;
He brought neither shield nor spearshaft to shove or to smite,
But instead he held in one hand a bough of the holly
That grows most green when all the groves are bare
And held in the other an ax, immense and unwieldy,
30 A pitiless battleblade terrible to tell of. . . .
King Arthur stared down at the stranger before the high dais[10]
And greeted him nobly, for nothing on earth frightened him.
And he said to him, "Sir, you are welcome in this place;[11]
I am the head of this court. They call me Arthur.
35 Get down from your horse, I beg you, and join us for dinner,
And then whatever you seek we will gladly see to."
But the stranger said, "No, so help me God on high,
My errand is hardly to sit at my ease in your castle!
But friend, since your praises are sung so far and wide,
40 Your castle the best ever built, people say, and your barons
The stoutest men in steel armor that ever rode steeds,

ANALYZE

Reread lines 18–36. Underline the details that make the Green Knight seem larger than life. Circle details that reveal King Arthur's chivalry.

---

6. **forelock:** the part of a horse's mane that falls between the ears.
7. **dock:** the fleshy part of an animal's tail.
8. **hauberk** (hô′bərk): a coat of chain mail (a type of armor).
9. **breastplate or gorget** (gôr′jĭt) **or iron cleats:** armor for the chest, the throat, or the shoulders and elbows.
10. **dais** (dā′ĭs): a raised platform where honored guests are seated.
11. **this place:** Camelot, Arthur's favorite castle and the site of his court of the Round Table.

Most mighty and most worthy of all mortal men

And tough devils to toy with in tournament games,[12]

And since courtesy is in flower[13] in this court, they say,

45 All these tales, in truth, have drawn me to you at this time.

You may be assured by this holly branch I bear

That I come to you in peace, not spoiling for[14] battle.

If I'd wanted to come in finery, fixed up for fighting,

I have back at home both a helmet and a hauberk,

50 A shield and a sharp spear that shines like fire,

And other weapons that I know pretty well how to use.

But since I don't come here for battle, my clothes are mere cloth.

Now if you are truly as bold as the people all say,

You will grant me gladly the little game that I ask

as my right."

55   Arthur gave him answer

And said, "Sir noble knight,

If it's a duel you're after,

We'll furnish you your fight." ▶

"Good heavens, I want no such thing! I assure you, Sire,

60 You've nothing but beardless babes about this bench!

If I were hasped[15] in my armor and high on my horse,

You haven't a man that could match me, your might is so feeble. ▶

And so all I ask of this court is a Christmas game,

For the Yule is here, and New Year's, and here sit young men;

65 If any man holds himself, here in this house, so hardy,

So bold in his blood—and so brainless in his head—

That he dares to stoutly exchange one stroke for another,

I shall let him have as my present this lovely gisarme,[16]

This ax, as heavy as he'll need, to handle as he likes,

70 And I will abide the first blow, bare-necked as I sit.

If anyone here has the daring to try what I've offered,

Leap to me lightly, lad; lift up this weapon;

I give you the thing forever—you may think it your own;

---

12. In medieval tournaments, knights on horseback fought one another for sport.

13. **courtesy is in flower:** the high standards of behavior expected in a king's court are currently flourishing.

14. **spoiling for:** eager for.

15. **hasped:** fastened.

16. **gisarme** (gĭ-zärm'): a battle-ax with a long shaft and a two-edged blade.

INTERPRET

In what way does the Green Knight's greeting appeal to King Arthur's sense of honor?

_____

_____

_____

_____

MAKE INFERENCES

Underline the insults the Green Knight makes. ✎ Why do you think he insults the knights in this way?

_____

_____

And I will stand still for your stroke, steady on the floor,
75 Provided you honor my right, when my inning comes,
     to repay.
  But let the respite be
  A twelvemonth and a day;[17]
  Come now, my boys, let's see
  What any here can say." ◄

80 If they were like stone before, they were stiller now,
 Every last lord in the hall, both the high and the low;
 The stranger on his destrier stirred in the saddle
 And ferociously his red eyes rolled around;
 He lowered his grisly eyebrows, glistening green,
85 And waved his beard and waited for someone to rise;
 When no one answered, he coughed, as if embarrassed,
 And drew himself up straight and spoke again:
 "What! Can this be King Arthur's court?" said the stranger,
 "Whose renown runs through many a realm, flung far and wide?
90 What has become of your chivalry and your conquest,
 Your greatness-of-heart and your grimness and grand words?
 Behold the radiance and renown of the mighty Round Table
 Overwhelmed by a word out of one man's mouth!
 You shiver and blanch before a blow's been shown!"
95 And with that he laughed so loud that the lord was distressed;
 In chagrin, his blood shot up in his face and limbs
     so fair; ◄
  More angry he was than the wind,
  And likewise each man there;
  And Arthur, bravest of men,
100   Decided now to draw near.

And he said, "By heaven, sir, your request is strange;
But since you have come here for folly,[18] you may as well find it.
I know no one here who's aghast of your great words.
Give me your gisarme, then, for the love of God,
105 And gladly I'll grant you the gift you have asked to be given."
Lightly the King leaped down and clutched it in his hand;

---

17. **let the respite . . . day:** let the period of delay be a year and a day.
18. **folly:** dangerous and foolish activity.

Then quickly that other lord alighted on his feet.
Arthur lay hold of the ax, he gripped it by the handle,
And he swung it up over him sternly, as if to strike.
110 The stranger stood before him, in stature higher
By a head or more than any man here in the house;
Sober and thoughtful he stood there and stroked his beard,
And with patience like a priest's he pulled down his collar,
No more unmanned[19] or dismayed by Arthur's might
115 Than he'd be if some baron on the bench had brought him a glass
of wine.

Then Gawain, at Guinevere's[20] side,
Made to the King a sign:
"I beseech you, Sire," he said,
"Let this game be mine.

120 "Now if you, my worthy lord," said Gawain to the King,
"Would command me to step from the dais and stand with you there,
That I might without bad manners move down from my place
(Though I couldn't, of course, if my liege lady[21] disliked it)
I'd be deeply honored to advise you before all the court;
125 For I think it unseemly, if I understand the matter,
That challenges such as this churl[22] has chosen to offer
Be met by Your Majesty—much as it may amuse you—
When so many bold-hearted barons sit about the bench: ▶
No men under Heaven, I am sure, are more hardy in will
130 Or better in body on the fields where battles are fought;
I myself am the weakest, of course, and in wit the most feeble
My life would be least missed, if we let out the truth.
Only as you are my uncle have I any honor,
For excepting your blood, I bear in my body slight virtue.
135 And since this affair that's befallen us here is so foolish,
And since I have asked for it first, let it fall to me.
If I've reasoned incorrectly, let all the court say,
without blame." ▶

MAKE INFERENCES

Reread the boxed text. What character traits does Gawain reveal through his words and actions?

_____

_____

_____

MAKE JUDGMENTS

Underline the modest comments Gawain makes about himself. ✎
Do you think he really believes he is the "weakest" and "feeblest" of the knights? Explain.

_____

_____

_____

---

19. **unmanned:** deprived of manly courage.

20. **Guinevere:** King Arthur's wife.

21. **liege** (lēj) **lady:** a lady to whom one owes loyalty and service; here used by Gawain to refer to Queen Guinevere.

22. **churl:** rude, uncouth person.

The nobles gather round
And all advise the same:
140   "Let the King step down
And give Sir Gawain the game!" . . .

Arthur grants Gawain's request to take on the Green Knight's challenge. The Green Knight asks Gawain to identify himself, and the two agree on their pact. Gawain then prepares to strike his blow against the Green Knight.

On the ground, the Green Knight got himself into position,
His head bent forward a little, the bare flesh showing,
His long and lovely locks laid over his crown
145 So that any man there might note the naked neck.
Sir Gawain laid hold of the ax and he hefted it high,
His pivot foot thrown forward before him on the floor,
And then, swiftly, he slashed at the naked neck;
The sharp of the battleblade shattered asunder[23] the bones
150 And sank through the shining fat and slit it in two,
And the bit of the bright steel buried itself in the ground.
The fair head fell from the neck to the floor of the hall
And the people all kicked it away as it came near their feet.
The blood splashed up from the body and glistened on the green,
155 But he never faltered or fell for all of that,
But swiftly he started forth upon stout shanks[24]
And rushed to reach out, where the King's retainers[25] stood,
Caught hold of the lovely head, and lifted it up,
And leaped to his steed and snatched up the reins of the bridle,
160 Stepped into stirrups of steel and, striding aloft,
He held his head by the hair, high, in his hand;
And the stranger sat there as steadily in his saddle
As a man entirely unharmed, although he was headless
        on his steed.
    He turned his trunk about,
165   That baleful[26] body that bled,
    And many were faint with fright
    When all his say was said. ◀

TESTSMART

What characteristics of a medieval romance are reflected in lines 154–167?

  Ⓐ a mistaken identity

  Ⓑ the code of chivalry

  Ⓒ a sense of honor

  Ⓓ a supernatural plot event

TIP A test question may ask what the characteristics of a particular genre are. To answer a question like this, mentally **review the characteristics of that genre.** Then reread the text to see which characteristic is reflected.

---

23. **asunder:** into pieces.
24. **shanks:** legs.
25. **retainers:** servants or attendants.
26. **baleful:** threatening evil; sinister.

He held his head in his hand up high before him,
Addressing the face to the dearest of all on the dais;
170 And the eyelids lifted wide, and the eyes looked out,
And the mouth said just this much, as you may now hear:
"Look that you go, Sir Gawain, as good as your word,
And seek till you find me, as loyally, my friend,
As you've sworn in this hall to do, in the hearing of the knights.
175 Come to the Green Chapel, I charge you, and take
A stroke the same as you've given, for well you deserve
To be readily requited on New Year's morn.
Many men know me, the Knight of the Green Chapel;
Therefore if you seek to find me, you shall not fail.
180 Come or be counted a coward, as is fitting."
Then with a rough jerk he turned the reins
And haled away through the hall-door, his head in his hand,
And fire of the flint flew out from the hooves of the foal.
To what kingdom he was carried no man there knew,
185 No more than they knew what country it was he came from.
          What then?
    The King and Gawain there
    Laugh at the thing and grin;
    And yet, it was an affair
    Most marvelous to men. ▶

MAKE INFERENCES

What can you infer about King Arthur's and Sir Gawain's feelings about their encounter with the Green Knight?

_____

_____

_____

_____

As the end of the year approaches, Gawain leaves on his quest to find the Green Chapel and fulfill his pledge. After riding through wild country and encountering many dangers, he comes upon a splendid castle. The lord of the castle welcomes Gawain and invites him to stay with him and his lady for a few days.

The lord proposes that he will go out to hunt each day while Gawain stays at the castle. At the end of the day, they will exchange what they have won. While the lord is out hunting, the lady attempts to seduce Gawain. Gawain resists her, however, and on the first two days accepts only kisses, which he gives to the lord at the end of each day in exchange for what the lord has gained in the hunt. On the third day Gawain continues to resist the lady, but she presses him to accept another gift.

190 She held toward him a ring of the yellowest gold
And, standing aloft on the band, a stone like a star

From which flew splendid beams like the light of the sun;
And mark you well, it was worth a rich king's ransom.
But right away he refused it, replying in haste,
195 "My lady gay, I can hardly take gifts at the moment;
Having nothing to give, I'd be wrong to take gifts in turn."
She implored[27] him again, still more earnestly, but again
He refused it and swore on his knighthood that he could take nothing.
Grieved that he still would not take it, she told him then:
200 "If taking my ring would be wrong on account of its worth,
And being so much in my debt would be bothersome to you,
I'll give you merely this sash that's of slighter value."
She swiftly unfastened the sash that encircled her waist,
Tied around her fair tunic, inside her bright mantle;[28]
205 It was made of green silk and was marked of gleaming gold
Embroidered along the edges, ingeniously stitched.
This too she held out to the knight, and she earnestly begged him
To take it, trifling as it was, to remember her by.
But again he said no, there was nothing at all he could take,
210 Neither treasure nor token, until such time as the Lord
Had granted him some end to his adventure.
"And therefore, I pray you, do not be displeased,
But give up, for I cannot grant it, however fair
                              or right.
        I know your worth and price,
215   And my debt's by no means slight;
        I swear through fire and ice
        To be your humble knight."

"Do you lay aside this silk," said the lady then,
"Because it seems unworthy—as well it may?
220 Listen. Little as it is, it seems less in value,
But he who knew what charms are woven within it
Might place a better price on it, perchance.
For the man who goes to battle in this green lace,
As long as he keeps it looped around him,
225 No man under Heaven can hurt him, whoever may try,
For nothing on earth, however uncanny, can kill him." ◄
The knight cast about in distress, and it came to his heart

---

27. **implored:** begged.
28. **tunic . . . mantle:** shirtlike garment worn under a sleeveless cloak.

This might be a treasure indeed when the time came to take
The blow he had bargained to suffer beside the Green Chapel.
230 If the gift meant remaining alive, it might well be worth it;
So he listened in silence and suffered the lady to speak,
And she pressed the sash upon him and begged him to take it,
And Gawain did, and she gave him the gift with great pleasure
And begged him, for her sake, to say not a word,
235 And to keep it hidden from her lord. And he said he would,
That except for themselves, this business would never be known
        to a man. ▶
    He thanked her earnestly,
    And boldly his heart now ran;
    And now a third time she
240   Leaned down and kissed her man.

*When the lord returns at the end of the third day, Gawain gives him a kiss but
does not reveal the gift of the sash.* ▶

*On New Year's Day Gawain must go to meet the Green Knight. Wearing the green
sash, he sets out before dawn. Gawain arrives at a wild, rugged place, where he
sees no chapel but hears the sound of a blade being sharpened. Gawain calls
out, and the Green Knight appears with a huge ax. The Green Knight greets
Gawain, who, with pounding heart, bows his head to take his blow.*

Quickly then the man in the green made ready,
Grabbed up his keen-ground ax to strike Sir Gawain;
With all the might in his body he bore it aloft
And sharply brought it down as if to slay him;
245 Had he made it fall with the force he first intended
He would have stretched out the strongest man on earth.
But Sir Gawain cast a side glance at the ax
As it glided down to give him his Kingdom Come,[29]
And his shoulders jerked away from the iron a little,
250 And the Green Knight caught the handle, holding it back,
And mocked the prince with many a proud reproof:
"*You* can't be Gawain," he said, "who's thought so good,
A man who's never been daunted on hill or dale!

---

29. **his Kingdom Come:** his death and entry into the afterlife; a reference to the
sentence "Thy kingdom come" in the Lord's Prayer.

For look how you flinch for fear before anything's felt!
255 I never heard tell that Sir Gawain was ever a coward!
I never moved a muscle when *you* came down;
In Arthur's hall I never so much as winced.
My head fell off at my feet, yet I never flickered;
But you! You tremble at heart before you're touched!
260 I'm bound to be called a better man than you, then,
                    my lord."[30]
              Said Gawain, "I shied once:
              No more. You have my word.
              But if my head falls to the stones
              It cannot be restored. ◀

INTERPRET

Reread the underlined text. What important difference is Gawain pointing out between the Green Knight and himself?

_____

_____

_____

265 "But be brisk, man, by your faith, and come to the point!
Deal out my doom if you can, and do it at once,
For I'll stand for one good stroke, and I'll start no more
Until your ax has hit—and that I swear."
"Here goes, then," said the other, and heaves it aloft
270 And stands there waiting, scowling like a madman;
He swings down sharp, then suddenly stops again,
Holds back the ax with his hand before it can hurt,
And Gawain stands there stirring not even a nerve;
He stood there still as a stone or the stock of a tree
275 That's wedged in rocky ground by a hundred roots.
O, merrily then he spoke, the man in green:
"Good! You've got your heart back! Now I can hit you.
May all that glory the good King Arthur gave you
Prove efficacious now—if it ever can—
280 And save your neck." In rage Sir Gawain shouted,
"*Hit* me, hero! I'm right up to here with your threats!
Is it *you* that's the cringing coward after all?"
"Whoo!" said the man in green, "he's wrathful, too!
No pauses, then; I'll pay up my pledge at once,
                    I vow!"
285   He takes his stride to strike
              And lifts his lip and brow;
              It's not a thing Gawain can like,
              For nothing can save him now! ◀

ANALYZE

What doesn't Sir Gawain know about the Green Knight at this point in the story?

_____

_____

_____

30. The Green Knight has proclaimed himself a better man than Gawain.

He raises that ax up lightly and flashes it down,
290 And that blinding bit bites in at the knight's bare neck—
But hard as he hammered it down, it hurt him no more
Than to nick the nape of his neck, so it split the skin;
The sharp blade slit to the flesh through the shiny hide,
And red blood shot to his shoulders and spattered the ground.
295 And when Gawain saw his blood where it blinked in the snow
He sprang from the man with a leap to the length of a spear;
He snatched up his helmet swiftly and slapped it on,
Shifted his shield into place with a jerk of his shoulders,
And snapped his sword out faster than sight; said boldly—
300 And, mortal born of his mother that he was,
There was never on earth a man so happy by half—
"No more strokes, my friend; you've had your swing!
I've stood one swipe of your ax without resistance;
If you offer me any more, I'll repay you at once
305 With all the force and fire I've got—as you
                    will see.
        I take one stroke, that's all,
        For that was the compact[31] we
        Arranged in Arthur's hall;
        But now, no more for me!"

310 The Green Knight remained where he stood, relaxing on his ax—
Settled the shaft on the rocks and leaned on the sharp end—
And studied the young man standing there, shoulders hunched,
And considered that staunch and doughty[32] stance he took,
Undaunted yet, and in his heart he liked it;
315 And then he said merrily, with a mighty voice—
With a roar like rushing wind he reproved the knight—
"Here, don't be such an ogre on your ground!
Nobody here has behaved with bad manners toward you
Or done a thing except as the contract said.
320 I owed you a stroke, and I've struck; consider yourself
Well paid. And now I release you from all further duties. ▶
If I'd cared to hustle, it may be, perchance, that I might

MAKE INFERENCES

Underline details that reveal the Green Knight's fondness and respect for Sir Gawain. Why does the Green Knight feel this way?

_____

_____

---

31. **compact**: binding agreement.
32. **staunch**: firm; **doughty** (dou′tē): brave.

SIR GAWAIN AND THE GREEN KNIGHT   53

Have hit somewhat harder, and then you might well be cross!
The first time I lifted my ax it was lighthearted sport,
325 I merely feinted[33] and made no mark, as was right,
For you kept our pact of the first night with honor
And abided by your word and held yourself true to me,
Giving me all you owed as a good man should.
I feinted a second time, friend, for the morning
330 You kissed my pretty wife twice and returned me the kisses;
And so for the first two days, mere feints, nothing more
            severe.
    A man who's true to his word,
    There's nothing he needs to fear;
    You failed me, though, on the third
335   Exchange, so I've tapped you here.

"That sash you wear by your scabbard[34] belongs to me;
My own wife gave it to you, as I ought to know.
I know, too, of your kisses and all your words
And my wife's advances, for I myself arranged them.
340 It was I who sent her to test you. I'm convinced
You're the finest man that ever walked this earth.
As a pearl is of greater price than dry white peas,
So Gawain indeed stands out above all other knights.
But you lacked a little, sir; you were less than loyal;
345 But since it was not for the sash itself or for lust
But because you loved your life, I blame you less." ◄
Sir Gawain stood in a study a long, long while,
So miserable with disgrace that he wept within,
And all the blood of his chest went up to his face
350 And he shrank away in shame from the man's gentle words.
The first words Gawain could find to say were these:
"Cursed be cowardice and covetousness both,
Villainy and vice that destroy all virtue!"
He caught at the knots of the girdle[35] and loosened them
355 And fiercely flung the sash at the Green Knight.

INTERPRET

Reread the boxed text. Why is the Green Knight able to forgive Gawain for accepting the sash from his wife?

_____

_____

_____

_____

_____

---

33. **feinted** (fān′tĭd): pretended to attack.
34. **scabbard** (skăb′ərd): a sheath for a dagger or sword.
35. **girdle**: sash.

"There, there's my fault! The foul fiend vex[36] it!
Foolish cowardice taught me, from fear of your stroke,
To bargain, covetous, and abandon my kind,
The selflessness and loyalty suitable in knights;
360   Here I stand, faulty and false, much as I've feared them,
Both of them, untruth and treachery; may they see sorrow
                    and care!
        I can't deny my guilt;
        My works shine none too fair!
        Give me your good will
365   And henceforth I'll beware."

At that, the Green Knight laughed, saying graciously,
"Whatever harm I've had, I hold it amended
Since now you're confessed so clean, acknowledging sins
And bearing the plain penance[37] of my point;[38]
370   I consider you polished as white and as perfectly clean
As if you had never fallen since first you were born.[39] ▶
And I give you, sir, this gold-embroidered girdle,
For the cloth is as green as my gown. Sir Gawain, think
On this when you go forth among great princes;
375   Remember our struggle here; recall to your mind
This rich token. Remember the Green Chapel.
And now, come on, let's both go back to my castle
And finish the New Year's revels with feasting and joy,
                    not strife,
        I beg you," said the lord,
380   And said, "As for my wife,
        She'll be your friend, no more
        A threat against your life."

"No, sir," said the knight, and seized his helmet
And quickly removed it, thanking the Green Knight,
385 "I've reveled too well already; but fortune be with you;
May He who gives all honors honor you well." . . .

CONTRAST

How does the Green Knight's attitude toward Gawain's moment of weakness differ from Gawain's attitude?

_____

_____

_____

_____

_____

---

36. **vex:** harass; torment.
37. **penance:** punishment accepted by a person to show sorrow for wrongdoing.
38. **point:** blade.
39. The Green Knight is saying that Gawain has paid for his fault by admitting it and offering his head to the ax.

And so they embraced and kissed and commended each other
To the Prince of Paradise, and parted then
              in the cold;
     Sir Gawain turned again
390   To Camelot and his lord;
     And as for the man of green,
     He went wherever he would. ◀

Big Question ?

Look back at the web you created on page 41. Which of the ideals you listed are most important to Gawain? Explain your answer.

_____

_____

_____

_____

Reading Comprehension

DIRECTIONS *Answer these questions about* Sir Gawain and the Green Knight *by filling in the correct ovals.*

1. The Green Knight comes to Camelot because he wants to

   Ⓐ seize the throne from King Arthur

   Ⓑ test the reputation of Arthur and his knights

   Ⓒ fight a duel with King Arthur

   Ⓓ get revenge against his wife's lover

2. What kind of conflict does Sir Gawain experience in lines 247–251?

   Ⓐ external

   Ⓑ internal

   Ⓒ both external and internal

   Ⓓ neither external nor internal

3. Why does Gawain volunteer to take on the Green Knight's challenge?

   Ⓐ He thinks Arthur is too important for the task.

   Ⓑ He has a long-standing grudge against the Green Knight.

   Ⓒ He wants to impress Queen Guinevere.

   Ⓓ He thinks he is the only one who can defeat the Green Knight.

4. Which lines contain an example of an internal conflict?

   Ⓐ lines 356–359

   Ⓑ lines 367–369

   Ⓒ lines 379–382

   Ⓓ lines 387–390

5. Which characteristic of medieval romance is reflected in lines 336–340?

   Ⓐ hero motivated by honor

   Ⓑ idealized characters

   Ⓒ exotic setting

   Ⓓ hidden identify

6. The Green Knight cut Gawain's neck on his third swing because Gawain

   Ⓐ boasted about King Arthur's greatness

   Ⓑ seduced the Green Knight's wife

   Ⓒ kept the gift of the sash a secret

   Ⓓ made insulting remarks about the Green Knight

7. Which word best describes Gawain's reaction when the Green Knight reveals why he cut his neck?

   Ⓐ shame Ⓒ fear

   Ⓑ anger Ⓓ confusion

8. Reread lines 377–388. Why does Gawain turn down the Green Knight's offer to come back to his castle?

   Ⓐ He promised Arthur to return home quickly.

   Ⓑ He is still ashamed of his own behavior.

   Ⓒ He fears another trick from the Green Knight.

   Ⓓ He is angry with the Green Knight.

GO ON

For help, use the **Test-Taker's Toolkit** below.

Responding in Writing

9. Short Response What message does *Sir Gawain and the Green Knight* convey about the ideals of chivalry? Write a paragraph analyzing the way chivalry is portrayed in this medieval romance.

_____

_____

_____

_____

_____

_____

TEST-TAKER'S TOOLKIT

GRAPHIC ORGANIZER Use the chart below to help you plan your response. Look back at the romance to help you remember details about how well Gawain lives up to the code of behavior known as chivalry.

	Element of Chivalry	Gawain's Actions
Bravery		
Modesty		
Courtesy		
Loyalty		
Honesty		

What's the Connection?

Sir Gawain and the Green Knight is a legendary tale of romantic chivalry. In "The Birth of Chivalry," an excerpt from Diane Ackerman's *A History of Love*, we learn about the origins of chivalry during the Middle Ages.

CHART IT In the K-W-L chart, write down what you know about chivalry and what you would like to learn about it. Then after you read the selection, complete the chart by writing down important information you have learned.

The Birth of Chivalry
BOOK EXCERPT

Use with Sir Gawain and the Green Knight, page 40

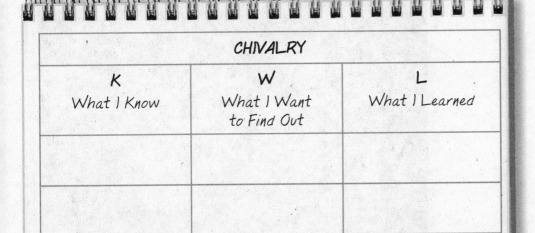

CHIVALRY

K What I Know	W What I Want to Find Out	L What I Learned

LEARN THE SKILL: ANALYZE AUTHOR'S PURPOSE

An **author's purpose** is the reason or reasons why he or she creates a particular work. Authors often write to explain or inform, to persuade, to entertain, or to express emotion and ideas. Writers may have more than one purpose in mind when they write a work. When you read nonfiction, look for the following clues to the author's purpose:

- What is the form of the writing (for example, a news article, magazine column, or book)? Why do writers usually use this form?
- What is the author's tone, or attitude toward a subject? How is a reader likely to react to this tone?

For more on author's purpose, see the Nonfiction Skills Handbook beginning on page R2.

The Birth of Chivalry

by Diane Ackerman

During the Middle Ages, France seethed with paradoxes. Plague, famine, and filth were Everyman's constant companions. So-called witches were regularly burned at the stake, and heretics of all stripes were tortured and driven from their homes. Nobles played chess by waging war with one another, in the process destroying crops, terrorizing towns, and killing legions of innocent families. Gangs of outlaws scoured the countryside, looting and burning. No one felt safe from nature or from one another. But, at the same time, a modern-feeling civilization was starting to take hold in Europe.

10 The population was growing, and new towns were being built, improved plows and other tools gave agriculture a boost, merchants had wares to sell, craftsmen busied themselves in the cities, and pilgrims traveled the roads and rivers. The world was in motion, and as Chaucer related so well, anyone could meet anyone on the crossroads to anywhere.[1] ◀

---

1. **Chaucer . . . to anywhere:** a reference to *The Canterbury Tales* by Geoffrey Chaucer, a collection of stories told by a group of travelers on a pilgrimage.

AUTHOR'S PURPOSE

Why do you think the author begins by describing what Europe was like during the Middle Ages?

It's no coincidence that spires began to appear on the churches. The entire era was gripped by the symbolism of the spire, which connected the earth and sky, the concrete with the abstract, the all-too-visible hovels—full of bodily functions, poverty, and fatigue—with the loftier realities of an invisible city. Could there be no relief from earth's sweat and decay? Was it possible that a poor life led only downward to a carnal circus underground? People aspired toward heaven, which they depicted as pure, clean, deodorized, and brightly lit. . . .

In this atmosphere of the lofty and the mundane, a ritualized code of manners, called chivalry, arose to reconcile the worlds of warfare and religion by giving them a common enemy. "A moral gloss was needed that would allow the Church to tolerate the warriors in good conscience and the warriors to pursue their own values in spiritual comfort." By making the warriors knights of the lord, they supposedly fought for truth, goodness, piety, and the Church. In a solemn dedication ceremony, a knight would purify his soul through confession, receive communion, and take his sacred vows. Then he was free to slaughter for a holy cause. ▶

It wasn't easy being a knight, whose sole occupation was warfare, which meant hand-to-hand combat while wearing a suit of armor that wasn't very flexible and weighed around fifty pounds. Lances, swords, and battle-axes were preferred weapons, and they were used during what amounted to traffic accidents—two riders galloping at each other at full speed. The ensuing crash usually hurled at least one rider to the ground, where getting up was like an overturned turtle's efforts to right itself. Being a knight took immense strength and energy; and, if you didn't exhibit plenty of what was called *prowess*, you were branded a sissy. Wounds were frequent, and they often became septic. Only the young could manage this lifestyle ▶ for long. Lest knights become unruly or psychopathic, chivalry's code required that they be courteous and kind when dealing with civilians. Dandies in later eras, who spread their capes over puddles so that women might pass with unsullied ankles, inherited their sense of gallantry from the knights. A knight's word was his bond; breaking it was an act of treason. This was the code, anyway. As often as not, the ideal differed from the reality. Soldiers were ruffians by trade, who settled disputes with violence, and they

AUTHOR'S PURPOSE

What tone does the author use in the boxed text?

_____

Why might she have chosen to use this tone?

_____

_____

SPECIALIZED Vocabulary

The word *septic* in line 45 describes an infected wound or body system. *Septic* is the adjective form of the noun *sepsis*, which refers to the presence of toxins in the blood or tissues. Septic conditions abound where sanitation is poor and medical treatment is scarce.

sometimes fought battles for lords whom they then murdered and robbed, or used the costume of chivalry to lure maidens whom they seduced or raped. According to one knight, La Tour Landry, he and his pals would ride into a village, lie like crazy to the local girls in order to bed them, then ride off like a band of armor-plated gigolos.

When they weren't at war, knights engaged in tournaments staged by
60 nobles with time to kill and a yen for a human version of a cockfight. As much as a week might be devoted to a tournament, with all sorts of events interspersed with the fighting. A hundred or so knights would contest with one another, in pairs or in groups. Just as a horse race or soccer match is usually surrounded by parties and ballyhoo, the tournaments justified feasts and merriment. They attracted people from all classes, including gamblers, conmen, prostitutes, souvenir sellers, and groupies. If a knight died during a tournament, the Church considered it suicide, which meant direct passage to hell. Even that didn't deter the knights, who had much to gain in prizes and fame, and
70 women to impress. Tournaments gave them a chance to win armor and horses, and rehearse the codes of chivalry in a small, safe setting. Faced with the rigors of all-out warfare, etiquette and form might be the last things on their minds.

During the first thirty years of the twelfth century, half the knights in France rode to the Crusades, joined by knights from England and Spain. The first Crusade was a blood-and-thunder success, driving the Muslims farther and farther south and out of Jerusalem. Knights returning from the Holy Land were conquering heroes. Imagine the wild temper of revelry and vindication they must have felt, not to
80 mention divine favor. All had seen friends die savagely at sword point. Many would be suffering from what we now call posttraumatic stress syndrome. Spirited young men full of spunk and mischief, they were accustomed to bloodshed, intrigue, and new hungers. They brought back a taste for the exotic spices of the Orient; brilliant silks and sensuous perfumes tempted the western appetite. The knights sang songs of conquest, bawdiness, bravery. At their most exquisite, they praised nature for allowing them pretty fields in which to slaughter their enemies. Heroic epics such as the *Song of Roland* celebrated the warriors' brotherhood, and since castles revolved around knights and
90 war, it was just these songs that rang from their parapets. . . . ◄

DRAW CONCLUSIONS

What were the harmful effects of the Crusades?

_____

_____

_____

In what ways did the Crusades benefit European society?

_____

_____

_____

Castles were islands of civility and culture, where a wandering knight could pause to refresh his spirit, much as a sailor might visit a bustling port after some time at sea. It must have seemed a dazzling mirage: the lady and her damsels, the children and other relatives, and all the servingmen and -women. Encountering such an island, a knight would choose a beautiful, remote, married "lady," whom he greatly idealized. At first he would hide in the bushes and worship his lady from afar, a voyeur excited by his invisible intimacy. The sweep of her skirt would make him flush. The revelation of her wrist would send gooseflesh down his neck. In time, he would present himself to her as a humble servant, pledging his heart and soul, his faithfulness and his valor. This is when cushions first appeared in the western world; a swain falling to his knees before a lady needed a soft place to land, and a lady expecting a swain always had a cushion handy. No doubt there was an enchanting coquetry in how far away she kept the cushion. Whatever trials she set him he swore to meet. Loving her would be a pilgrimage of her own devising. In a feudal world, where serfs bowed down to a lord, he would be her serfdom, she his master. . . .

The lady loved the knight only if he merited her love. This notion—of the female putting the male through tests before she accepts him as a lover—is not a supercivilized human conceit; it is a ritual played throughout the animal kingdom, from insects to bowerbirds to elks. The knight, on the other hand, loved his lady because of her innate beauty. . . . Knights were warriors; how thrilling for a lady to force them to be gentle and refined in her name, knowing what violence was being reined in. "Service" was everything. The Romans and Greeks despised men who served anyone, especially a woman. Now we find service raised to an art form, and knights longing to be humiliated by love. If so ordered, a knight would even be willing to lose a joust intentionally, telling no one that he had thrown the fight, slinking away like a fool. ▶

AUTHOR'S PURPOSE

What do you think was the author's main purpose in writing "The Birth of Chivalry"? Explain.

_____

_____

_____

_____

_____

Reading Comprehension

DIRECTIONS *Answer these questions about the two selections in this lesson by filling in the correct ovals.*

1. According to "The Birth of Chivalry," chivalry filled the need to

   (A) reconcile past and future

   (B) cure poverty and disease

   (C) save lives on the battlefield

   (D) reconcile ideals and reality

2. Which of the following did *not* motivate knights to fight in tournaments?

   (A) prize money

   (B) training opportunities

   (C) religion

   (D) fame

3. According to "The Birth of Chivalry," many knights were traumatized by

   (A) being defeated at tournaments

   (B) their experiences during the Crusades

   (C) disputes with civilians

   (D) humiliating service to a married lady

4. Reread lines 110–122 of "The Birth of Chivalry." The main purpose of this paragraph is to

   (A) inform readers about how knights were tested by women

   (B) persuade readers to be more gentle and refined

   (C) entertain readers by describing the humiliation of knights

   (D) express ideas about chivalry and service

5. Which aspect of medieval life does Sir Gawain represent?

   (A) common enemies

   (B) the mundane world

   (C) the carnal circus

   (D) lofty ideals

6. Which detail from "The Birth of Chivalry" explains Sir Gawain's embarrassment over his lie?

   (A) A knight fights for his king.

   (B) A knight's word is his bond.

   (C) A knight purifies his soul.

   (D) A knight fights for a cause.

7. From its context in line 49 of "The Birth of Chivalry," you can tell that *unsullied* means

   (A) unwilling

   (B) ungrateful

   (C) unstained

   (D) unashamed

8. The most likely meaning for the word *ruffians* in line 53 of "The Birth of Chivalry" is

   (A) petty thugs

   (B) gallant souls

   (C) poor merchants

   (D) murderous criminals

Timed Writing Practice

PROMPT

Chivalry may be dead, as the saying goes, but the world of medieval knighthood is still a popular subject for fiction. Write a short story about a knight who faces an important challenge. The knight can be a famous hero such as Gawain or a new character you create, such as a young person training to become a knight. Use details from both selections to help you portray the story's setting and characters.

BUDGET YOUR TIME

You have **45 minutes** to respond. Decide how much time to spend on each step.

Analyze _____

Plan _____

Write _____

Review _____

45

TEST-TAKER'S TOOLKIT

1. ANALYZE THE PROMPT

A. Identify the type of writing you are asked to do.

B. Circle key words that indicate the topic of your writing. One phrase has been circled for you.

C. Restate the prompt in your own words on the lines to the right.

_____

_____

_____

_____

_____

2. PLAN YOUR RESPONSE

A. **Make notes** Think about interesting characters, settings (such as a castle or a forest), plots, and conflicts. Write down whatever comes into your mind. Circle the ideas that interest you the most.

B. **Organize your information** Fill out this chart to help you organize your ideas.

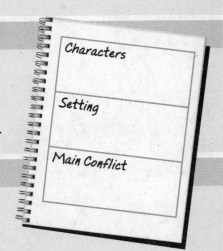

Characters

Setting

Main Conflict

3. WRITE AND REVIEW

A. Make sure that you provide clues at the beginning of the story to let readers know that your story is set in the Middle Ages. For example, you might include sensory details to create a vivid description of a knight's armor.

B. Be sure to leave time to check your spelling and grammar.

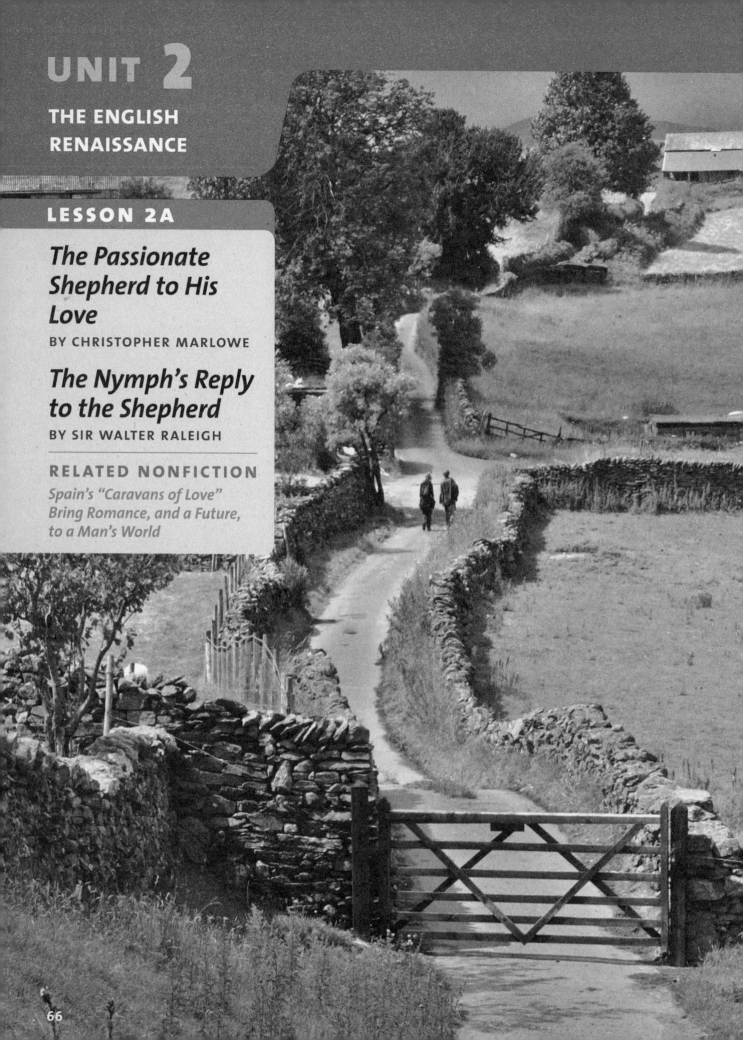

LESSON 2A

The Passionate Shepherd to His Love

BY CHRISTOPHER MARLOWE

The Nymph's Reply to the Shepherd

BY SIR WALTER RALEIGH

RELATED NONFICTION

Spain's "Caravans of Love" Bring Romance, and a Future, to a Man's World

Is PASSION *overrated?*

Throughout the ages, writers have composed poems and songs describing the passion of new love. But have people placed too much emphasis on intensely romantic love? Are other aspects of love more important?

LIST IT Which of the qualities listed here are most important for love to thrive? Which ones do you value less? Number the list of qualities from 1 to 10, with 1 being the most important and 10 being the least. Then share reasons for your opinions with a partner.

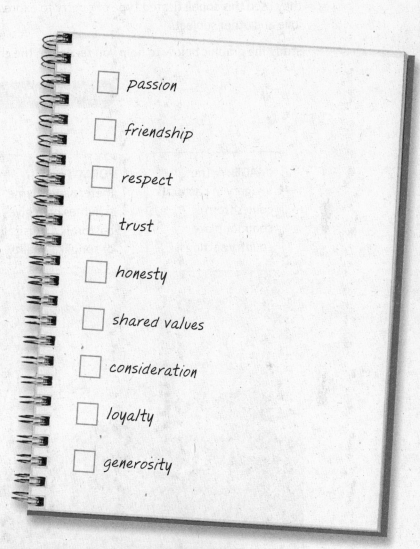

☐ passion

☐ friendship

☐ respect

☐ trust

☐ honesty

☐ shared values

☐ consideration

☐ loyalty

☐ generosity

ASSESSMENT GOALS

By the end of this lesson, you will be able to . . .

- analyze the characteristics of pastoral poetry
- apply critical thinking strategies to analyze text
- analyze cause and effect in a work of nonfiction
- analyze a writing prompt and plan an opinion essay

Pastoral

A **PASTORAL** is a poem that presents shepherds in idealized rural settings. Pastorals were very popular during the English Renaissance. Poets like Marlowe and Raleigh did not write pastorals to show how people in the country really lived and spoke. Instead, they used this sophisticated type of poetry to express their feelings and thoughts about love and other subjects.

Study the graphic below to help you recognize the characteristics of pastoral poetry.

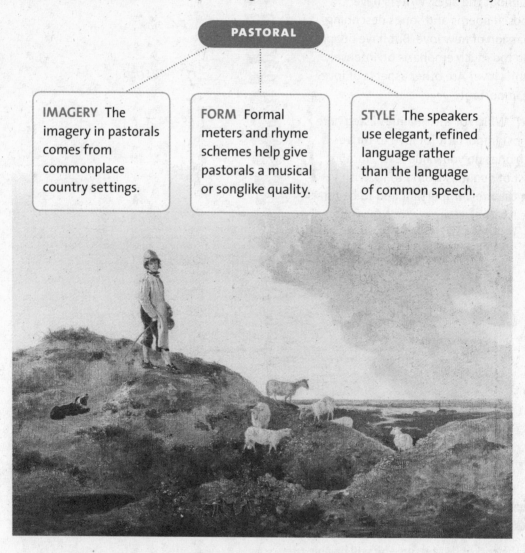

PASTORAL

IMAGERY The imagery in pastorals comes from commonplace country settings.

FORM Formal meters and rhyme schemes help give pastorals a musical or songlike quality.

STYLE The speakers use elegant, refined language rather than the language of common speech.

ADDITIONAL TERM FOR CRITICAL ANALYSIS

A poem's **SPEAKER** is the voice that addresses the reader. A poet may use a speaker to express ideas or tell a story from a specific point of view. The speaker and the poet are not necessarily the same, even when the words *I* and *me* are used.

The Passionate Shepherd to His Love

Christopher Marlowe

MARK & ANALYZE

Read the poems once on your own, marking the text in any way that is helpful to you.

Then read the poems a second time, using the questions in the margins to help you analyze the literature. When you see this pencil ✐, you'll be asked to mark up the text.

BACKGROUND Christopher Marlowe is best known as a playwright, but he also distinguished himself as a poet. His poem "The Passionate Shepherd to His Love" was so popular that it inspired responses in verse, including Sir Walter Raleigh's "The Nymph's Reply to the Shepherd." The two poems present sharply contrasting views on love.

Come live with me and be my love,
And we will all the pleasures prove[1]
That valleys, groves, hills, and fields,
Woods, or steepy mountain yields.

5 And we will sit upon the rocks,
Seeing the shepherds feed their flocks,
By shallow rivers to whose falls
Melodious birds sing madrigals.[2] ▶

And I will make thee beds of roses
10 And a thousand fragrant posies,
A cap of flowers, and a kirtle[3]
Embroidered all with leaves of myrtle;

ANALYZE

What characteristics of **pastoral poetry** do you find in the boxed text? Identify specific examples.

_____

_____

_____

_____

_____

1. **prove:** experience.
2. **madrigals:** songs of a type popular during the Renaissance.
3. **kirtle:** skirt or dress.

How would you characterize the **speaker's** portrayal of love in the poem? Explain.

_____

_____

_____

_____

_____

A gown made of the finest wool
Which from our pretty lambs we pull;
15 Fair lined slippers for the cold,
With buckles of the purest gold;

A belt of straw and ivy buds,
With coral clasps and amber studs:
And if these pleasures may thee move,
20 Come live with me, and be my love.

The shepherds' swains⁴ shall dance and sing
For thy delight each May morning:
If these delights thy mind may move,
Then live with me and be my love. ◄

4. **swains:** country youths.

The Nymph's Reply to the Shepherd

Sir Walter Raleigh

If all the world and love were young,
And truth in every shepherd's tongue,
These pretty pleasures might me move
To live with thee and be thy love.

5 Time drives the flocks from field to fold[1]
When rivers rage and rocks grow cold,
And Philomel[2] becometh dumb;[3]
The rest complains of cares to come.

The flowers do fade, and wanton[4] fields
10 To wayward winter reckoning yields;
A honey tongue, a heart of gall,
Is fancy's spring, but sorrow's fall. ▶

Thy gowns, thy shoes, thy beds of roses,
Thy cap, thy kirtle, and thy posies
15 Soon break, soon wither, soon forgotten—
In folly ripe, in reason rotten. ▶

Thy belt of straw and ivy buds,
Thy coral clasps and amber studs,
All these in me no means can move
20 To come to thee and be thy love.

---

1. **fold:** a pen for animals, especially sheep.
2. **Philomel:** the nightingale
3. **dumb:** silent.
4. **wanton:** here, producing abundant crops; luxuriant.

TESTSMART

Which message is conveyed by the imagery in the boxed text?

(A) True love is everlasting.

(B) Time does not affect love.

(C) Feelings change over time.

(D) Each season has its special beauty.

TIP A test question may ask you to interpret the meaning conveyed by a poem's **imagery. Look for patterns** in the imagery to determine what message it conveys. In this case, what natural process does the imagery describe, and how does this description relate to the subject of the poem?

INTERPRET

What does the **speaker** suggest with the phrase "In folly ripe, in reason rotten" in line 16?

_____

_____

_____

How would you describe
the **speaker's** views on the
following subjects?

• lovers' words

_____

_____

• the value of love tokens

_____

_____

• planning for the future

_____

_____

But could youth last and love still breed,
Had joys no date[5] nor age no need,
Then these delights my mind might move
To live with thee and be thy love. ◄

5. **date:** ending.

Reading Comprehension

DIRECTIONS *Answer these questions about the poems by filling in the correct ovals.*

1. What will the speaker of "The Passionate Shepherd to His Love" seek in the different places he describes in lines 2–4?

   Ⓐ a woman who loves him

   Ⓑ a location to build a home

   Ⓒ grazing areas for his sheep

   Ⓓ different types of pleasure

2. Which detail in "The Passionate Shepherd to His Love" is the *best* example of how nature is idealized in the pastoral form?

   Ⓐ beds made from roses

   Ⓑ a belt of straw and ivy buds

   Ⓒ melodious birds singing madrigals

   Ⓓ swains dancing and singing

3. What does the speaker of "The Passionate Shepherd to His Love" suggest will happen if his love comes to live with him?

   Ⓐ They will have great wealth.

   Ⓑ All of their needs will be taken care of.

   Ⓒ They will need to work hard.

   Ⓓ He will always be faithful to her.

4. Which of the following senses does the imagery in lines 6–7 of "The Nymph's Reply to the Shepherd" appeal to?

   Ⓐ sight and smell

   Ⓑ sight and taste

   Ⓒ touch and hearing

   Ⓓ touch and taste

5. Who is the speaker in "The Nymph's Reply to the Shepherd"?

   Ⓐ Sir Walter Raleigh

   Ⓑ a young woman

   Ⓒ a young shepherd

   Ⓓ an outside observer

6. In "The Nymph's Reply to the Shepherd," the speaker says that the gifts the shepherd has promised are

   Ⓐ likely to break or wither

   Ⓑ too fancy for a country girl

   Ⓒ things she already owns

   Ⓓ not fashionable enough for her

7. The speaker of "The Nymph's Reply to the Shepherd" hints that the shepherd

   Ⓐ is simple-minded

   Ⓑ needs to work harder

   Ⓒ might try to deceive her

   Ⓓ has grown too old

8. At the end of "The Nymph's Reply to the Shepherd," the speaker

   Ⓐ decides that she loves the shepherd after all

   Ⓑ renounces all hope of love and happiness

   Ⓒ finds another man to move in with

   Ⓓ explains what it would take to change her mind

GO ON ➤

For help, use the **Test-Taker's Toolkit** below.

Responding in Writing

9. **Short Response** Write a paragraph **comparing and contrasting** the views of love and life expressed in "The Passionate Shepherd to His Love" and "The Nymph's Reply to the Shepherd." Make sure to discuss Marlowe's and Raleigh's use of pastoral imagery.

_____

_____

_____

_____

_____

TEST-TAKER'S TOOLKIT

GRAPHIC ORGANIZER Use the chart below to help you plan your response. Reread the poems to help you remember the details.

Pastoral Imagery Used to Convey Ideas	
Shepherd	Nymph

What's the Connection?

The speakers in "The Passionate Shepherd to His Love" and "The Nymph's Reply to the Shepherd" present two different views of romantic love. The newspaper article you are about to read describes how one man's belief in the power of love inspired him to become a matchmaker for lonely bachelors in rural Spain.

CHART IT Love has been a popular topic for writers throughout the ages. Read the three famous quotes about love below. Write what you think each one means. Then write whether you agree or disagree with each quote, and why. Discuss your answers with a partner.

Spain's "Caravans of Love" Bring Romance, and a Future, to a Man's World
NEWSPAPER ARTICLE

Use with "The Passionate Shepherd to His Love" and "The Nymph's Reply to the Shepherd," p. 66

Quote	Why I Agree or Disagree
"Love conquers all." —Virgil, Roman poet **Meaning:** _____	
"Love is blind." —William Shakespeare **Meaning:** _____	
"'Tis better to have loved and lost Than never to have loved at all." —Alfred Lord Tennyson, English poet **Meaning:** _____	

LEARN THE SKILL: ANALYZE CAUSE AND EFFECT

The events described in works of nonfiction are often related by cause and effect. These tips can help you recognize **cause-and-effect relationships:**

- Writers may use **clue words** to indicate a cause or an effect. *Because, since,* and *due to* indicate a cause. *As a result, consequently,* and *therefore* suggest an effect.

- A cause-and-effect relationship may be **stated directly** or may be **implied.**

- More than one cause can lead to a single effect; more than one effect can stem from a single cause.

For more on analyzing cause and effect, see the Nonfiction Skills Handbook beginning on page R2.

_____

_____

_____

ANALYZE CAUSE AND EFFECT

What effect did seeing the 1955 film *Caravana de Mujeres* have on the bachelors in the village of Plan?

_____

_____

_____

Underline one effect of the men's newspaper ad. ✏

SPECIALIZED Vocabulary

Sometimes articles use words from another language without translating them. The Spanish word *solterónes* in line 57 means "confirmed bachelor." The word's context can help you figure out its meaning. Another clue is that *solterónes* is related to the English word *solitary*.

LIFESTYLE Section B1

Spain's "Caravans of Love" Bring Romance, and a Future, to a Man's World

by Elizabeth Nash
from The Independent

"Repopulating villages through love"—that is the ambitious task an insurance salesman from Madrid has set himself. He organizes "caravanas de amor" (love caravans)—busloads of women that roll periodically into Spain's remote rural outposts to be greeted with enthusiasm, tinged with apprehension, by scores of single men. Manuel Gozalo holds fast to his utopian dream in the face of today's cynical commercialism, as he prepares his latest "caravan," the sixth this year, that heads next weekend to the village of Cabezuela de Segovia.

It all started 22 years ago when a handful of single men in the Pyrenean village of Plan saw the American film *Westward the Women,* released in Spain in 1955 as *Caravana de Mujeres* (Caravan of Women). The film told of wagonloads of women heading west as potential wives for frontiersmen.

Plan (pop. 170) was no vibrant frontier town, rather a rural backwater that women had deserted in search of livelier company and less drudgery. But the movie gave Plan's lonely bachelors an idea, and they put an ad in the regional newspaper: "Women wanted between 20 and 40 for matrimonial purposes in a village in the foothills of the Pyrenees." They received 57 replies within the week. ◀

Spain's first busload of women trundled into Plan on March 7, 1985. Five more "love caravans" followed in four years. The plan from Plan produced 40 marriages.

And there it might have remained, a poignant attempt by solitary farmers to find a wife, with little impact beyond the mountain valleys of north-east Spain. But in 1995, another lonely chap yearned not only to find love, but also to stem the decline of his own small village, Fuentesauco, near Segovia, north of Madrid. Inspired by Plan, Manuel Gozalo revived the caravanas de amor, and 12 years on is organizing his 32nd trip.

"There were 30 *solterones* and one ◀ widow in Fuentesauco," recalls Mr.

Single women from Madrid dancing with bachelors in a Spanish village.

Gozalo with a smile. "It was
60 dying. The young women had
left to work in offices or shops
in town, and the only people
left were single men who farmed
their piece of land and tended
cattle. There were no children,
no school. In winter it was very
sad." ▶

Mr. Gozalo, 50, joined the
flight from the land 30 years ago
70 to sell insurance in Madrid, but
he travels home frequently and
still considers himself at heart a
country boy. He mobilized some
friends, put out the word in villages around Fuentesauco, and
persuaded 30 women—with the
promise of a day out and the
chance of romance—to board
the bus on June 15, 1995.

80 "At first the idea was just to
have fun, and it wasn't easy to
find the women. We had music
and dancing in the park, then
dinner in the bar of Fuentesauco
station, paid for by the men.
There was a great atmosphere."
By popular demand, another
caravan was organized a month
later in nearby Laguna village. ▶
90 His enthusiasm undimmed,
he squeezes in front of his computer in his tiny flat in a workers'
suburb of Madrid, fielding calls
on three telephones from town
halls, bus companies and appli-
cants for tickets. His minuscule
balcony accommodates a printer,
a scanner, petunias, scarlet gera-
niums and bulging files.

DRAW CONCLUSIONS

Reread the boxed text.
What conclusion can you
draw regarding Manuel
Gozalo's view of family and
community? Explain.

_____

_____

_____

_____

ANALYZE CAUSE
AND EFFECT

Underline the effect the
successful caravan of love
in Fuentesauco had on a
neighboring village. ✎

ANALYZE CAUSE
AND EFFECT

Reread the boxed text.
Underline two **causes** for the
exodus from Spain's villages to
its cities.

What three things did people
who moved to cities hope to
find there?

1. _____

2. _____

3. _____

INTERPRET

Why are Gozalo's "love
caravans" only a symbolic
contribution to his dream
that rural villages will be
repopulated?

_____

_____

_____

100   It wasn't easy at first. "I nearly threw in the towel. In 1997 we organized only one caravan. No one seemed interested." Interest picked up following the success in 2000 of Iciar Bollain's sympathetic film about the *caravanas*— *Flores de Otro Mundo* (Flowers of Another World)—that won the critics' prize at Cannes. Today his
110 Association of Women's Caravans has hundreds of affiliates, and a thriving bush telegraph ensures that there are always men willing to pay €50 ($68)—women pay €18—for the day.

    "Town halls in tiny villages call me constantly asking me to send women. But they must be within 350 km (220 miles) of Madrid,
120 so we can return the same day. Sometimes the bus doesn't get back till dawn, which is tiring for elderly participants. The local town hall, bars and restaurants pay for the band, the lamb stew, the wine and sangria. That takes the pressure off me. At first I was paying for everything. The idea is to have a day out in the coun-
130 try, a fiesta and the promise of romance."

    It worked for him. Bustling around our conversation is Venecia Alcantara, whom he met in 1995 on the third caravan, a feisty woman from the Dominican Republic who gives him the affection he craved. But Mr. Gozalo aspires to be more than Cupid

140 of the countryside. He wants to repopulate Spain's dying villages.

    The statistics are stark: Up to 96 percent of Spaniards live in cities or on the coast, with just 4 percent in tiny isolated communities. Some 5,000 towns are inhabited by fewer than a thousand people. More than 2,500 villages are deserted.

150   The exodus started in the 1950s, the "hungry years" of Franco's dictatorship, and accelerated with the industrialization of the sixties and seventies. Millions moved to the cities, where there was work, company and the prospect of education. ◄

    Many townies still return to their home village—"el pueblo"—
160 for holidays or weekends, but countless more abandoned their birthplace forever. "The situation is desperate. The only people left in the villages are old people and single men who tend the family plot. If you want work you have to be in the city," Mr. Gozalo says. He admits his "love cara-vans" offer a symbolic rather than
170 real contribution to his dream that couples will return and repopulate abandoned villages. "The truth is that rural depopulation is irreversible." . . . ◄

    Few receive Cupid's dart immediately, but some strike lucky: "Once a young woman missed the bus," chuckles Mr. Gozalo, "and I took her in my car and we arrived

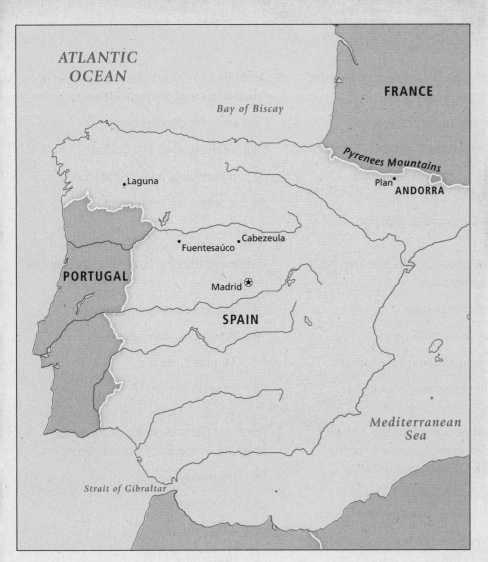

ATLANTIC OCEAN

Bay of Biscay

FRANCE

Pyrenees Mountains

Plan
ANDORRA

Laguna

Cabezeula
Fuentesaúco

PORTUGAL

Madrid ✪

SPAIN

Mediterranean Sea

Strait of Gibraltar

TESTSMART

Which factor is an implied cause for the men's shyness?

- Ⓐ The men are afraid of being laughed at.
- Ⓑ Country farmers are rough.
- Ⓒ The women are boisterous.
- Ⓓ The men aren't used to women.

TIP A test question may ask you about an **implied cause-and-effect relationship.** You must use what you know to **infer the answer.** Three of the answer choices are directly stated in the text. The correct answer to the question is implied—you can infer it by thinking about what the men's lives are like in general.

180 late. But she met a young man and stayed the night. Last to arrive, she was the first to score. It was love at first sight."

The men are shy when confronted with an exuberant busload of mostly Latin American women, and they are afraid of being laughed at, Mr. Gozalo said. "Country farmers are a bit rough. They make earthy 190 comments about the women. But they are straightforward, and gentlemanly in their way. ▶

"Most are genuinely looking for a companion," Mr. Gozalo said. "And the women are not very educated, despite their clothes and make-up. They're mostly immigrants, working as cleaners or care assistants, 200 often from small villages themselves. They'd like a home in a safe village with someone to care for. Everyone has a right to happiness." ▶

MAKE JUDGMENTS

Do you think the women who visit the villages are good matches for the men? Why or why not?

_____

_____

_____

_____

Reading Comprehension

DIRECTIONS *Answer these questions about the article and the poems in this lesson by filling in the correct ovals.*

1. What inspired Manuel Gozalo to revive the "caravans of love" in 1995?

   (A) the film *Westward the Women*

   (B) the efforts of the bachelors in Plan

   (C) the efforts of the bachelors of Fuentesauco

   (D) the film *Caravana de Mujeres*

2. According to Manuel Gozalo, the love caravans *cannot* provide

   (A) a chance of marriage

   (B) multiple visits to villages

   (C) bus transportation from Madrid

   (D) a solution to rural depopulation

3. Reread the last paragraph of the article. Which factor is an implied cause for the women's interest in village life?

   (A) The women have experienced poverty and faced danger in the city.

   (B) The women are not very educated.

   (C) The women are mostly immigrants.

   (D) The women work as cleaners or care assistants.

4. Which of the following is *not* a reason why Spaniards moved from rural villages to cities?

   (A) better education

   (B) more companionship

   (C) better climate

   (D) more job opportunities

5. According to the article, most people in Spain think that pastoral life is

   (A) ideal for couples

   (B) sophisticated and desirable

   (C) undesirable and old-fashioned

   (D) a dream for retirement

6. Who would probably agree with the statement that the land fulfills all human needs?

   (A) Marlowe's shepherd speaker

   (B) Raleigh's nymph speaker

   (C) Manuel Gozalo

   (D) Venecia Alcantara

7. The most likely meaning of the word *poignant* in line 45 of the article is

   (A) troubling

   (B) unsuccessful

   (C) awkward

   (D) touching

8. The most likely meaning of the word *exuberant* in line 185 is

   (A) bashful

   (B) confused

   (C) lively

   (D) exhausted

Timed Writing Practice

PROMPT

In their pastoral poems, Christopher Marlowe and Sir Walter Raleigh present sharply contrasting views of rural life. Which view is closer to your own? Write a personal essay in which you express your opinion about (life in the country.) You can, like Marlowe's shepherd, idealize nature, or you can offer a more realistic view in the manner of Raleigh's nymph. Provide at least three reasons and one or two examples to support each reason. Draw examples from your own experiences as well as the two poems and other works you have read.

BUDGET YOUR TIME

You have **45 minutes** to respond. Decide how much time to spend on each step.

Analyze _____

Plan _____

Write _____

Review _____

TEST-TAKER'S TOOLKIT

1. ANALYZE THE PROMPT

A. Underline the question in the prompt and circle key words in the sentences that follow the question. One phrase has been circled for you.

_____

_____

B. Jot down a list of the key elements you need to include in your essay.

_____

_____

2. PLAN YOUR RESPONSE

A. **Make notes** In a chart like the one shown here, list three good reasons for your opinion and examples to support your reasons.

B. **Organize your information** In the introduction, identify the topic of your essay and present a thesis statement that clearly identifies your personal opinion. Then you can write a paragraph for each reason you noted in your chart. Use your examples to support each reason. Be sure to include a conclusion in which you wrap up your ideas.

Reason 1: ___	Example(s):
Reason 2: ___	Example(s):
Reason 3: ___	Example(s):

3. WRITE AND REVIEW

A. An attention-grabbing opener gets readers interested in your ideas. Try beginning with an anecdote or a question:

_____

_____

B. Be sure to leave time to revise and to check your spelling and grammar.

LESSON 2B

Selected Poetry

BY WILLIAM SHAKESPEARE

RELATED NONFICTION

All You Need Is Love

Can LOVERS *see clearly?*

"Love is blind," according to an old saying. To what extent is this true? The thrill of falling in love can cloud one's perceptions of a lover, but usually those clouds drift away over time. Is it possible to see a person's faults clearly and still love him or her?

CHART IT With a partner, identify three fictional couples from books, movies, or plays. For each couple, answer the question, "How clearly did they see each other?" Discuss the reasons for your answers. What conclusions can you draw about the way love is portrayed in fiction?

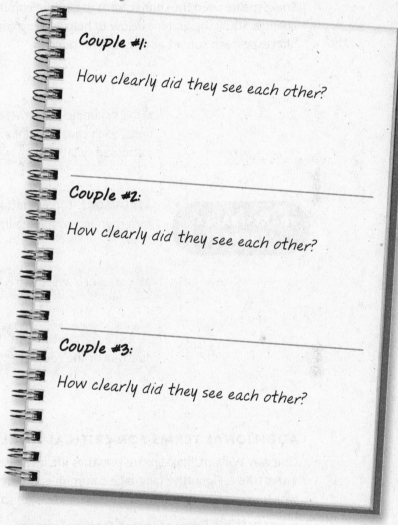

Couple #1:

How clearly did they see each other?

Couple #2:

How clearly did they see each other?

Couple #3:

How clearly did they see each other?

ASSESSMENT GOALS

By the end of this cluster, you will be able to . . .

- analyze the Shakespearean sonnet form
- apply critical thinking skills to analyze text
- analyze text features in a work of nonfiction
- analyze a writing prompt and plan a character description

Shakespearean Sonnet

During the Renaissance, love poems often came in the form of sonnets. A SONNET is a 14-line lyric poem with a complicated rhyme scheme and a defined structure. There are several varieties of sonnets. The most common variety used in England is called the SHAKESPEAREAN SONNET, which is also known as the English sonnet.

Shakespeare used the sonnet form to explore complex ideas about love, loss, and change. Study the graphic below to help you recognize characteristics of the Shakespearean sonnet as you read his poems.

SHAKESPEAREAN SONNET

METER: iambic pentameter lines containing five metrical units, each consisting of an unstressed syllable followed by a stressed syllable

STRUCTURE: three quatrains (stanzas of 4 lines) followed by a rhyming couplet (2 lines)

RHYME SCHEME: *abab cdcd efef gg*

TURN: a shift in thought that often occurs in the third quatrain or the couplet

ADDITIONAL TERMS FOR CRITICAL ANALYSIS

One way William Shakespeare breathes life into his sonnets is by using FIGURATIVE LANGUAGE. Figurative language communicates ideas beyond the literal meaning of the words to express emotions and abstract ideas, or to create rich images in readers' minds.

- A SIMILE is a figure of speech that compares two things using the word *like* or *as*.
  Example: "Death lies on her like an untimely frost." (*Romeo and Juliet*)

- A METAPHOR is a figure of speech that compares two things without using the word *like* or *as*.
  Example: "Juliet is the sun!" (*Romeo and Juliet*)

Sonnet 18

William Shakespeare

MARK & ANALYZE

Read this selection once on your own, marking the text in any way that is helpful to you.

Then read the narrative a second time, using the questions in the margins to help you analyze the literature. When you see this pencil ✎, you'll be asked to mark up the text.

BACKGROUND Shakespeare expressed a great variety of thoughts and feelings in his 154 sonnets. The four sonnets you will read illustrate that variety. The first two celebrate the joy that love can bring. The third offers a definition of love. The fourth makes fun of the exaggerations that poets sometimes use in describing love.

Shall I compare thee to a summer's day?
Thou art more lovely and more temperate:
Rough winds do shake the darling buds of May,
And summer's lease hath all too short a date:
5 Sometime too hot the eye of heaven shines,
And often is his gold complexion dimmed;
And every fair from fair sometime declines,
By chance or nature's changing course untrimmed;[1]
But thy eternal summer shall not fade, ▶
10 Nor lose possession of that fair thou owest;[2]
Nor shall Death brag thou wander'st in his shade,
When in eternal lines to time thou growest:[3]
    So long as men can breathe, or eyes can see,
    So long lives this, and this gives life to thee. ▶

CONTRAST

Circle two ways in which the subject of the poem is different from a summer's day. ✎

ANALYZE

Why do you think the poet chooses to focus on ways in which his love and a summer day are different, instead of describing their similarities?

_____

_____

---

1. **fair from . . . untrimmed:** beauty eventually fades, due to misfortune or natural aging.
2. **thou owest:** you own; you possess.
3. **When . . . growest:** when in immortal poetry you become a part of time.

Sonnet 29

William Shakespeare

CONNECT

Read the first two **quatrains**. Do you think the poet is expressing feelings most people have at one time or another? Explain.

_____

_____

_____

_____

When in disgrace with Fortune and men's eyes
I all alone beweep my outcast state,
And trouble deaf heaven with my bootless[1] cries,
And look upon myself and curse my fate,
5 Wishing me like to one more rich in hope,
Featur'd like him,[2] like him with friends possess'd,
Desiring this man's art, and that man's scope,[3]
With what I most enjoy contented least; ◄
Yet in these thoughts myself almost despising,
10 Haply[4] I think on thee, and then my state,
Like to the lark[5] at break of day arising
From sullen earth, sings hymns at heaven's gate,
    For thy sweet love rememb'red such wealth brings,
    That then I scorn to change my state with kings. ◄

ANALYZE

Draw a box around the section of the poem where the **turn** occurs. Then underline the **simile** in that section.

1. **bootless:** futile; useless.
2. **Featur'd like him:** with his handsome features.
3. **this man's art . . . scope:** this man's skill and that man's intelligence.
4. **Haply:** by chance.
5. **lark:** the English skylark, noted for its beautiful singing while soaring in flight.

Sonnet 116

William Shakespeare

Let me not to the marriage of true minds
Admit impediments;[1] love is not love
Which alters when it alteration finds,
Or bends with the remover to remove.
5 O no, it is an ever-fixéd mark[2]
That looks on tempests and is never shaken;
It is the star to every wand'ring bark,
Whose worth's unknown, although his height be taken.[3]
Love's not Time's fool, though rosy lips and cheeks
10 Within his bending sickle's compass come,[4]
Love alters not with his brief hours and weeks,
But bears it out even to the edge of doom.[5] ▶

  If this be error and upon me proved,
  I never writ, nor no man ever loved. ▶

TestSmart

Which line of "Sonnet 116" contains a metaphor?

A line 2

B line 5

C line 11

D line 13

TIP A test may ask you to identify a **metaphor.** To answer, remember that a metaphor is a **figure of speech** in which one thing is described as if it were something else. The words *is* or *are* often signal a metaphor.

ANALYZE

Underline references to time in the sonnet. ✎

What message does the poet convey about the effects of time on love?

_____

_____

---

1. **impediments:** obstacles.

2. **mark:** a landmark seen from the sea and used by sailors as a guide in navigation.

3. **the star . . . taken:** the star—usually the North Star—whose altitude sailors measure in order to help guide their ships. A **bark** is a sailing ship.

4. **within . . . come:** come within range of Time's curving sickle.

5. **bears . . . doom:** endures even to Judgment Day, the time when, Christian teachings predict, the world will end and God will make his final judgment of all people.

Sonnet
130

William Shakespeare

COMPARE

Compare the views of beauty in "Sonnet 18" and "Sonnet 130." Which one do you think is more complimentary of the poem's subject?

_____

_____

_____

Underline examples in each poem that support your answer.

Big Question

Do you think any of the speakers in these poems see love clearly? Explain.

_____

_____

_____

_____

My mistress' eyes are nothing like the sun;
Coral is far more red than her lips' red;
If snow be white, why then her breasts are dun;[1]
If hairs be wires, black wires grow on her head.
5 I have seen roses damask'd,[2] red and white,
But no such roses see I in her cheeks,
And in some perfumes is there more delight
Than in the breath that from my mistress reeks.[3]
I love to hear her speak, yet well I know
10 That music hath a far more pleasing sound;
I grant I never saw a goddess go,[4]
My mistress when she walks treads on the ground.
    And yet, by heaven, I think my love as rare
    As any she belied with false compare.[5] ◀

---

1. **dun:** grayish brown.
2. **damask'd:** mottled; spotted or streaked with different colors.
3. **reeks:** is exhaled (used here without the word's present reference to offensive odors).
4. **go:** walk.
5. **As any . . . compare:** as any woman misrepresented by exaggerated comparisons.

Reading Comprehension

DIRECTIONS *Answer these questions about the poems by filling in the correct ovals.*

1. Which line from "Sonnet 18" contains a metaphor?

   (A) line 3

   (B) line 5

   (C) line 13

   (D) line 14

2. What does the speaker of "Sonnet 18" say will "give life" to the person he addresses?

   (A) the speaker's love

   (B) this sonnet

   (C) the warmth of summer

   (D) physical beauty

3. What condition does the speaker of "Sonnet 29" express in the simile in lines 10–12?

   (A) his musical talent

   (B) the lifting of his depression

   (C) his soaring fortune

   (D) his love of nature

4. What idea does the speaker of "Sonnet 29" express in the poem's couplet?

   (A) He is filled with jealousy.

   (B) He has grown wealthy over time.

   (C) He hates all kings.

   (D) Love allows him to accept himself.

5. What do the metaphors in lines 5 and 7 of "Sonnet 116" suggest about the nature of love?

   (A) Love is full of obstacles.

   (B) Love is often stormy.

   (C) Love can doom people.

   (D) Love never changes.

6. What does the phrase "Love's not Time's fool" in line 9 of "Sonnet 116" suggest?

   (A) Love lasts forever.

   (B) Fools can never love.

   (C) Love is not foolish.

   (D) Lovers should be cautious.

7. What idea does the speaker express about his mistress in lines 11–12 of "Sonnet 130"?

   (A) She is like a goddess to him.

   (B) She will be immortal.

   (C) She is merely human.

   (D) She walks too slowly.

8. What does the speaker reveal in lines 13–14 of "Sonnet 130"?

   (A) He has deep love for his mistress.

   (B) He rarely loves his mistress

   (C) His mistress has been false to him.

   (D) His mistress rarely tells lies.

GO ON

For help, use the **Test-Taker's Toolkit** below.

Responding in Writing

9. Short Response Write a summary of one of Shakespeare's sonnets, breaking it down into the four parts of its structure. Identify where the turn occurs.

_____

_____

_____

_____

_____

TEST-TAKER'S TOOLKIT

❂ **GRAPHIC ORGANIZER** Use the chart below to help you plan your response. Reread the poems to help you remember details.

SONNET: _____	
First Quatrain	**Third Quatrain**
Second Quatrain	**Couplet**

What's the Connection?

Shakespeare suggests that just thinking about someone you love can turn depression into joy. The article "All You Need Is Love" offers scientific evidence that loving and being loved have positive effects on health.

THINK ABOUT LOVE With a partner, brainstorm three positive effects you think love might have on a person's health. List those effects in the boxes below. After you have read the article, compare what you have learned to your responses.

All You Need Is Love
MAGAZINE ARTICLE

Use with Selected Poetry by William Shakespeare, p. 82

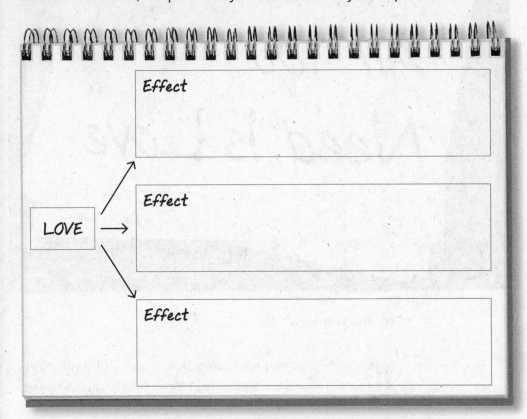

LOVE

Effect

Effect

Effect

LEARN THE SKILL: ANALYZE TEXT FEATURES

You can use the **text features** in a nonfiction selection to preview a text, identify its main ideas, understand how information is organized, and get a deeper understanding of the topic.

- The **title** suggests an article's topic.
- **Subheadings** usually name the selection's main ideas.
- **Sidebars** provide additional information related to the main text.
- **Graphic aids** such as diagrams, charts, and maps provide information in visual form.

For more on analyzing text features, see the Nonfiction Skills Handbook beginning on page R2.

SET A PURPOSE

_____

_____

_____

Medical Associates

All You Need Is Love

Refill 0 1 2 3 4 5 PRN   M.D.

TEXT FEATURES

Preview the article. Which text features appear in the selection? Check all that apply.

- [ ] title
- [ ] subheading
- [ ] sidebar
- [ ] map

Based on your preview, what do you think you'll learn about love?

_____

_____

_____

by Jill Neimark

Imagine getting a prescription that reads: "100 milligrams of love, twice daily, unlimited renewals." Caring, of course, can't be put in a capsule, but it can heal as powerfully as medicine. "Love is a basic human need," says Dean Ornish, M.D., author of *Love and Survival: 8 Pathways to Intimacy and Health.* "When we don't get it, we pay a price in how long we live and how likely we are to get sick."

We may also pay a price if we don't give love. According to Stephen Post, Ph.D., professor of bioethics and religion at Ohio's
10 Case Western University, research shows that loving acts neutralize the kind of negative emotions that adversely affect immune, endocrine and cardiovascular function. Studies published over the past five years show that loving and helping others has health benefits, says Post. There may even be a physiological response or "helper's high" that makes people feel stronger and more energetic and counters some of the harmful effects of stress.

But beyond our need to get and give it, what is love? How do we define something as essential and invisible as air? Researchers often look at human connection as the cardinal signal of love.

20 Loving Ties

Fifty years ago at the University of Wisconsin, psychologist Harry Harlow believed that affection and connection were the foundations of life. In a landmark experiment, Harlow took baby monkeys from their real mothers, giving them wire "moms" devised to deliver milk. But the youngsters would only cuddle when their surrogates were covered in a furry cloth. These monkeys thrived, while those with the bare-wire models didn't. The results proved Harlow's theory that attachment to another is as crucial a drive as thirst, hunger and sex.

30 In the ensuing decades, scientists have taken the study of love in new directions, examining everything from the impact of a mother's smile on her baby to the healing power of hugs. An interesting discovery has been how many kinds of connections count. Ties to friends, family, work, neighbors and community can all bolster health and happiness. One example: After hundreds of students at Carnegie Mellon University were exposed to a cold virus, those who had one to three types of social bonds were four times more likely to develop a cold than those with six or more types.

Disruptions to connections also affect health, as shown by research in primate bonding, which remains a template for its human counter-part. Sally Mendoza, Ph.D., professor of psychology at the University of
40 California at Davis, found that isolating one squirrel monkey from its group caused a sudden spike not only in that animal's stress hormones, but in the stress hormones of its fellows as well. ▶

Meanwhile, social support appears to prolong life. A Duke University study of 1,400 people with heart disease found that those with a spouse or confidant died at one-third the rate of those who felt isolated. And Dartmouth Medical School researchers noted that participation in church or civic activities extended the lives of open-heart surgery patients.

"Other studies have since confirmed that social isolation increases the risk of early death up to five times," Ornish says. "Connection is the foun-
50 dation of health. You can be sure that if a drug or a new surgical technique came out that increased survival that much, every doctor in the country would be using it." ▶

SPECIALIZED Vocabulary

The word *template*, which appears in line 38, has specialized meanings in several fields. For example, in computer science a template is a formatted document that functions as a starting point in software programs. But *template* also has a more general meaning; it describes something used as a pattern for making something similar. Underline words and phrases in lines 29–42 that suggest this meaning. ✎

SYNTHESIZE

The author cites six studies or groups of studies on this page. Number them 1–6. ✎

What conclusion do you draw from these studies?

Beyond Romance

A powerful shift is occurring in the understanding of love, declares Deborah Blum, Pulitzer Prize–winning science writer and author of *Love at Goon Park*: *Harry Harlow and the Science of Affection*. "The science of today puts kindness ahead of romance," she says. "The field of psychology has shifted away from Freud and sexuality to an adult view of love as responsibility and caring. The message is very clear: Taking care of each other is the nature of love."

Post couldn't agree more. His Institute for Research on Unlimited Love awards grants to study altruism in action. "My hypothesis is that voluntary, generous, helping behavior enhances health, self-esteem and happiness," he says.

Giving love allows you to ascertain who you are. "I define love as the unsought-for discovery of self through giving," Post says. He sees love as our indestructible core, an insight he confirmed when he began to work with Alzheimer's sufferers. "People with cognitive deficits are incredibly sensitive to affection. Any person can respond profoundly to love." ◄

Post recalls one Alzheimer's patient who handed him a twig with a big smile. "If love was wind, you'd have been blown off your chair by the love in his eyes," he says. "I learned that when he was a little boy he adored his father, and his morning chore was to bring in kindling for the fireplace."

COMPARE AND CONTRAST

Reread lines 54–70. Underline two definitions of love. 🖉

How are the definitions similar?

_____

_____

How are they different?

_____

_____

TEXT FEATURES

How does the **sidebar** on this page support the main text?

_____

_____

_____

Your Rx for Love

Here are some simple actions to bring more love into your life.

Do small things with great kindness.   To get started in a more generous life, be a sincerely attentive presence and a good and empathetic listener wherever you are, says bioethicist Stephen Post.

Volunteer. Anything that will help us freely transcend the boundaries of separateness is joyful, according to cardiologist and author Dean Ornish. Studies of volunteers have determined that not only do they tend to live longer, they often feel better, sometimes reporting a burst of feel-good endorphins as they're helping others. ◄

Extend and Connect

So how do we "self-medicate" with love? You can begin with a simple exercise in awareness: Choose a neutral person in your world, perhaps someone who sells you a morning coffee, and think of that person with compassion. "This practice awakens feelings of resonance and joy, which actually changes your biology [by releasing the chemical dopamine in the brain]," says Sally Severino, M.D., professor of psychiatry at the University of New Mexico.

Move on to visualizing those closest to you with compassion. "The key is to cultivate a feeling of joy when you connect with others," says University of California at Los Angeles psychiatrist Jeffrey Schwartz, M.D. His brain-imaging studies have shown that compassionate practices stabilize and balance brain function, sometimes as effectively as medications such as antidepressants. ▶

Finally, remember that love takes many forms, and that connection is more than romantic love. Expand your circle of love into a friendship toward all living things.

"I used to feel loved because I thought I was special," says Ornish. "Now I feel special because I am loved and because I can love."

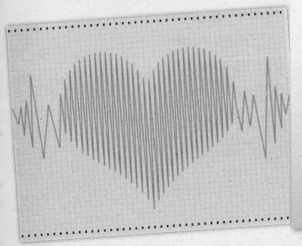

More Rx for Love

Touch and be touched. "Touching is intimate," says Ornish. "Lack of human contact can lead to profound isolation and illness. Give someone a pat on the back or a hug when they've done a good job—or even when they haven't. Get a massage or manicure or shampoo. Shake hands when you see a colleague. Hold hands with your beloved—and don't forget to kiss."

Avoid rudeness. Realize that when you are rude to people, they feel as if they don't matter. It reverberates down to the very core of their being, says Post. "Instead, be courteous to others, affirming that their existence is meaningful and worthy of attention."

Love, and do what you will. Echoing the philosophy of St. Augustine, psychiatrist Sally Severino says, "If you can get yourself into a state of love, no matter what you do, it's going to be good." ▶

EVALUATE

Underline two examples of scientific data that support the idea that love is a form of "medication." ✎

Do you think these facts provide adequate support for this idea? Explain.

_____

_____

_____

TESTSMART

The purpose of the sidebar is to

A give relevant tips

B give supporting details

C state the article's topic

D restate the main ideas

TIP A test question may ask you about the **purpose** of a particular **text feature**. In this case, think about which answer describes information that an author might feel is not essential to include in the main text of an article.

Reading Comprehension

DIRECTIONS *Answer these questions about the article and the poems in this lesson by filling in the correct ovals.*

1. The main idea in "All You Need Is Love" is that

   Ⓐ romantic love is important

   Ⓑ giving love is better than receiving it

   Ⓒ small kindnesses are important

   Ⓓ love helps keep people healthy

2. The main idea of the section "Loving Ties" is that

   Ⓐ surrogate monkeys should be furry

   Ⓑ people and animals need love

   Ⓒ hugs have healing power

   Ⓓ squirrel monkeys need their mothers

3. The purpose of the subheadings in "All You Need Is Love" is to

   Ⓐ explain types of love

   Ⓑ give practical advice

   Ⓒ sum up main ideas

   Ⓓ present results of studies

4. Which of these terms does *not* define love as it is described in "All You Need Is Love"?

   Ⓐ caring

   Ⓑ touching

   Ⓒ kind

   Ⓓ everlasting

5. Which statement would both Shakespeare and the author of "All You Need Is Love" agree with?

   Ⓐ Love is timeless.

   Ⓑ Love has a positive effect on a people.

   Ⓒ Lovers should be immortalized.

   Ⓓ Isolation shortens life.

6. Which idea from "All You Need Is Love" is supported by "Sonnet 29"?

   Ⓐ Love can diminish depression.

   Ⓑ Volunteering feels good.

   Ⓒ Relationships prolong life.

   Ⓓ Kindness is important.

7. In line 62 of "All You Need Is Love," *altruism* means

   Ⓐ unselfish concern

   Ⓑ perpetual selfishness

   Ⓒ unending happiness

   Ⓓ eternal truth

8. The word *cognitive* in line 74 of "All You Need Is Love" has to do with

   Ⓐ physical activity

   Ⓑ thinking

   Ⓒ health

   Ⓓ religion

Timed Writing Practice

PROMPT

Many literary works portray love as a powerful force that can change people's lives. Describe someone you have read about, real or fictional, whose (life was transformed by love.) The love doesn't have to be romantic—it could be the love between a parent and child or between close friends. Try to make your character description so vivid that your readers will feel that they know this person. Use an appropriate quote from one of Shakespeare's sonnets or the related nonfiction to help introduce your topic.

TEST-TAKER'S TOOLKIT

1. ANALYZE THE PROMPT

A. Identify the type of writing you are asked to do.

B. Circle any key words that describe the topic or indicate what you are required to include in your writing. One phrase has been circled for you.

2. PLAN YOUR RESPONSE

A. **Make notes** Decide which person or character you will write about. Brainstorm a list of events in his or her life, and choose examples that illustrate your ideas about love. Use this chart to list examples that you plan to include.

B. **Organize your information** Your description should begin with an introduction in which you use a quote to help convey the point you wish to make about your subject. Then you can write a paragraph for each event you included in your chart. You may not be able to describe your subject's entire life; focus on key events that relate to your topic.

Event	Importance of Love

3. WRITE AND REVIEW

A. Write a conclusion that vividly summarizes the portrait you have created of your subject. You might ask a thought-provoking question that encourages readers to relate your description to their own lives.

B. Be sure to leave time to check your spelling and grammar.

JUST-STARVE-US.
WORKHOUSE

Tell Ah! Tell us, can aught be worse?
Than hungry Maw & empty Purse!!
MERCY SHOW & PITY US,
GREAT OVERSEER.

How can we fight INJUSTICE?

There's an old proverb that states, "The pen is mightier than the sword." Jonathan Swift wielded his pen like a rapier, using it to slash away at injustice. Though some may claim that the power of the pen is greatly diminished these days, people still fight injustice with words—in speeches, in newspapers and magazines, and on the Internet.

CHART IT With a small group, brainstorm some contemporary examples of injustice. Write three of them down in the chart. For each example, identify some tactics that people can use to fight the injustice.

Examples of Injustice	Tactics for Fighting Injustice

ASSESSMENT GOALS

By the end of this lesson, you will be able to . . .

- analyze satire
- apply critical thinking skills to analyze text
- evaluate news articles
- analyze a writing prompt and plan a problem-solution essay

Satire

SATIRE is a literary technique in which behaviors or institutions are ridiculed for the purpose of improving society. What sets satire apart from other forms of social and political protest is humor. For example, Swift used his savage wit to attack prominent British politicians and to protest unjust policies in Ireland.

The following chart shows three types of IRONY that Swift used in his satires. Look for examples of these techniques as you read "A Modest Proposal."

TECHNIQUE	EXAMPLE
SITUATIONAL IRONY a contrast between what is expected and what actually occurs	After safely completing a dangerous mountain climb, a climber slips in the shower and hurts herself.
VERBAL IRONY when a writer or character says one thing but means the opposite	A football player fumbles the ball and loses the game. When he reaches the sideline, his coach tells him, "Nice play!"
UNDERSTATEMENT a form of irony that creates emphasis by saying less than what is true or appropriate	Reporting from a town that was hit by a hurricane, a reporter describes the place as "a bit messy."

ADDITIONAL TERMS FOR CRITICAL ANALYSIS

The selection you are about to read is an example of JUVENALIAN SATIRE. This kind of satire bitterly condemns human wrongdoing and foolishness, and reflects moral outrage on the part of the speaker. In contrast, HORATIAN SATIRE is a more tolerant treatment of human folly. Instead of expressing anger, Horatian satire reflects the speaker's ironic amusement toward the subject.

A Modest Proposal

FOR PREVENTING THE CHILDREN OF POOR PEOPLE IN IRELAND
FROM BEING A BURDEN TO THEIR PARENTS OR COUNTRY,
AND FOR MAKING THEM BENEFICIAL TO THE PUBLIC

JONATHAN SWIFT

BACKGROUND By 1700, Ireland was completely dominated by England. The Catholic majority could not vote, hold public office, buy land, or receive an education—policies that reduced most Irish people to poverty. When crops failed, many faced starvation. Jonathan Swift, outraged by England's treatment of Ireland, wrote a satirical attack on this injustice in "A Modest Proposal."

It is a melancholy object to those who walk through this great town[1] or travel in the country, when they see the streets, the roads, and cabin doors, crowded with beggars of the female sex, followed by three, four, or six children, all in rags and importuning every passenger for an alms.[2] These mothers, instead of being able to work for their honest livelihood, are forced to employ all their time in strolling to beg **sustenance** for their helpless infants, who, as they grow up, either turn thieves for want[3] of work, or leave their dear native country to fight for the Pretender[4] in Spain, or sell themselves to the Barbadoes.[5] ▶

10   I think it is agreed by all parties that this prodigious number of children in the arms, or on the backs, or at the heels of their mothers, and

---

1. **this great town:** Dublin, Ireland.
2. **importuning** (ĭm'pôr-to͞on'ĭng) **. . . alms** (ämz): begging from every passerby for a charitable handout.
3. **want:** lack; need.
4. **Pretender:** James Edward Stuart, who claimed the English throne, from which his now deceased father, James II, had been removed in 1688. Because James II and his son were Roman Catholic, the common people of Ireland were loyal to them.
5. **sell . . . Barbadoes:** To escape poverty, some Irish migrated to the West Indies, obtaining money for their passage by agreeing to work as slaves on plantations there for a set period.

MARK & ANALYZE

Read this selection once on your own, marking the text in any way that is helpful to you.

Then read the narrative a second time, using the questions in the margins to help you analyze the literature. When you see this pencil ✏, you'll be asked to mark up the text.

sustenance (sŭs'tə-nəns) *n.* a means of support or nourishment

ANALYZE

Underline the generalizations the speaker makes about poor children in lines 1–9. ✏

How do these statements help set up the proposal to come?

_____

_____

_____

_____

frequently of their fathers, is in the present deplorable state of the kingdom a very great additional grievance; and therefore whoever could find out a fair, cheap, and easy method of making these children sound, useful members of the commonwealth would deserve so well of the public as to have his statue set up for a preserver of the nation.

But my intention is very far from being confined to provide only for the children of professed beggars; it is of a much greater extent, and shall take in the whole number of infants at a certain age who are born of
20 parents in effect as little able to support them as those who demand our charity in the streets.

As to my own part, having turned my thoughts for many years upon this important subject, and maturely weighed the several schemes of other projectors,[6] I have always found them grossly mistaken in their computation. It is true, a child just dropped from its dam[7] may be supported by her milk for a solar year, with little other nourishment; at most not above the value of two shillings, which the mother may certainly get, or the value in scraps, by her lawful occupation of begging; and it is exactly at one year old that I propose to provide for them in such a manner
30 as instead of being a charge upon their parents or the parish, or wanting food and raiment for the rest of their lives, they shall on the contrary contribute to the feeding, and partly to the clothing, of many thousands. ◄

There is likewise another great advantage in my scheme, that it will prevent those voluntary abortions, and that horrid practice of women murdering their bastard children, alas, too frequent among us, sacrificing the poor innocent babes, I doubt,[8] more to avoid the expense than the shame, which would move tears and pity in the most savage and inhuman breast.

The number of souls in this kingdom being usually reckoned one
40 million and a half, of these I calculate there may be about two hundred thousand couple whose wives are breeders; from which number I subtract thirty thousand couples who are able to maintain their own children, although I apprehend there cannot be so many under the present distresses of the kingdom; but this being granted, there will remain an hundred and seventy thousand breeders. I again subtract fifty thousand for those women who miscarry, or whose children die by accident or disease within the year. There only remain an hundred and twenty thousand children of poor parents annually born. The question therefore is, how this number ◄

INTERPRET

Reread lines 25–26, in which the author refers to a new mother as a "dam." What effect does this choice of words have?

_____

_____

_____

_____

ANALYZE

Reread the boxed text. Why does the speaker use mathematical language when discussing the poor?

_____

_____

_____

_____

6. **projectors:** persons who propose public projects or plans.
7. **dam** (dăm): female parent. The term is used mostly for farm animals.
8. **doubt:** suspect.

shall be reared and provided for, which, as I have already said, under the
50 present situation of affairs, is utterly impossible by all the methods hitherto
proposed. For we can neither employ them in handicraft or agriculture;
we neither build houses (I mean in the country) nor cultivate land. They
can very seldom pick up a livelihood by stealing till they arrive at six years
old, except where they are of towardly parts;[9] although I confess they learn
the <u>rudiments</u> much earlier, during which time they can however be
looked upon only as probationers, as I have been informed by a principal
gentleman in the county of Cavan, who protested to me that he never
knew above one or two instances under the age of six, even in a part of the
kingdom so renowned for the quickest proficiency in that art.

60   I am assured by our merchants that a boy or girl before twelve years old
is no salable commodity; and even when they come to this age they will
not yield above three pounds, or three pounds and half a crown at most on
the Exchange; which cannot turn to account[10] either to the parents or the
kingdom, the charge of nutriment and rags having been at least four times
that value.

    I shall now therefore humbly propose my own thoughts, which I hope
will not be liable to the least objection.

    I have been assured by a very knowing American of my acquaintance
in London, that a young healthy child well nursed is at a year old a most
70 delicious, nourishing, and wholesome food, whether stewed, roasted,
baked, or boiled; and I make no doubt that it will equally serve in a
fricassee or a ragout.[11]

    I do therefore humbly offer it to public consideration that of the
hundred and twenty thousand children, already computed, twenty
thousand may be reserved for breed,[12] whereof only one fourth part to
be males, which is more than we allow to sheep, black cattle, or swine;
and my reason is that these children are seldom the fruits of marriage, a
circumstance not much regarded by our savages, therefore one male will
be sufficient to serve four females. That the remaining hundred thousand
80 may at a year old be offered in sale to the persons of quality and fortune
through the kingdom, always advising the mother to let them suck
plentifully in the last month, so as to render them plump and fat for a
good table. A child will make two dishes at an entertainment for friends; ▶
and when the family dines alone, the fore or hind quarter will make a

rudiment (rōō′də-mənt) *n.* a
basic principle or element

CONTRAST

Reread the boxed text.
Compare the way the speaker
describes the poor with the
way he describes the rich.

_____

_____

_____

_____

Underline details that support
your answer. 🖉

---

9. **are of towardly** (tôrd′lē) **parts:** have a promising talent.
10. **turn to account:** earn a profit; benefit; prove useful.
11. **fricassee** (frĭk′ə-sē′) **. . . ragout** (ră-gōō′): types of meat stews.
12. **reserved for breed:** kept for breeding (instead of being slaughtered).

ANALYZE

Reread the boxed text. In
what way does this passage
reflect the characteristics of
Juvenalian satire?

_____

_____

_____

_____

collateral (kə-lăt′ər-əl) *adj.*
accompanying as a parallel or
subordinate factor; related

INTERPRET

Why is the sentence in
lines 111–113 an example of
understatement?

_____

_____

_____

_____

reasonable dish, and seasoned with a little pepper or salt will be very good
boiled on the fourth day, especially in winter.

I have reckoned upon a medium that a child just born will weigh
twelve pounds, and in a solar year if tolerably nursed increaseth to twenty-
eight pounds.

90   I grant this food will be somewhat dear, and therefore very proper for
landlords, who, as they have already devoured most of the parents, seem to
have the best title to the children. ◄

Infant's flesh will be in season throughout the year, but more plentiful
in March, and a little before and after. For we are told by a grave author,
an eminent French physician,[13] that fish being a prolific[14] diet, there are
more children born in Roman Catholic countries about nine months after
Lent[15] than at any other season; therefore, reckoning a year after Lent, the
markets will be more glutted than usual, because the number of popish
infants is at least three to one in this kingdom; and therefore it will have
100 one other <u>collateral</u> advantage, by lessening the number of Papists[16]
among us.

I have already computed the charge of nursing a beggar's child (in
which list I reckon all cottagers, laborers, and four fifths of the farmers),
to be about two shillings per annum, rags included; and I believe no
gentleman would repine to give ten shillings for the carcass of a good fat
child, which, as I have said, will make four dishes of excellent nutritive
meat, when he hath only some particular friend or his own family to dine
with him. Thus the squire will learn to be a good landlord, and grow
popular among the tenants; the mother will have eight shillings net profit,
110 and be fit for work till she produces another child.

Those who are more thrifty (as I must confess the times require) may
flay the carcass; the skin of which artificially dressed will make admirable
gloves for ladies, and summer boots for fine gentlemen. ◄

As to our city of Dublin, shambles[17] may be appointed for this purpose
in the most convenient parts of it, and butchers we may be assured
will not be wanting; although I rather recommend buying the children
alive, and dressing them hot from the knife as we do roasting pigs.

---

13. **grave . . . physician:** François Rabelais (răb′ə-lā′), a 16th-century French satirist.
14. **prolific:** promoting fertility.
15. **Lent:** Catholics traditionally do not eat meat during Lent, the 40 days leading up
     to Easter, and instead eat a lot of fish.
16. **popish** (pō′pǐsh) **. . . Papists:** hostile or contemptuous terms referring to Roman
     Catholics.
17. **shambles:** slaughterhouses.

A very worthy person, a true lover of his country, and whose virtues I highly esteem, was lately pleased in discoursing on this matter to offer a refinement upon my scheme. He said that many gentlemen of this kingdom, having of late destroyed their deer, he conceived that the want of venison might be well supplied by the bodies of young lads and maidens, not exceeding fourteen years of age nor under twelve, so great a number of both sexes in every county being now ready to starve for want of work and service; and these to be disposed of by their parents, if alive, or otherwise by their nearest relations. But with due **deference** to so excellent a friend and so deserving a patriot, I cannot be altogether in his sentiments; for as to the males, my American acquaintance assured me from frequent experience that their flesh was generally tough and lean, like that of our schoolboys, by continual exercise, and their taste disagreeable; and to fatten them would not answer the charge. Then as to the females, it would, I think with humble submission, be a loss to the public, because they soon would become breeders themselves; and besides, it is not improbable that some scrupulous people might be apt to censure such a practice (although indeed very unjustly) as a little bordering upon cruelty; which, I confess, hath always been with me the strongest objection against any project, how well soever intended.

But in order to justify my friend, he confessed that this **expedient** was put into his head by the famous Psalmanazar, a native of the island Formosa,[18] who came from thence to London above twenty years ago, and in conversation told my friend that in his country when any young person happened to be put to death, the executioner sold the carcass to persons of quality as a prime dainty; and that in his time the body of a plump girl of fifteen, who was crucified for an attempt to poison the emperor, was sold to his Imperial Majesty's prime minister of state, and other great mandarins of the court, in joints from the gibbet,[19] at four hundred crowns. Neither indeed can I deny that if the same use were made of several plump young girls in this town, who without one single groat[20] to their fortunes cannot stir abroad without a chair,[21] and appear at the playhouse and assemblies in foreign fineries which they never will pay for, the kingdom would not be the worse. ▶

---

18. **Psalmanazar** (săl′mə-năz′ər) ... **Formosa** (fôr-mō′sə): a French imposter in London who called himself George Psalmanazar and pretended to be from Formosa (now Taiwan), where, he said, cannibalism was practiced.

19. **gibbet** (jĭb′ĭt): gallows.

20. **groat:** an old British coin worth four pennies.

21. **cannot stir ... chair:** cannot go outside without using an enclosed chair carried on poles by two men.

deference (dĕf′ər-əns) *n.* a yielding or courteous regard toward the opinion, judgment, or wishes of others; respect

expedient (ĭk-spē′dē-ənt) *n.* something useful in achieving the desired effect; a convenience; an advantage

ANALYZE

How would you describe the speaker's **tone** in lines 138–151? Check one.

☐ matter-of-fact
☐ appalled
☐ disapproving

What effect does this tone have on the subject matter being discussed?

_____

_____

_____

Some persons of a desponding spirit are in great concern about that vast number of poor people who are aged, diseased, or maimed, and I have been desired to employ my thoughts what course may be taken to ease the nation of so grievous an **encumbrance**. But I am not in the least pain upon that matter, because it is very well known that they are every day dying and rotting by cold and **famine**, and filth and vermin, as fast as can be reasonably expected. And as to the younger laborers, they are now in almost as hopeful a condition. They cannot get work, and consequently pine away for want of nourishment to a degree that if at any time they are accidentally hired to common labor, they have not strength to perform it; and thus the country and themselves are happily delivered from the evils to come. ◀

I have too long digressed, and therefore shall return to my subject. I think the advantages by the proposal which I have made are obvious and many, as well as of the highest importance.

For first, as I have already observed, it would greatly lessen the number of Papists, with whom we are yearly overrun, being the principal breeders of the nation as well as our most dangerous enemies; and who stay at home on purpose to deliver the kingdom to the Pretender, hoping to take their advantage by the absence of so many good Protestants, who have chosen rather to leave their country than stay at home and pay tithes against their conscience to an Episcopal curate.[22]

Secondly, the poorer tenants will have something valuable of their own, which by law may be made liable to distress,[23] and help to pay their landlord's rent, their corn and cattle being already seized and money a thing unknown.

Thirdly, whereas the maintenance of an hundred thousand children, from two years old and upwards, cannot be computed at less than ten shillings a piece per annum, the nation's stock will be thereby increased fifty thousand pounds per annum, besides the profit of a new dish introduced to the tables of all gentlemen of fortune in the kingdom who have any refinement in taste. And the money will circulate among ourselves, the goods being entirely of our own growth and manufacture.

Fourthly, the constant breeders, besides the gain of eight shillings sterling per annum by the sale of their children, will be rid of the charge of maintaining them after the first year.

160

170

180

22. **Protestants . . . curate** (kyŏŏr′ĭt): Swift is criticizing absentee Anglo-Irish landowners who lived—and spent their income from their property—in England.
23. **distress:** seizure of a person's property for the payment of debts.

Fifthly, this food would likewise bring great custom to taverns, where the vintners will certainly be so prudent as to procure the best receipts[24] for dressing it to perfection, and consequently have their houses frequented by all the fine gentlemen, who justly value themselves upon their knowledge in good eating; and a skillful cook, who understands how to oblige his guests, will contrive to make it as expensive as they please.

Sixthly, this would be a great inducement to marriage, which all wise nations have either encouraged by rewards or enforced by laws and penalties. It would increase the care and tenderness of mothers toward their children, when they were sure of a settlement for life to the poor babes, provided in some sort by the public, to their annual profit instead of expense. We should see an honest emulation among the married women, which of them could bring the fattest child to the market. Men would become as fond of their wives during the time of their pregnancy as they are now of their mares in foal, their cows in calf, or sows when they are ready to farrow; nor offer to beat or kick them (as is too frequent a practice) for fear of a miscarriage. ▶

Many other advantages might be enumerated. For instance, the addition of some thousand carcasses in our exportation of barreled beef, the **propagation** of swine's flesh, and improvement in the art of making good bacon, so much wanted among us by the great destruction of pigs, too frequent at our tables, which are no way comparable in taste or magnificence to a well-grown, fat, yearling child, which roasted whole will make a considerable figure at a lord mayor's feast or any other public entertainment. But this and many others I omit, being studious of brevity. ▶

Supposing that one thousand families in this city would be constant customers for infants' flesh, besides others who might have it at merry meetings, particularly weddings and christenings, I compute that Dublin would take off annually about twenty thousand carcasses, and the rest of the kingdom (where probably they will be sold somewhat cheaper) the remaining eighty thousand.

I can think of no one objection that will possibly be raised against this proposal, unless it should be urged that the number of people will be thereby much lessened in the kingdom. This I freely own, and it was indeed one principal design in offering it to the world. I desire the reader will observe, that I calculate my remedy for this one individual kingdom of Ireland and for no other that ever was, is, or I think ever can be upon

---

24. **receipts:** recipes.

EVALUATE
How convincing do you find the speaker's argument in lines 194–204 that his proposal would improve family life? Explain.

_____

_____

_____

_____

propagation (prŏp′ə-gā′shən) *n.* the act of reproducing, multiplying, or increasing

TESTSMART

VOCABULARY
The most likely meaning of the word *brevity* in line 212 is

Ⓐ courageous approach to problems

Ⓑ concise use of language

Ⓒ ironic discourse

Ⓓ the act of making merry

TIP Use **context clues** to figure out the meaning of an unfamiliar word. Reread lines 205–212, and underline any words or phrases that provide clues to the meaning of the word *brevity*. ✏

earth. Therefore let no man talk to me of other expedients: of taxing our absentees at five shillings a pound: of using neither clothes nor household furniture except what is of our own growth and manufacture: of utterly rejecting the materials and instruments that promote foreign luxury: of curing the expensiveness of pride, vanity, idleness, and gaming in our

230 women: of introducing a vein of parsimony,[25] prudence, and temperance: of learning to love our country, in the want of which we differ even from Laplanders and the inhabitants of Topinamboo:[26] of quitting our animosities and factions, nor acting any longer like the Jews, who were murdering one another at the very moment their city was taken:[27] of being a little cautious not to sell our country and conscience for nothing: of teaching landlords to have at least one degree of mercy toward their tenants: lastly, of putting a spirit of honesty, industry, and skill into our shopkeepers; who, if a resolution could now be taken to buy only our native goods, would immediately unite to cheat and exact upon us in the

240 price, the measure, and the goodness, nor could ever yet be brought to make one fair proposal of just dealing, though often and earnestly invited to it.

Therefore I repeat, let no man talk to me of these and the like expedients,[28] till he hath at least some glimpse of hope that there will ever be some hearty and sincere attempt to put them in practice. ◀

But as to myself, having been wearied out for many years with offering vain, idle, visionary thoughts, and at length utterly despairing of success, I fortunately fell upon this proposal, which, as it is wholly new, so it hath something solid and real, of no expense and little trouble, full in our own

250 power, and whereby we can incur no danger in disobliging England. For this kind of commodity will not bear exportation, the flesh being of too tender a consistence to admit a long continuance in salt, although perhaps I could name a country which would be glad to eat up our whole nation without it.

After all, I am not so violently bent upon my own opinion as to reject any offer proposed by wise men, which shall be found equally innocent, cheap, easy, and effectual. But before something of that kind shall be

ANALYZE

Reread lines 243–245 and footnote 28. What is **ironic** about Swift's dismissal of the "expedients" in the previous paragraph?

25. **parsimony** (pär′sə-mō′nē): frugality; thrift.
26. **Topinamboo** (tŏp′ĭ-năm′boō): an area in Brazil supposedly inhabited by wild savages.
27. **Jews . . . taken:** In A.D. 70, during a Jewish revolt against Roman rule, the inhabitants of Jerusalem, by fighting among themselves, made it easier for the Romans to capture the city.
28. **let no man . . . expedients:** In his writings, Swift had suggested "other expedients" without success.

advanced in contradiction to my scheme, and offering a better, I desire the
author or authors will be pleased maturely to consider two points. First, as
things now stand, how they will be able to find food and raiment for an
hundred thousand useless mouths and backs. And secondly, there being
a round million of creatures in human figure throughout this kingdom,
whose sole subsistence put into a common stock[29] would leave them in
debt two millions of pounds sterling, adding those who are beggars by
profession to the bulk of farmers, cottagers, and laborers, with their wives
and children who are beggars in effect; I desire those politicians who
dislike my overture, and may perhaps be so bold to attempt an answer,
that they will first ask the parents of these mortals whether they would not
at this day think it a great happiness to have been sold for food at a year
old in the manner I prescribe, and thereby have avoided such a perpetual
scene of misfortunes as they have since gone through by the oppression
of landlords, the impossibility of paying rent without money or trade, the
want of common sustenance, with neither house nor clothes to cover them
from the inclemencies of the weather, and the most inevitable prospect of
entailing the like or greater miseries upon their breed forever. ▶

   I profess, in the sincerity of my heart, that I have not the least personal
interest in endeavoring to promote this necessary work, having no other
motive than the public good of my country, by advancing our trade,
providing for infants, relieving the poor, and giving some pleasure to the
rich. I have no children by which I can propose to get a single penny; the
youngest being nine years old, and my wife past childbearing.

Which of the following
words *best* characterizes the
suggestion that poor adults
would have been better off
if they had been sold for
food as babies?

(A) prudent

(B) immoral

(C) forceful

(D) unusual

TIP Notice that the
question asks which is the
best answer. This tells you
that more than one answer
may be possible. Reread
lines 266–275, and **decide
which choice best fits the
message** of Swift's satire.

Big Question

Think about the
contemporary examples
of injustice that you listed
on page 99. How effective
would a **satire** similar to
"A Modest Proposal" be in
fighting these injustices?
Explain your answer.

_____

_____

_____

Reading Comprehension

DIRECTIONS *Answer these questions about "A Modest Proposal" by filling in the correct ovals.*

1. Suggesting that infants should be served at christenings (lines 213–218) is ironic because christenings

   Ⓐ are held by the rich

   Ⓑ celebrate a baby's birth

   Ⓒ are not held in Ireland

   Ⓓ commemorate privilege

2. Which word *best* describes the satire in lines 174–177?

   Ⓐ verbal irony

   Ⓑ situational irony

   Ⓒ understatement

   Ⓓ Juvenalian satire

3. Which of the following is an example of verbal irony?

   Ⓐ the title of the essay

   Ⓑ the speaker's description of mothers begging for food

   Ⓒ the estimate of 200,000 "breeders" in Ireland

   Ⓓ the argument that the proposal will encourage marriage

4. What technique does Swift use to create satire in lines 133–137, where the speaker suggests that some people might consider slaughtering and eating girls 12 to 14 years old "a little bordering upon cruelty"?

   Ⓐ situational irony

   Ⓑ verbal irony

   Ⓒ understatement

   Ⓓ hyperbole

5. Why does the speaker lack faith in the alternative solutions listed near the end of the essay?

   Ⓐ Similar proposals have been ignored in the past.

   Ⓑ These solutions have been tried and they didn't work.

   Ⓒ He is jealous of the people who have proposed these solutions.

   Ⓓ He thinks his own proposal is the most humane.

6. Which word *best* describes the effect that Swift wanted to have on his readers?

   Ⓐ exciting

   Ⓑ persuasive

   Ⓒ convincing

   Ⓓ horrifying

7. The word *prodigious* in line 10 means

   Ⓐ impoverished

   Ⓑ athletic

   Ⓒ enormous

   Ⓓ insignificant

8. What does the word *procure* mean in line 189?

   Ⓐ heal

   Ⓑ obtain

   Ⓒ prohibit

   Ⓓ cook

For help, use the **Test-Taker's Toolkit** below.

Responding in Writing

9. Short Response Does the real message of "A Modest Proposal" come across clearly, or could Swift's use of irony confuse readers into mistaking the satire for a sincere proposal? Write a brief evaluation of the essay, referring to at least two examples of irony to support your opinion.

_____

_____

_____

_____

_____

TEST-TAKER'S TOOLKIT

- ⊗ **ACADEMIC VOCABULARY** Remember that **situational irony** is a contrast between what is expected and what actually occurs; **verbal irony** occurs when a writer says one thing but means the opposite; and **understatement** is saying less than what is true or appropriate.

- ⊗ **GRAPHIC ORGANIZER** Use the chart below to help you plan your response.

Example of Irony	How It Relates to Swift's Message

Use with "A Modest Proposal," p. 98

What's the Connection?

In "A Modest Proposal," satirist Jonathan Swift presents a scathing commentary on the mistreatment and neglect of the poor in 18th-century Ireland. The news article you are about to read describes the plight of poor children in modern-day Honduras.

HELPING HANDS Poverty is a difficult problem to tackle in any society, even one far wealthier than Honduras. With a partner, brainstorm ways to help people who are living on the street. Consider measures that can be taken by governments, charitable organizations, and concerned individuals. For each idea, note possible objections to the measure.

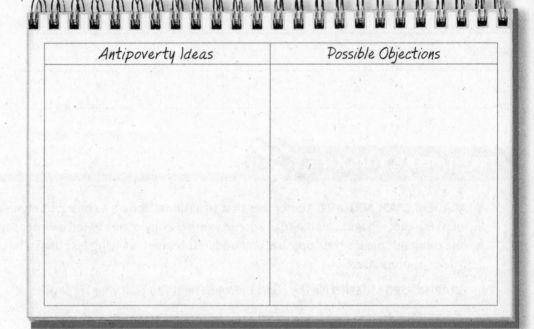

Antipoverty Ideas	Possible Objections

LEARN THE SKILL: EVALUATE NEWS ARTICLES

How do you know if a **news article** can be trusted? Use the following criteria to help you evaluate news articles.

Criteria	Look for . . .
The article is **objective.**	a balanced point of view, not a biased one
The information is **accurate.**	verifiable facts
The article is **thorough.**	background that tells who, what, when, where, why; representations of all sides of the story

For more on evaluating news articles, see the Evaluate Evidence entry in the Nonfiction Skills Handbook beginning on page R2.

Guilty of Poverty, Youth: "Street Kids" in Honduras

by Malcolm Garcia

EVALUATE NEWS ARTICLES

Is the headline of the article **objective,** or does it convey the author's opinion about his topic? Explain.

_____
_____
_____
_____
_____

TEGUCIGALPA, HONDURAS— When Honduran police snatched 11-year-old Roberto Alvarez off the street this summer, he was just about to buy candy with money he earned polishing shoes.

"I don't know where my family is," he said from a bare dormitory room at Hogares de Proteccion 10 Kennedy, a rundown facility of cement block buildings and a garbage-strewn playground that houses about 130 street children. A black metal bunk bed without mattresses stood in one corner slashed with light coming through a barred window. "I don't like it here," Roberto said.

Faced with chronic poverty and 20 a soaring crime rate, the Honduran government last spring began a sweep of street children such as Roberto, removing them to government-sponsored centers.

The centers, authorities say, offer the children a future by providing them with counseling and referrals to agencies. As of September, more than 1,000 children had been 30 picked up and sheltered for varying lengths of stays in one of four centers in the country. Each center

EXAMINE PERSPECTIVES

Do Jose Manuel Capellin and Eduardo Villanueva view the policy of rounding up street children from a similar perspective? Explain why or why not.

_____

_____

_____

_____

EVALUATE NEWS ARTICLES

Underline information in the boxed text that is factual. Circle information that is not factual.

Explain why the circled information cannot be verified.

_____

_____

_____

has room for 150 children, and all are full, according to Lesbia Lagos, director of Hogares de Proteccion Kennedy.

Children—some as young as 6—are taken to the centers by teams of police and social workers if they are seen begging, prostituting themselves or just walking the streets alone at night. Lagos said children who have families are returned home only if their parents have an income and the children attend school. Otherwise they are referred to nongovernmental organizations that work with children.

But many of these agencies won't accept the referrals, and the children stay much longer, possibly years, until they turn 18 and are considered adults.

"We won't take them if they've been taken by force because the child will just go back to the streets and hide," said Jose Manuel Capellin, national director of Casa Alianza, a nonprofit organization that assists poor and homeless children in Honduras and other parts of Central America.

"It is an impossible situation," said attorney Eduardo Villanueva, who represents children in the courts. "It is criminalizing poverty." ◀

The roundups reflect the tremendous social problems in one of the poorest and youngest democracies in the Western Hemisphere.

In Honduras, half the population of 6.5 million is under 18. The average monthly income is about $65, and the unemployment rate hovers at 28 percent. There are no reliable estimates as to the numbers of street children in Honduras. They are believed by government officials and advocates alike to be in the thousands. ◀

The sweeps come at a time when police are arresting hundreds of teenagers and young adults in a crackdown on gangs. Membership in gangs is now considered an "illicit association," which carries a sentence of up to seven years in jail. The law is a response to an increase of violent crime over the past decade by young gangs that have carved up major cities into their turf.

Human rights advocates argue that these initiatives violate civil rights, break up families and do little to improve the lives of impoverished children. Many families live in makeshift homes of aluminum siding or in cramped, single-room apartments above the clogged din of downtown.

"The people now feel they are living in a police state," said lawyer Gustavo Zelaya. "Is the solution always to have severe punishment?"

Business owners, however, support the crackdown. "Street children used to be all over downtown,"

HONDURAS FACTS

Government type: republic

Capital: Tegucigalpa

Economic rank: 2nd poorest country in Central America

Per Capita Gross Domestic Product: $3,100 ▶

Population below poverty line: 53%

Unemployment rate: 28%

Agricultural products: bananas, coffee, citrus, beef, timber, shrimp

Industries: sugar, coffee, textiles, clothing, wood products

Source: CIA: The World Factbook

said Gina Burgos, 48, general manager of the posh, castle-shaped Medieval Bar and Restaurant. "You couldn't go anywhere without them following you, coming into businesses asking for money, grabbing you. It's better now but a little strange. Where have they gone? They just disappeared from downtown."

Some apparently have not gone far. The government estimates that about 1,000 street children struggle to survive in barrios not far from downtown Tegucigalpa. They scavenge in the open-air markets, competing with feral dogs for scraps of food discarded by vendors.

Countless other children spend hours on the streets working to help support their families. They earn about $1 to $2 a day. However, they also fall under the government's definition of street children.

"Some of these children are helping their mothers and fathers, I know this," Lagos said. "But to work only, without education, they will become like their mothers and fathers. Nothing." ▶

Reading Comprehension

DIRECTIONS *Answer these questions about the two selections in this lesson by filling in the correct ovals.*

1. Gustavo Zelaya's statement in lines 103–107 supports the perspective that the street sweeps

   Ⓐ criminalize poverty

   Ⓑ are necessary

   Ⓒ help impoverished children

   Ⓓ improve downtown areas

2. Which person interviewed for the news article would be *least* likely to agree that street sweeps criminalize poverty?

   Ⓐ Roberto Alvarez

   Ⓑ Eduardo Villanueva

   Ⓒ Lesbia Lagos

   Ⓓ Gustavo Zelaya

3. Which statistic provided in the article helps explain why Hondurans are so poor?

   Ⓐ unemployment rate: 28%

   Ⓑ location: Central America

   Ⓒ industries: sugar, coffee, textiles

   Ⓓ population: 6.5 million

4. The graphic on page 115 adds to the article's credibility by providing

   Ⓐ a map of Honduras

   Ⓑ verifiable facts

   Ⓒ a balanced view

   Ⓓ background on street children

5. Modern-day Honduras and 18th-century Ireland are alike because in both places, poverty is

   Ⓐ sanitized

   Ⓑ ignored

   Ⓒ ridiculed

   Ⓓ widespread

6. Which societal element does *not* exist in both 18th-century Ireland and modern-day Honduras?

   Ⓐ generations of poverty

   Ⓑ a problem with theft

   Ⓒ anti-Catholic laws

   Ⓓ a business class

7. The word *hovers* in line 76 of the news article means

   Ⓐ floats above

   Ⓑ remains near

   Ⓒ watches closely

   Ⓓ threatens ominously

8. The most likely meaning of *barrios* in line 124 of the news article is

   Ⓐ garbage pits

   Ⓑ government agencies

   Ⓒ suburban sprawl

   Ⓓ urban slums

Timed Writing Practice

BUDGET YOUR TIME

You have **45 minutes** to respond. Decide how much time to spend on each step.

Analyze _____

Plan _____

Write _____

Review _____

45

PROMPT

Swift wasn't serious about the plan he outlined in "A Modest Proposal," but he took the problem of Irish poverty very seriously. Write a problem-solution essay in which you propose one step that should be taken to help the poor. Narrow the focus of your essay to address a specific example of poverty. You can focus on the conditions described in one of the selections you have read, or you can choose another example of poverty that you are familiar with. Provide at least three reasons for your solution, and one or two details to support each reason.

TEST-TAKER'S TOOLKIT

1. ANALYZE THE PROMPT

A. Underline the type of writing you are being asked to do.

B. Circle any key words that describe what should be included in your writing. One example has been circled for you.

2. PLAN YOUR RESPONSE

A. **Make notes** Decide which example of poverty you will focus on, and brainstorm a list of possible solutions. Choose the solution you will propose in your essay. In the chart here, list three reasons why your solution will help the poor, and list details to support your reasons.

B. **Organize your information** In the introductory paragraph, describe the specific problem of poverty that you will address in the essay, and clearly state a solution. Then you can write a paragraph for each reason you noted in your chart. Use your details to support each reason. End the essay with a conclusion in which you sum up your ideas.

Reason 1	Detail(s)
Reason 2	Detail(s)
Reason 3	Detail(s)

3. WRITE AND REVIEW

A. Capture your readers' attention by including a vivid description or a striking question in your introduction.

B. Be sure to leave time to check your spelling and grammar.

LESSON 3B

from *A Vindication
of the Rights of
Woman*

BY MARY WOLLSTONECRAFT

RELATED NONFICTION
Everyday Equality

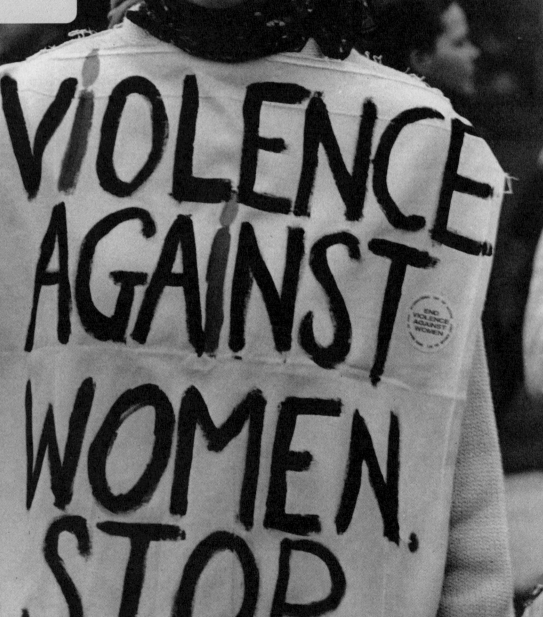

What makes EQUALITY *elusive?*

Thomas Jefferson wrote that "all men are created equal," but he and the other Founding Fathers left out many men and all women when they first considered rights in the new United States. Writing 16 years after the Declaration of Independence, Mary Wollstonecraft was one of the first to confront the issue of equality for women, although even she confined her arguments to education.

DISCUSS With a partner, consider why the issue of equal rights has historically been so difficult to achieve. Respond to the questions in the notebook, and then share your thoughts with a classmate.

Issues of Equality

1. What policies and actions can help promote equal rights among all citizens in a nation?

_____

_____

_____

_____

2. Why are groups of people sometimes opposed to these measures?

_____

_____

_____

_____

ASSESSMENT GOALS

By the end of this lesson, you will be able to. . .

- recognize the elements of an argument
- apply critical thinking skills to analyze text
- determine the author's message in a work of nonfiction
- analyze a writing prompt and plan a position paper

Argument

Mary Wollstonecraft has been called everything from a "hyena in petticoats" to "the mother of feminism." Both of these titles came in reaction to her arguments concerning women's rights. An ARGUMENT is speech or writing that expresses a position on an issue and then supports it with reasons and evidence.

Sound arguments include the elements listed in the chart below. You can practice answering questions about argument as you read the excerpt from *A Vindication of the Rights of Woman*.

ELEMENTS OF AN ARGUMENT	STRATEGIES FOR EVALUATION
CLAIM: the writer's position on an issue or problem	The claim is often stated directly in the introduction or conclusion of an argument. Make sure to look for clues in the title as well.
REASONS: statements that explain or justify the claim	Watch for errors in logic, such as overgeneralizations—conclusions that are too broad to be valid.
EVIDENCE: facts, statistics, examples, or the views of experts	Does the information come from trustworthy sources? Is there enough to support the claim?

ADDITIONAL TERM FOR CRITICAL ANALYSIS

Mary Wollstonecraft strengthens her argument by using COUNTERARGUMENTS— that is, she anticipates opposing views and logically responds to them in her essay. Counterarguments help convince readers that a writer has fully thought through a controversial or complex issue.

A VINDICATION of the RIGHTS of WOMAN

MARY WOLLSTONECRAFT

BACKGROUND In the late 18th century, daughters of English gentlemen were educated at home before being sent away to school for a few years. In addition to reading and studying foreign languages, girls learned how to play the piano, sing, draw, and do needlework. Young women were expected to marry. Barred from any profession, an unmarried woman could only support herself as a servant, a nurse, a governess, or some similar occupation.

vindication (vĭn′dĭ-kā′shən) *n.* clearing from criticism, blame, guilt, or suspicion; justification

FROM THE INTRODUCTION

After considering the historic page, and viewing the living world with anxious solicitude, the most melancholy emotions of sorrowful indignation have depressed my spirits, and I have sighed when obliged to confess, that either nature has made a great difference between man and man, or that the civilization which has hitherto taken place in the world has been very partial. I have turned over various books written on the subject of education, and patiently observed the conduct of parents and the management of schools; but what has been the result?—a profound conviction that the neglected education of my fellow-creatures is the grand
10 source of the misery I deplore; and that women, in particular, are rendered weak and wretched by a variety of concurring causes, originating from one hasty conclusion. The conduct and manners of women, in fact, evidently prove that their minds are not in a healthy state; for, like the flowers which are planted in too rich a soil, strength and usefulness are sacrificed to beauty; and the flaunting leaves, after having pleased a fastidious eye, fade, disregarded on the stalk, long before the season when they ought to have arrived at maturity. One cause of this barren blooming I attribute to a false system of education, gathered from the books written on this subject by men who, considering females rather as women than human

ANALYZE

Reread lines 1–25. Restate Wollstonecraft's claim in your own words.

_____

_____

_____

_____

_____

_____

prerogative (prĭ-rŏg'ə-tĭv) *n.* a privilege or distinctive advantage

TESTSMART

What is Wollstonecraft's counterargument in lines 40–49 to the idea that women are naturally inferior to men?

A Men and women are equal in every way.

B Women are actually superior to men.

C Women are inferior physically but not mentally.

D Women can achieve physical superiority over men.

TIP When answering a test question about **argument, reread the passage** to make sure you understand the author's logical point. Keep in mind that a **counterargument** does not need to entirely refute an opposing view.

20 creatures, have been more anxious to make them alluring mistresses than affectionate wives and rational mothers; and the understanding of the sex has been so bubbled by this specious homage,[1] that the civilized women of the present century, with a few exceptions, are only anxious to inspire love, when they ought to cherish a nobler ambition, and by their abilities and virtues exact respect. ◀

In a treatise,[2] therefore, on female rights and manners, the works which have been particularly written for their improvement must not be overlooked; especially when it is asserted, in direct terms, that the minds of women are enfeebled by false refinement; that the books of instruction, 30 written by men of genius, have had the same tendency as more frivolous productions; and that . . . they are treated as a kind of subordinate beings, and not as a part of the human species, when improvable reason is allowed to be the dignified distinction which raises men above the brute creation, and puts a natural scepter in a feeble hand.

Yet, because I am a woman, I would not lead my readers to suppose that I mean violently to agitate the contested question respecting the quality or inferiority of the sex; but as the subject lies in my way, and I cannot pass it over without subjecting the main tendency of my reasoning to misconstruction, I shall stop a moment to deliver, in a few words, my 40 opinion. In the government of the physical world it is observable that the female in point of strength is, in general, inferior to the male. This is the law of nature; and it does not appear to be suspended or abrogated in favor of woman. A degree of physical superiority cannot, therefore, be denied—and it is a noble **prerogative**! But not content with this natural pre-eminence, men endeavor to sink us still lower merely to render us alluring objects for a moment; and women, intoxicated by the adoration which men, under the influence of their senses, pay them, do not seek to obtain a durable interest in their hearts, or to become the friends of the fellow creatures who find amusement in their society. ◀

50 I am aware of an obvious inference: from every quarter have I heard exclamations against masculine women; but where are they to be found? If by this appellation men mean to inveigh against their ardor[3] in hunting, shooting, and gaming, I shall most cordially join in the cry; but if it be against the imitation of manly virtues, or, more properly speaking, the attainment of those talents and virtues, the exercise of which ennobles the

---

1. **bubbled by this specious homage** (spē'shəs hŏm'ĭj): deceived by this false honor.

2. **treatise**: a formal, detailed article or book on a particular subject.

3. **If by . . . inveigh** (ĭn-vā') **against their ardor**: if by this term ("masculine women") men mean to condemn some women's enthusiasm.

human character, and which raise females in the scale of animal being, when they are comprehensively termed mankind; all those who view them with a philosophic eye must, I should think, wish with me, that they may every day grow more and more masculine. . . .

60 My own sex, I hope, will excuse me, if I treat them like rational creatures, instead of flattering their *fascinating* graces, and viewing them as if they were in a state of perpetual childhood, unable to stand alone. I earnestly wish to point out in what true dignity and human happiness consists—I wish to persuade women to endeavor to acquire strength, both of mind and body, and to convince them that the soft phrases, susceptibility of heart, delicacy of sentiment, and refinement of taste, are almost synonymous with epithets[4] of weakness, and that those beings who are only the objects of pity and that kind of love, which has been termed its sister, will soon become objects of contempt. . . . ▶

70 The education of women has, of late, been more attended to than formerly; yet they are still reckoned a frivolous sex, and ridiculed or pitied by the writers who endeavor by satire or instruction to improve them. It is acknowledged that they spend many of the first years of their lives in acquiring a smattering of accomplish-ments;[5] meanwhile strength of body and mind are sacrificed to libertine[6] notions of beauty, to the desire of establishing themselves—the only way women can rise in the world—by marriage. And this desire making mere animals of them, when they marry they act as such children may be expected to act: they dress; they paint, and nickname God's creatures. Surely these weak beings are only fit for a
80 seraglio![7] Can they be expected to govern a family with judgment, or take care of the poor babes whom they bring into the world?

If then it can be fairly deduced from the present conduct of the sex, from the prevalent fondness for pleasure which takes place of ambition and those nobler passions that open and enlarge the soul; that the instruction which women have hitherto received has only tended, with the constitution of civil society, to render them insignificant objects of desire—mere propagators of fools!—if it can be proved that in aiming to accomplish them, without cultivating their understandings, they are taken out of their sphere of duties, and made ridiculous and useless when
90 the short-lived bloom of beauty is over, I presume that *rational* men will

---

4. **epithets** (ĕp′ə-thĕts′): descriptive terms.
5. **accomplishments:** This term, when applied to women, designated only those achievements then considered suitable for middle- and upper-class women, such as painting, singing, playing a musical instrument, and embroidery.
6. **libertine** (lĭb′ər-tēn′): indecent or unseemly.
7. **seraglio** (sə-răl′yō): harem.

ANALYZE

Underline words and phrases in lines 60–69 that Wollstonecraft uses to describe the state of most women in her time. Circle words and phrases that describe admirable qualities she wants women to develop. ✐

excuse me for endeavoring to persuade them to become more masculine and respectable.

Indeed the word masculine is only a bugbear:[8] there is little reason to fear that women will acquire too much courage or fortitude; for their apparent inferiority with respect to bodily strength, must render them, in some degree, dependent on men in the various relations of life; but why should it be increased by prejudices that give a sex to virtue, and confound simple truths with sensual reveries?[9]

FROM CHAPTER 2

Youth is the season for love in both sexes; but in those days of thoughtless
100 enjoyment provision should be made for the more important years of life, when reflection takes place of sensation. But Rousseau,[10] and most of the male writers who have followed his steps, have warmly **inculcated** that the whole tendency of female education ought to be directed to one point: to render them[11] pleasing.

Let me reason with the supporters of this opinion who have any knowledge of human nature, do they imagine that marriage can eradicate the habitude of life? The woman who has only been taught to please will soon find that her charms are oblique sunbeams, and that they cannot have much effect on her husband's heart when they are seen every day,
110 when the summer is passed and gone. Will she then have sufficient native energy to look into herself for comfort, and cultivate her dormant faculties? or, is it not more rational to expect that she will try to please other men; and, in the emotions raised by the expectation of new conquests, endeavor to forget the mortification her love or pride has received? When the husband ceases to be a lover—and the time will inevitably come, her desire of pleasing will then grow languid, or become a spring of bitterness; and love, perhaps, the most **evanescent** of all passions, gives place to jealousy or vanity. ◀

I now speak of women who are restrained by principle or prejudice;
120 such women, though they would shrink from an intrigue with real abhorrence, yet, nevertheless, wish to be convinced by the homage of gallantry that they are cruelly neglected by their husbands; or, days and

inculcate (ĭn-kŭl′kāt′) v. to impress on the mind by frequent repetition; to teach; to instill

INTERPRET

Reread the underlined sentence in lines 107–110. Circle the two metaphors, and number them 1 and 2. 🖉

What point is the author making in this sentence?

_____

_____

_____

_____

_____

evanescent (ĕv′ə-nĕs′ənt) adj. quick to disappear

---

8. **bugbear:** an object of exaggerated fear.
9. **confound . . . reveries** (rĕv′ə-rēz): confuse simple truths with men's sexual daydreams.
10. **Rousseau** (rōō-sō′): The Swiss-born French philosopher Jean-Jacques Rousseau (1712–1778) presented a plan for female education in his famous 1762 novel *Émile*.
11. **them:** that is, females.

weeks are spent in dreaming of the happiness enjoyed by congenial souls till their health is undermined and their spirits broken by discontent. How then can the great art of pleasing be such a necessary study? it is only useful to a mistress; the chaste wife, and serious mother, should only consider her power to please as the polish of her virtues, and the affection of her husband as one of the comforts that render her talk less difficult and her life happier. But, whether she be loved or neglected, her first wish
130 should be to make herself respectable, and not to rely for all her happiness on a being subject to like infirmities with herself. ▶

    The worthy Dr. Gregory fell into a similar error. I respect his heart; but entirely disapprove of his celebrated Legacy to his Daughters.[12] . . .

    He actually recommends dissimulation, and advises an innocent girl to give the lie to her feelings, and not dance with spirit, when gaiety of heart would make her feet eloquent without making her gestures immodest. In the name of truth and common sense, why should not one woman acknowledge that she can take more exercise than another? or, in other words, that she has a sound constitution; and why, to damp innocent
140 vivacity, is she darkly to be told that men will draw conclusions which she little thinks of? Let the libertine draw what inference he pleases; but, I hope, that no sensible mother will restrain the natural frankness of youth by instilling such indecent cautions. Out of the abundance of the heart the mouth speaketh; and a wiser than Solomon[13] hath said, that the heart should be made clean, and not trivial ceremonies observed, which it is not very difficult to fulfil with scrupulous exactness when vice reigns in the heart. ▶

    Women ought to endeavor to purify their heart; but can they do so when their uncultivated understandings make them entirely dependent
150 on their senses for employment and amusement, when no noble pursuit sets them above the little vanities of the day, or enables them to curb the wild emotions that agitate a reed over which every passing breeze has power? To gain the affections of a virtuous man, is affectation necessary? Nature has given woman a weaker frame than man; but, to ensure her husband's affections, must a wife, who by the exercise of her mind and body whilst she was discharging the duties of a daughter, wife, and mother,

---

12. **Dr. Gregory . . . Daughters:** In his 1774 work *A Father's Legacy for His Daughters*, John Gregory (1724–1773) offered a plan for female education that remained popular for decades.

13. **a wiser than Solomon:** King David, reputed author of many psalms in the Bible and the father of King Solomon, who was known for his wisdom. The words that follow draw on ideas in Psalm 24, which states that only those with "clean hands, and a pure heart" shall ascend into Heaven.

TestSmart

VOCABULARY
The word *infirmities* in line 131 means
  (A) weaknesses
  (B) complications
  (C) principles
  (D) charms

TIP To help you figure out the meaning of an unfamiliar word in a difficult sentence, first **paraphrase** the sentence, restating it in your own words. The correct answer choice is the one that would make the most sense in place of the vocabulary word.

ANALYZE

What **counterargument** does Wollstonecraft make in response to Dr. Gregory's argument that girls should use dissimulation?

_____

_____

_____

feign (fān) *v.* to make a false show of; pretend

has allowed her constitution to retain its natural strength, and her nerves a healthy tone, is she, I say, to condescend to use art and **feign** a sickly delicacy in order to secure her husband's affection? Weakness may excite
160 tenderness, and gratify the arrogant pride of man; but the lordly caresses of a protector will not gratify a noble mind that pants for, and deserves to be respected. Fondness is a poor substitute for friendship! . . .

Besides, the woman who strengthens her body and exercises her mind will, by managing her family and practicing various virtues, become the friend, and not the humble dependent of her husband; and if she, by possessing such substantial qualities, merit his regard, she will not find it necessary to conceal her affection, nor to pretend to an unnatural coldness of constitution to excite her husband's passions. . . .

If all the faculties of woman's mind are only to be cultivated as they
170 respect her dependence on man; if, when a husband be obtained, she have arrived at her goal, and meanly proud rests satisfied with such a paltry crown, let her grovel contentedly, scarcely raised by her employments above the animal kingdom; but, if, struggling for the prize of her high calling, she look beyond the present scene, let her cultivate her understanding without stopping to consider what character the husband may have whom she is destined to marry. Let her only determine, without being too anxious about present happiness, to acquire the qualities that ennoble a rational being, and a rough inelegant husband may shock her taste without destroying her peace of mind. She will not model her soul
180 to suit the frailties of her companion, but to bear with them: his character may be a trial, but not an impediment to virtue. . . .

These may be termed Utopian dreams. Thanks to that Being who impressed them on my soul, and gave me sufficient strength of mind to dare to exert my own reason, till, becoming dependent only on him for the support of my virtue, I view, with indignation, the mistaken notions that enslave my sex. ◀

I love man as my fellow; but his scepter, real, or usurped, extends not to me, unless the reason of an individual demands my homage; and even then the submission is to reason, and not to man. In fact, the conduct
190 of an accountable being must be regulated by the operations of its own reason; or on what foundation rests the throne of God?

It appears to me necessary to dwell on these obvious truths, because females have been insulated, as it were; and, while they have been stripped of the virtues that should clothe humanity, they have been decked with artificial graces that enable them to exercise a short-lived tyranny. Love, in their bosoms, taking place of every nobler passion, their sole ambition is to be fair, to raise emotion instead of inspiring respect; and this ignoble

CONNECT

Reread Wollstonecraft's **counterargument** in lines 182–186 to the view that her ideas are "Utopian dreams." Are her ideas still Utopian, or have they become more widely accepted in Western society? Explain.

desire, like the servility in absolute monarchies, destroys all strength of character. Liberty is the mother of virtue, and if women be, by their very
200 constitution, slaves, and not allowed to breathe the sharp invigorating air of freedom, they must ever languish like exotics,[14] and be reckoned beautiful flaws in nature. ▶

---

14. **languish** (lăng′gwĭsh) **like exotics:** wilt like plants grown away from their natural environment.

Reading Comprehension

DIRECTIONS *Answer these questions about the excerpt from* A Vindication of the Rights of Woman *by filling in the correct ovals.*

1. Wollstonecraft provided counterarguments to Rousseau's conviction that female education should aim to make women

   (A) stronger   (C) pleasing

   (B) weaker   (D) rational

2. According to Wollstonecraft, why do most women go along with the "false system of education" that fails to develop their mental and physical abilities?

   (A) They are anxious to get married.

   (B) They don't know any better.

   (C) They prefer to be weak and ignorant.

   (D) They would rather be alluring mistresses than dutiful wives.

3. In response to the argument that education would make women more masculine, Wollstonecraft says that it would make them

   (A) less masculine and thus more pleasing

   (B) better wives, mothers, and companions

   (C) the physical and mental equals of men

   (D) better at hunting and gaming

4. Which statement *best* sums up Wollstonecraft's argument in this essay?

   (A) Men will never allow women to improve their status.

   (B) Women's education needs to focus more on improving their physical and mental abilities.

   (C) Intelligent women find it easier to attract good husbands.

   (D) Women should become physically and mentally equal to men.

5. Which reason does Wollstonecraft *not* use to support her claim?

   (A) Strengthening their bodies and minds makes women better mothers.

   (B) Developing character through education enables women to be better partners to their husbands.

   (C) Women raised only to be pleasing to men are at the mercy of their own senses.

   (D) Women who are allowed to participate in sports and hunting activities make better, more playful wives.

6. Wollstonecraft's comparison of women to exotic flowers in lines 12–17 emphasizes her point that

   (A) women are raised to be pleasing at the expense of their strength and intelligence

   (B) women should be beautiful and healthy, like carefully tended flowers

   (C) though beauty fades, women, like flowers, can bloom again

   (D) women who receive too much education can wither, just like flowers that receive too much water

7. In the context of line 42, *abrogated* means

   (A) praised   (C) deceived

   (B) abolished   (D) imposed

8. In line 153, *affectation* means

   (A) tender feeling   (C) depression

   (B) bias   (D) false behavior

Responding in Writing

9. Short Response In a paragraph, summarize Wollstonecraft's argument about women's rights in this excerpt from *A Vindication of the Rights of Woman*. Be sure to discuss her views on education and explain what she thought women should strive for. Use quotations from the essay to support your summary.

_____

_____

_____

_____

_____

_____

TEST-TAKER'S TOOLKIT

- **ACADEMIC VOCABULARY** When you **summarize** an author's ideas, you restate his or her most important points in your own words. Unlike a paraphrase, a summary is usually shorter than the original text. It also often uses simpler language.

- **GRAPHIC ORGANIZER** Use the chart below to organize your thoughts and gather evidence before you begin your response.

WOLLSTONECRAFT ON WOMEN'S RIGHTS

The Author's Ideas	Support from the Essay
Wollstonecraft believed that women's place in society was a miserable one, and that lack of female education was largely to blame.	"... the neglected education of my fellow-creatures is the grand source of the misery I deplore ..." (lines 9–10)

Everyday Equality
MAGAZINE COLUMN

*Use with the excerpt
from* A Vindication of
the Rights of Woman,
p. 118

What's the Connection?

Mary Wollstonecraft wrote *A Vindication of the Rights of Woman* at a time when there were very few opportunities for women to develop their talents. In "Everyday Equality," journalist Anna Quindlen reflects on the great advancements that were made possible by her generation's struggle for gender equality.

CHART IT In the first column of the chart below, write some notes about the freedoms and opportunities available to the women of Mary Wollstonecraft's generation. In the third column, make notes about the same topic for your own generation. After reading the article, complete the second column for Anna Quindlen's generation.

WOLLSTONECRAFT'S GENERATION	QUINDLEN'S GENERATION	MY GENERATION
Educational opportunities:	Educational opportunities:	Educational opportunities:
Careers:	Careers:	Careers:
Domestic life:	Domestic life:	Domestic life:

LEARN THE SKILL: DETERMINE AUTHOR'S MESSAGE

An **author's message** is the main idea that the author wishes to convey about a topic. It can be helpful to keep the following points in mind when determining an author's message:

- In many nonfiction works, the author's message is expressed directly in a **thesis statement.** Often the thesis statement appears in the introduction and is one sentence, although it may be two or more.

- Sometimes the message of a nonfiction work is not directly stated, but you can infer it from details in the work.

For more on author's message, see the Main Ideas and Supporting Details entry in the Nonfiction Skills Handbook beginning on page R2.

from *Newsweek*

Everyday Equality

by Anna Quindlen

Each of us rose on the shoulders of women who had come before us.

I came to feminism the way some people come to social movements in their early years: out of self-interest. <u>As a teenager, I was outspoken and outraged, which paired with a skirt was once considered arrogance.</u> When I was expelled from convent school I was furious.
10 Now I am more understanding. Would you have wanted to be the nun teaching me typing? ▶

I got on the equality band-wagon because I was a young woman with a streak of ambition a mile wide, and without a change in the atmosphere I thought I was going to wind up living a life that would make me crazy. As my
20 father said not long ago, "Can you imagine what it would have been like if you had been born 50 years earlier? Your life would have been miserable."

The great thing was that it was possible to do good for all while you were doing well for yourself. Each of us rose on the shoulders of women who had come before
30 us. Move up, reach down: that was the motto of those who were

Reread the underlined sentence. What does it say about gender roles at the time when the author was growing up?

---

worth knowing. But it was not just other women we elevated, but entire enterprises. More women on the staffs and the mastheads of the country's largest publications changed them. It resulted in newspapers and magazines that covered women as more 40 than an amalgam of recipes and fashion collections. They simply became more reflective of the world around them, and therefore better.

I remember a page-one meeting in which I told my colleagues that it was fine if a story about Geraldine Ferraro recounted what she wore as long as her male 50 Republican vice-presidential opponent—George Bush I— got the same sartorial treatment. I envisioned daily tie dispatches: foulards, regimental stripes, embroidered Labradors and tiny tennis rackets. But I was conspicuously pregnant at the time, and no one really wanted to set me off; the references to the Ferraro skirt 60 suit were deleted, leaving a bit of room for something of more substance. All in all, a very satisfactory day at the office. ◀

There's one question that always lurks around the margins of the battle for equal rights:

how will we know when we've won? Sometimes it seems like a classic dance of two steps for- 70 ward, one back. Indra Nooyi, an Indian-born numbers cruncher, was recently named CEO of Pepsi. But that makes her one of only 11 women now running a Fortune 500 company, which works out to slightly more than 2 percent. CBS appointed the first woman solo network news anchor. But some genius Photoshopped a publicity 80 still of Katie Couric even though Walter Cronkite had long ago made clear that a person with a normal face and physique can read a teleprompter. And *Forbes* magazine just published an essay titled "Don't Marry Career Women," by a male writer who couldn't see the advantages of a wife who could pay the mortgage and support 90 the children even if her husband lost his job or suffered a massive coronary.

That kind of nonsense takes you back in time, to the early days when women dumped babies on the desk of the mayor of Syracuse to protest the lack of child care and picketed male-only press clubs. Maybe it was the classic 100 protest slogan "Don't cook dinner—starve a rat today," but the

> But the battle was really against waste, the waste of talent, the waste to society, the waste of women who had certain gifts and goals and had to suppress both.

perception was that the fight for equality was a war against men. But the battle was really against waste, the waste of talent, the waste to society, the waste of women who had certain gifts and goals and had to suppress both. The point was not to take over male terrain but to change it because it badly needed changing. The depth and breadth of that transformation is what reflects the success of the movement, and by that measure, women are doing well. And so is everyone else. ▶

Fathers take a far larger role in the daily raising of their kids. Companies feel more pressure to be sensitive to medical and family emergencies. Sex crimes are prosecuted; so is domestic violence. Patients demand more personal care from their doctors. Readers want more human-interest stories from magazines. Even the bottom line has benefited. Catalyst, the research organization that tracks women at work, reported in 2004 that the Fortune 500 corporations with the most women in top positions yielded, on average, a 35 percent higher return on equity than those with the fewest female corporate officers. ▶

When I was told 40 years ago that I should learn to type so I could someday type papers for my boyfriend, I didn't know what I wanted, but I knew it wasn't that. It's an act of hubris to think that things can be truly different, but hubris was what I had—hubris, and the millions of other women who knew that there must be more to life than waxy buildup and a frost-free freezer. In 1970, 46 women at this magazine charged it with workplace discrimination; today *Newsweek* publishes an annual issue on women's leadership. That marks one of countless unremarked everyday distinctions between an old world and a better one, and, on a personal level, between a girl who would have been a mad housewife and a woman whose typing has been on her own terms.

AUTHOR'S MESSAGE

What message does the author convey in lines 104–116? Summarize this idea in one sentence.

_____

_____

_____

_____

SPECIALIZED *Vocabulary*

The terms *bottom line* (lines 126–127) and *return on equity* (line 133) come from the business world. Circle the financial result that proves women are good at running corporations. ✎

Based on this clue, what do you think the "bottom line" is?

_____

_____

Reading Comprehension

DIRECTIONS *Answer these questions about the two selections in this lesson by filling in the correct ovals.*

1. The motto "Move up, reach down" in line 30 of "Everyday Equality" means

   (A) women should seek high positions

   (B) women should not suppress their talents

   (C) newspapers need to hire more women

   (D) women should help each other become successful

2. The details given in lines 117–126 of "Everyday Equality" convey the message that the fight for equality

   (A) is over

   (B) is a battle against men

   (C) has benefited society as a whole

   (D) has improved health care

3. Anna Quindlen's style is *best* described as

   (A) formal and impersonal

   (B) old fashioned and dry

   (C) descriptive and flowery

   (D) informal and conversational

4. The description of Katie Couric's appointment in lines 76–84 supports the idea that

   (A) women still face discrimination

   (B) Couric is less atttractive than Walter Cronkite

   (C) most viewers prefer male anchors

   (D) CBS is disappointed in Couric

5. The authors of *A Vindication of the Rights of Woman* and "Everyday Equality" share the viewpoint that women

   (A) have made great advances toward equality

   (B) have equal educational opportunities

   (C) should use dissimulation as a tool

   (D) should be self-reliant

6. How do the two selections in this lesson differ?

   (A) Wollstonecraft does not suggest that women can pursue important careers.

   (B) Quindlen disputes Wollstonecraft's claim that women are physically inferior to men.

   (C) Wollstonecraft is more optimistic about the role of women in society.

   (D) Quindlen feels that education has little impact on a woman's development.

7. In line 34 of "Everyday Equality," *enterprises* means

   (A) fashion magazines

   (B) business organizations

   (C) social movements

   (D) business colleagues

8. The most likely meaning of the word *hubris* in line 141 of "Everyday Equality" is

   (A) feelings of insecurity

   (B) unrealistic goals

   (C) inappropriate conduct

   (D) exaggerated pride

Timed Writing Practice

PROMPT

If you were the head of a government, business, or university, what would you do to ensure that all members of your community had equal rights, regardless of gender? Imagine yourself in one of the three roles above. Write a position paper in which you (explain your policy) and tell what it does to ensure equality.

BUDGET YOUR TIME

You have 45 minutes to respond. Decide how much time to spend on each step.

Analyze _____

Plan _____

Write _____

Review _____

45

TEST-TAKER'S TOOLKIT

1. ANALYZE THE PROMPT

A. Underline the question that the prompt asks you to answer.

B. Circle key words and phrases that tell you what to include. One phrase has been circled for you.

C. Restate the prompt in your own words.

2. PLAN YOUR RESPONSE

A. **Make Notes** Choose which role you will imagine yourself in. Then think about the equality issues your specific institution might face. For example, if you were the head of a university, you might have to make sure that men's and women's sports teams receive equal funding and equal publicity. Brainstorm a list of issues you might face in your chosen role, and note how you might solve each one.

B. **Organize your information** Your position paper should start with a strong introduction that explains why you think it is important to strive for equality. You should tell what position you've chosen to promote. You might also give an overview of your policy—that is, a summary of the ways you fight discrimination at your institution. Each paragraph that follows your introduction can go into more detail about one issue and how you solve it.

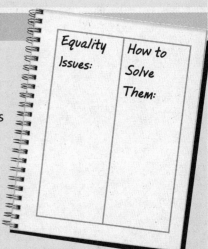

3. WRITE AND REVIEW

A. Write your full response on a separate piece of paper.

B. Be sure to leave time to review your work and to check your spelling and grammar.

UNIT 4

THE FLOWERING OF ROMANTICISM

LESSON 4A

Selected Poetry
BY WILLIAM WORDSWORTH

RELATED NONFICTION

Happy by Nature: Fondness for Plants and Animals May Be Hard-Wired, Healthy

Where do we find
PEACE?

When filled with the stresses and strains of everyday life, people sometimes go to a particular place to regain a sense of peace. Like William Wordsworth, many people seek peace in a natural setting. Others find comfort in a grandparent's home or in a place of worship.

SKETCH IT What place gives you a peaceful feeling? In the notebook shown, draw a simple sketch of that place. Then complete the sentences. Share your work with a partner.

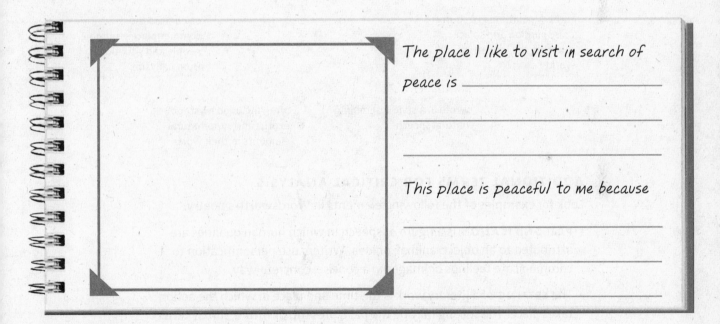

The place I like to visit in search of peace is _____

_____

_____

This place is peaceful to me because

_____

_____

_____

ASSESSMENT GOALS

By the end of this lesson, you will be able to . . .

- analyze romantic poetry
- apply critical thinking skills to analyze text
- analyze evidence in a work of nonfiction
- analyze a writing prompt and plan a descriptive essay

Romantic Poetry

In England, **ROMANTICISM** was a literary and artistic movement that began in the late 18th century and lasted through the first few decades of the 19th century. Romantic poets stressed the importance of the individual's subjective experiences, paying more attention to their inner lives than to social issues. Unlike most 18th-century poets, the romantics valued emotion, spontaneity, and imagination over reason and orderliness.

William Wordsworth helped launch the romantic movement in England, and he was the most influential poet of the period. Review the methods used by romantic poets in the graphic below to help you analyze Wordsworth's poetry.

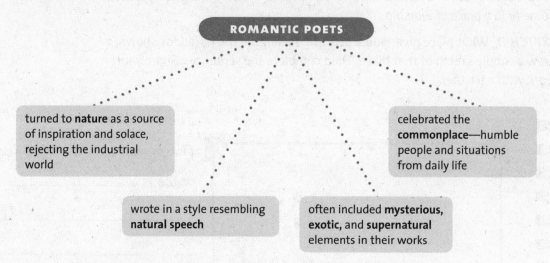

ROMANTIC POETS

turned to **nature** as a source of inspiration and solace, rejecting the industrial world

wrote in a style resembling **natural speech**

often included **mysterious, exotic,** and **supernatural** elements in their works

celebrated the **commonplace**—humble people and situations from daily life

ADDITIONAL TERMS FOR CRITICAL ANALYSIS

Look for examples of the following elements in Wordsworth's poetry:

- **PERSONIFICATION** is a figure of speech in which human qualities are attributed to an object, animal, or idea. Writers use personification to communicate feelings or images in a concise, concrete way.

- The **SETTING** of a literary work is the time and place in which the action takes place. The setting may be the past, present, or future; it may reflect the work's cultural or historical context.

Lines Composed a Few Miles Above
Tintern Abbey

William Wordsworth

BACKGROUND In many of his poems, Wordsworth explores his thoughts and feelings about a particular setting. He wrote "Tintern Abbey" five years after his first visit to a ruined medieval abbey in the Wye River valley in Wales. In the poem, he describes returning to the site accompanied by his beloved sister, Dorothy. Another of his poems, "I Wandered Lonely As a Cloud," was inspired by a walk he took with Dorothy near their home in the picturesque Lake District.

Five years have passed; five summers, with the length
Of five long winters! and again I hear
These waters, rolling from their mountain-springs
With a soft inland murmur. Once again
5 Do I behold these steep and lofty cliffs,
That on a wild secluded scene impress
Thoughts of more deep seclusion; and connect
The landscape with the quiet of the sky. ▶
The day is come when I again repose[1]
10 Here, under this dark sycamore, and view
These plots of cottage ground, these orchard tufts,
Which at this season, with their unripe fruits,
Are clad in one green hue, and lose themselves
'Mid groves and copses.[2] Once again I see
15 These hedgerows, hardly hedgerows, little lines
Of sportive wood run wild; these pastoral[3] farms,

INTERPRET

What do lines 1–8 convey about the speaker's return to the landscape near Tintern Abbey? Cite words and phrases to support your answer.

_____

_____

_____

_____

_____

1. **repose:** lie at rest.
2. **copses** (kŏp'sĭz): thickets of small trees.
3. **pastoral** (păs'tər-əl): rural and serene.

Green to the very door; and wreaths of smoke
Sent up, in silence, from among the trees!
With some uncertain notice, as might seem
20 Of vagrant[4] dwellers in the houseless woods,
Or of some Hermit's cave, where by his fire
The Hermit sits alone.
                    These beauteous forms,
Through a long absence, have not been to me
As is a landscape to a blind man's eye;
25 But oft, in lonely rooms, and 'mid the din
Of towns and cities, I have owed to them,
In hours of weariness, sensations sweet,
Felt in the blood, and felt along the heart;
And passing even into my purer mind,
30 With tranquil restoration—feelings too
Of unremembered pleasure; such, perhaps,
As have no slight or trivial influence
On that best portion of a good man's life,
His little, nameless, unremembered, acts
35 Of kindness and of love. Nor less, I trust,
To them I may have owed another gift,
Of aspect more sublime; that blessed mood,
In which the burthen[5] of the mystery,
In which the heavy and the weary weight
40 Of all this unintelligible world,
Is lightened—that serene and blessed mood,
In which the affections gently lead us on—
Until, the breath of this corporeal[6] frame
And even the motion of our human blood
45 Almost suspended, we are laid asleep
In body, and become a living soul;
While with an eye made quiet by the power
Of harmony, and the deep power of joy,
We see into the life of things. ◀

                        If this
50 Be but a vain belief, yet, oh! how oft—

---

4. **vagrant:** wandering.
5. **burthen:** burden.
6. **corporeal** (kôr-pôr′ē-əl): bodily.

In darkness and amid the many shapes
Of joyless daylight; when the fretful stir
Unprofitable, and the fever of the world,
Have hung upon the beatings of my heart—
55 How oft, in spirit, have I turned to thee,
O sylvan[7] Wye![8] thou wanderer through the woods,
How often has my spirit turned to thee! ▶

    And now, with gleams of half-extinguished thought
With many recognitions dim and faint,
60 And somewhat of a sad perplexity,
The picture of the mind revives again;
While here I stand, not only with the sense
Of present pleasure, but with pleasing thoughts
That in this moment there is life and food
65 For future years. And so I dare to hope,
Though changed, no doubt, from what I was when first
I came among these hills; when like a roe[9]
I bounded o'er the mountains, by the sides
Of the deep rivers, and the lonely streams,
70 Wherever nature led—more like a man
Flying from something that he dreads than one
Who sought the thing he loved. For nature then
(The coarser pleasures of my boyish days,
And their glad animal movements all gone by)
75 To me was all in all.—I cannot paint
What then I was. The sounding cataract[10]
Haunted me like a passion; the tall rock,
The mountain, and the deep and gloomy wood,
Their colors and their forms, were then to me
80 An appetite; a feeling and a love,
That had no need of a remoter charm,
By thought supplied, nor any interest
Unborrowed from the eye.—That time is past,
And all its aching joys are now no more,
85 And all its dizzy raptures. Not for this ▶

INTERPRET

What feelings about urban life does the speaker express in lines 49–57? Underline words and phrases that support your answer. 🖊

_____

_____

_____

DRAW CONCLUSIONS

Reread the boxed text. How would you characterize the speaker's experiences in **nature** when he was younger? Cite details in your response.

_____

_____

_____

_____

---

7. **sylvan:** located in a wood or forest.
8. **Wye:** a river near Tintern Abbey.
9. **roe:** deer.
10. **cataract** (kăt′ə-răkt′): waterfall.

Faint I,[11] nor mourn nor murmur; other gifts
Have followed; for such loss, I would believe,
Abundant recompense.[12] For I have learned
To look on nature, not as in the hour
90 Of thoughtless youth; but hearing oftentimes
The still, sad music of humanity,
Nor harsh nor grating, though of ample power
To chasten[13] and subdue. And I have felt
A presence that disturbs me with the joy
95 Of elevated thoughts; a sense sublime
Of something far more deeply interfused,
Whose dwelling is the light of setting suns,
And the round ocean and the living air,
And the blue sky, and in the mind of man:
100 A motion and a spirit, that impels
All thinking things, all objects of all thought,
And rolls through all things. Therefore am I still ◀
A lover of the meadows and the woods,
And mountains; and of all that we behold
105 From this green earth; of all the mighty world
Of eye, and ear—both what they half create,
And what perceive; well pleased to recognize
In nature and the language of the sense
The anchor of my purest thoughts, the nurse,
110 The guide, the guardian of my heart, and soul
Of all my moral being.

Nor perchance,[14]
If I were not thus taught, should I the more
Suffer my genial[15] spirits to decay:
For thou art with me here upon the banks
115 Of this fair river; thou my dearest Friend,[16]
My dear, dear Friend; and in thy voice I catch

ANALYZE

Reread the boxed text. What "gifts" have compensated for the speaker's lost youth?

_____

_____

_____

_____

---

11. **Faint I:** I lose heart.
12. **recompense** (rĕk′əm-pĕns′): compensation.
13. **chasten** (chā′sən): scold; make modest.
14. **perchance:** by chance; perhaps.
15. **genial** (jēn′yəl): relating to genius; creative.
16. **thou my dearest Friend:** Wordsworth's sister, Dorothy.

The language of my former heart, and read
My former pleasures in the shooting lights
Of thy wild eyes. Oh! yet a little while
120 May I behold in thee what I was once,
My dear, dear Sister! and this prayer I make, ▶
Knowing that Nature never did betray
The heart that loved her; 'tis her privilege,
Through all the years of this our life, to lead
125 From joy to joy: for she can so inform
The mind that is within us, so impress
With quietness and beauty, and so feed
With lofty thoughts, that neither evil tongues,
Rash judgments, nor the sneers of selfish men,
130 Nor greetings where no kindness is, nor all
The dreary intercourse of daily life,
Shall e'er prevail against us, or disturb
Our cheerful faith, that all which we behold
Is full of blessings. Therefore let the moon
135 Shine on thee in thy solitary walk;
And let the misty mountain winds be free
To blow against thee: and, in after years,
When these wild ecstasies shall be matured
Into a sober pleasure; when thy mind
140 Shall be a mansion for all lovely forms,
Thy memory be as a dwelling place
For all sweet sounds and harmonies; oh! then,
If solitude, or fear, or pain, or grief
Should be thy portion, with what healing thoughts
145 Of tender joy wilt thou remember me,
And these my exhortations![17] Nor, perchance— ▶
If I should be where I no more can hear
Thy voice, nor catch from thy wild eyes these gleams
Of past existence[18]—wilt thou then forget
150 That on the banks of this delightful stream
We stood together; and that I, so long
A worshiper of Nature, hither came
Unwearied in that service; rather say

---

17. **exhortations:** words of encouraging advice.
18. **past existence:** the speaker's own past experience five years before
    (see lines 116–119).

COMPARE

Reread lines 111–121. What similarity does the speaker see between himself and his sister Dorothy?

_____

_____

_____

_____

TestSmart

In lines 121–146, the speaker prays that nature will always provide his sister with

Ⓐ wild ecstasies

Ⓑ sounds and harmonies

Ⓒ inspiration and protection

Ⓓ a memorable dwelling place

TIP On some test questions, the answer is not stated directly in the text. You need to **infer the answer** by combining clues from the text with your own knowledge. In this case, underline all the things the speaker says **nature** might provide as life goes on. ✏

With warmer love—oh! with far deeper zeal
155 Of holier love. Nor wilt thou then forget,
That after many wanderings, many years
Of absence, these steep woods and lofty cliffs,
And this green pastoral landscape, were to me
More dear, both for themselves and for thy sake!

Composed upon
Westminster Bridge,
September 3, 1802

William Wordsworth

Earth has not anything to show more fair:
Dull would he be of soul who could pass by
A sight so touching in its majesty;
This City now doth, like a garment, wear
5 The beauty of the morning; silent, bare,
Ships, towers, domes, theaters, and temples lie
Open unto the fields, and to the sky;
All bright and glittering in the smokeless air. ▶
Never did sun more beautifully steep[1]
10 In his first splendor, valley, rock, or hill;
Ne'er saw I, never felt, a calm so deep!
The river[2] glideth at his own sweet will:
Dear God! the very houses[3] seem asleep;
And all that mighty heart is lying still!

ANALYZE

Reread the boxed text. Underline an example of **personification.** ✏

How does this device enhance the description?

_____

_____

_____

_____

---

1. **steep:** soak; saturate.
2. **the river:** the Thames (tĕmz)—the principal river in London.
3. **houses:** possibly a pun on the Houses of Parliament, near Westminster Bridge.

The World
Is Too Much with Us

William Wordsworth

The world is too much with us; late and soon,
Getting and spending, we lay waste our powers;
Little we see in Nature that is ours;
We have given our hearts away, a sordid boon!¹
5 This Sea that bares her bosom to the moon,
The winds that will be howling at all hours,
And are up-gathered now like sleeping flowers,
For this, for everything, we are out of tune;
It moves us not.—Great God! I'd rather be ◀
10 A Pagan² suckled in a creed outworn;³
So might I, standing on this pleasant lea,⁴
Have glimpses that would make me less forlorn;
Have sight of Proteus rising from the sea;
Or hear old Triton⁵ blow his wreathèd horn. ◀

ANALYZE

Underline phrases in lines 1–9 that reveal the speaker's unhappiness with modern life. ✎

MAKE INFERENCES

Why does the speaker say he would rather be a pagan than live in his present state?

---

1. **sordid boon:** tarnished or selfish gift.
2. **Pagan** (pā′gən): someone who is not Christian, Jewish, or Muslim.
3. **suckled in a creed outworn:** raised in an outdated faith or belief system.
4. **lea:** meadow.
5. **Proteus** (prō′tē-əs) . . . **Triton** (trīt′n): sea gods of Greek mythology.

I Wandered
Lonely As a Cloud

William Wordsworth

I wandered lonely as a cloud
That floats on high o'er vales¹ and hills,
When all at once I saw a crowd,
A host, of golden daffodils;
5 Beside the lake, beneath the trees,
Fluttering and dancing in the breeze.

Continuous as the stars that shine
And twinkle on the milky way,
They stretched in never-ending line
10 Along the margin of a bay:
Ten thousand saw I at a glance,
Tossing their heads in sprightly dance.

The waves beside them danced; but they
Outdid the sparkling waves in glee;
15 A poet could not but be gay,
In such a jocund² company;
I gazed—and gazed—but little thought
What wealth the show to me had brought:

For oft, when on my couch I lie
20 In vacant or in pensive mood,
They flash upon that inward eye
Which is the bliss of solitude;
And then my heart with pleasure fills,
And dances with the daffodils. ▶

ANALYZE

Underline phrases that describe the two **settings** in the poem.

How does the poet's experience in the first setting influence his experiences in the second setting?

Big Question

Think about the peaceful place you sketched on page 137. How have you been affected by memories of that place?

_____

_____

_____

_____

_____

1. **vales:** valleys.
2. **jocund** (jŏk′ənd): merry.

Reading Comprehension

DIRECTIONS *Answer these questions about the selected poetry by filling in the correct ovals.*

1. Which poem shows that Wordsworth can appreciate the beauty of urban landscapes as well as natural ones?

   (A) "Lines Composed a Few Miles Above Tintern Abbey"

   (B) "Composed upon Westminster Bridge"

   (C) "The World Is Too Much with Us"

   (D) "I Wandered Lonely As a Cloud"

2. The speaker of "Tintern Abbey" values his memories from five years earlier because they have

   (A) inspired some of his poems

   (B) comforted him when he was lonely

   (C) made him feel close to his sister

   (D) taught him to appreciate nature

3. Which statement *best* describes how the speaker of "Tintern Abbey" currently responds to nature?

   (A) He no longer takes pleasure in nature's beauty.

   (B) His response has remained the same over time.

   (C) He senses the spiritual power of nature.

   (D) He wishes he felt at home in nature.

4. Which characteristic of romantic poetry does the speaker of "Tintern Abbey" emphasize to his sister in lines 119–134?

   (A) turning to nature for inspiration and solace

   (B) celebrating the commonplace

   (C) style resembling natural speech

   (D) exotic and supernatural elements

5. Which line from "The World Is Too Much with Us" contains an example of personification?

   (A) line 5

   (B) line 8

   (C) line 10

   (D) line 14

6. What does the speaker complain about in "The World Is Too Much with Us"?

   (A) Too many people are powerless.

   (B) The weather has become harsh.

   (C) People have lost touch with nature.

   (D) Pagan gods are no longer worshipped.

7. When the speaker of "I Wandered Lonely As a Cloud" says that the daffodils "flash upon that inward eye / Which is the bliss of solitude" in lines 21–22, he means that they

   (A) bring tears to his eyes

   (B) become very bright

   (C) make him feel alone

   (D) form a picture in his mind

8. Which phrase from "I Wandered Lonely As a Cloud" is the *best* example of his use of a style resembling natural speech?

   (A) "That floats on high o'er vales and hills"

   (B) "Beside the lake, beneath the trees"

   (C) "Tossing their heads in sprightly dance"

   (D) "For oft, when on my couch I lie"

For help, use the **Test-Taker's Toolkit** below.

Responding in Writing

9. Short Response The romantic poets stressed the importance of the individual's subjective experiences. How is this emphasis reflected in the poems of William Wordsworth? Provide at least three examples in your response.

_____

_____

_____

_____

_____

_____

TEST-TAKER'S TOOLKIT

⊗ **GRAPHIC ORGANIZER** Use the chart below to help you plan your response.

Experience Described in Poem	How It Affects Speaker

Use with selected poetry by William Wordsworth, p. 136

What's the Connection?

In his poetry, William Wordsworth celebrates nature's healing power. The newspaper article "Happy by Nature" discusses recent scientific research that shows people really do benefit from exposure to nature.

NATURE TO THE RESCUE Are you feeling stressed? lonely? anxious? Is your blood pressure off the charts? Some people insist that exposure to nature can help people with these and other kinds of health problems. With a partner, consider each nature-related activity in the chart below. Write the possible benefit of that experience in the spaces provided.

Activity	Benefits		
	Physical	Psychological	Emotional
gazing at gardens			
petting a cat			
watching aquarium fish			
playing with a dog			
taking a long walk			

LEARN THE SKILL: ANALYZE EVIDENCE

Writers use different kinds of **evidence** to support their ideas, such as:

- opinions of experts on the topic under discussion
- opinions of experts in other fields
- results of studies or surveys

Analyzing the kind of evidence a writer uses and the reliability of that evidence can help you decide whether the points the writer makes are credible.

For more on analyzing evidence, see the Nonfiction Skills Handbook beginning on page R2.

Section D LIFESTYLES

Happy by Nature: Fondness for Plants and Animals May Be Hard-Wired, Healthy

by Beth Baker

Intuitively, we know something in us responds to nature, even as most of us live our workaday lives further and further removed from flora and fauna. . . . Now a growing body of research suggests that this human affinity to nature—plants, animals and landscapes—is something hard-wired into us. Scientists
10 call it "biophilia." ▶

Credit for the idea properly goes to eminent sociobiologist E. O. Wilson, who popularized the term in his 1984 book *Biophilia: The Human Bond with Other Species* (Harvard University Press), defining it as "the connections that human beings subconsciously seek with the rest of life."

20 "Our existence depends on this propensity," he wrote. "Our spirit is woven from it, hopes rise on its currents." Biophilia, Wilson says, may explain why millions of us have pets, fill our homes with plants and flock to zoos and national parks when we're away from work. ▶

Wilson was by no means the first
30 to observe that we draw comfort and sustenance from the natural world: The ancient Egyptians created gardens to restore the spirit; Emerson, Whitman and Thoreau wrote memorably of the serenity that comes from being in nature.

But in recent years the focus has turned from the poetic to the

SPECIALIZED Vocabulary

The word *biophilia* contains the prefix *bio-*, meaning "life," and the suffix *–philia*, meaning "tendency toward." Underline phrases in lines 1–10 that suggest the term's meaning. ✎

INTERPRET

What do you think sociobiologist E. O. Wilson meant when he wrote, "Our existence depends on this propensity" (lines 20–21)?

> "We should pay attention to the access people have to the sight of trees and open space and recognize that this is not merely recreational."

scientific. Contact with animals, plants and nature may be a potent antidote to stress, credible research suggests, distracting us from worrisome thoughts, reducing anxiety and lowering blood pressure.

"We should pay attention to the access people have to the sight of trees and open space and recognize that this is not merely recreational," says Aaron Katcher, associate professor emeritus at the University of Pennsylvania in Philadelphia and a biophilia researcher. "It may be contributing to our well-being.". . .

In an analysis of biophilia-related literature published in the peer-reviewed *American Journal of Preventive Medicine,* Howard Frumkin, chair of the Department of Environmental and Occupational Health at Emory University in Atlanta, found evidence that contact with the natural world—including animals, plants, landscapes and wilderness—may offer health benefits. While he acknowledged that many of the studies lacked scientific rigor, Frumkin says, "I became convinced it's an important and researchable area."

Among results from what researchers judge to be some of the more credible studies: ▶

- In experiments conducted at Purdue University in West Lafayette, Ind., participants experienced a clinically significant decline in blood pressure after gazing at fish in an aquarium for 20 minutes. Other studies have found that aquarium watching reduces stress and anxiety for patients awaiting dental surgery.

- Researchers in Japan compared brain wave activity for a group of participants who viewed a hedge of greenery and then a concrete fence. While watching the hedge, the subjects had a higher relaxation response, while the concrete provoked a stressful effect. In another study, similar brain wave patterns occurred when subjects watched a pot filled with flowers, then an empty pot.

- In a study of children with autism and other pervasive development disorders, University of Washington researchers found that including a dog in therapy sessions led children to be more verbal and more engaged with therapists.

Some of the most consistent findings link companion animals with enhanced physical, mental and emotional well-being. One of the first such studies, conducted in 1977 at the University of Maryland, followed 92 patients with heart disease for a year. Patients with pets outlived their counterparts without pets.

The finding stunned the researchers, says Alan Beck, director of the Center for Applied Ethology and Human-Animal Interaction at Purdue University and a pioneer in companion animal research. Even after they eliminated dogs from the study—to ensure that exercise from dog-walking wasn't skewing the results—patients who owned iguanas, fish and gerbils had the same survival advantage. Subsequent studies found that pet owners tended to have lower cholesterol, triglycerides and blood pressure than their petless peers. ▶

ANALYZE EVIDENCE

Reread lines 72–74. How can you tell that the results of some biophilia studies are not to be trusted?

_____

_____

_____

_____

_____

TESTSMART

Eliminating dogs from the study described in lines 109–118 made the results

(A) more credible

(B) less credible

(C) scientifically questionable

(D) scientifically certain

TIP A test question may require you to **synthesize information** from more than one part of a text. In this case, you need to think about the description of the study itself in lines 109–118 and the part of the text that tells *why* dogs were removed from the experiment.

Reading Comprehension

DIRECTIONS *Answer these questions about the article and the poems
in this lesson by filling in the correct ovals.*

1. What new development is the focus of the article?

   (A) the basic idea of biophilia

   (B) scientific research into biophilia

   (C) how stress affects our health

   (D) the increasing popularity of pets

2. The author of the article suggests that a love of nature is

   (A) something humans must be taught

   (B) only recently being written about

   (C) part of our biological makeup

   (D) no longer necessary for our health

3. According to the article, Aaron Katcher and Howard Frumkin both believe that

   (A) increased contact with nature may make us healthier

   (B) biophilia has been proven to be true

   (C) all scientific studies of biophilia are flawed

   (D) biophilia is not a promising field of research

4. In the Japanese study described in lines 86–94 of the article, researchers had subjects look at a concrete fence

   (A) because blank walls are soothing

   (B) to prepare them for relaxation therapy

   (C) to see if isolation from nature is stressful

   (D) for two hours at a time

5. From the article's description of a study in lines 100–108, you can infer that children who have autism

   (A) have a strong appreciation of nature

   (B) like to solve math problems

   (C) develop social skills at an early age

   (D) find it hard to communicate with others

6. Which lines from Wordsworth's poem "I Wandered Lonely As a Cloud" are the most relevant to the information in the article?

   (A) lines 1–6

   (B) lines 7–12

   (C) lines 13–18

   (D) lines 19–24

7. The most probable meaning of *rigor* in line 69 of the article is

   (A) adherence to standards

   (B) difficulty of subject matter

   (C) a state of rigidity

   (D) harsh treatment

8. The phrase *clinically significant* in lines 78–79 implies that the observed decline in blood pressure

   (A) was not enough to matter

   (B) was not a random occurrence

   (C) differed from clinic to clinic

   (D) made some patients ill

Timed Writing Practice

PROMPT

Whether describing a natural landscape or a view of London, Wordsworth creates vivid word pictures in his poems. Write a descriptive essay about a place that has made a strong impression on you. (Use different types of sensory details), and explain how the place you are describing makes you feel. In your essay, refer to at least one idea from the selections you have read.

TEST-TAKER'S TOOLKIT

1. ANALYZE THE PROMPT

A. Identify the type of writing you are asked to do.

B. Circle any key words that describe the topic or indicate what you are required to include in your writing. One example has been circled for you.

2. PLAN YOUR RESPONSE

A. **Make notes** Decide which place you will write about. In the chart, list sensory details about that place.

B. **Organize your information** Choose a logical pattern for your description. You may present details in spatial order—the order in which they appear, such as near to far or inside to outside. Or you may present details in the order in which you experience them, starting out with the one that you first notice.

3. WRITE AND REVIEW

A. Begin your essay with a strong introductory paragraph that catches your readers' attention. You might start off with a humorous observation or a question.

B. Write out your response. Leave enough time to read through it and make sure you have met all the requirements of the prompt.

LESSON 4B

Selected Poetry

BY PERCY BYSSHE SHELLEY

RELATED NONFICTION
The Science of Color in Autumn Leaves

What can NATURE teach us?

Romantic poets thought that profound lessons could be learned from observing nature. They believed that there was no greater beauty than that found in nature, and they saw higher truths reflected in natural scenes.

VISUALIZE IT Visualize one of the following elements of nature—a sand dune, the wind, or a bird. Think deeply about it. What lessons about life could it suggest to you? Contemplating the wind, for example, might make you realize that any life circumstance can suddenly change, as the wind does. Note which element you chose to visualize in the notebook. Jot down one possible lesson about life that it suggests to you.

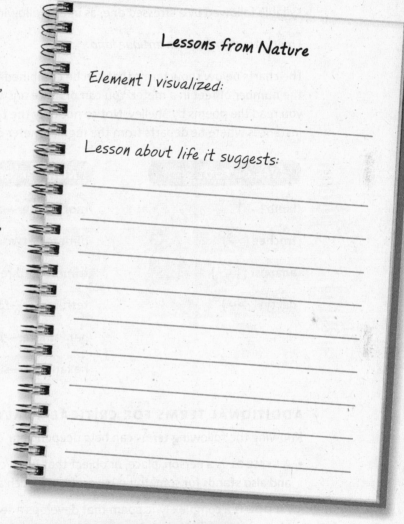

Lessons from Nature

Element I visualized:

_____

Lesson about life it suggests:

_____

_____

_____

_____

_____

_____

_____

_____

ASSESSMENT GOALS

By the end of this lesson, you will be able to . . .

- analyze rhythmic patterns in poetry
- apply critical thinking skills to analyze text
- summarize a work of nonfiction
- analyze a writing prompt and plan an analysis of poetry

Rhythmic Patterns

A poem's RHYTHM, or pattern of stressed and unstressed syllables, can help give it a musical quality. In most English poetry prior to the 20th century, the rhythm follows a regular pattern called a METER. Each unit of meter, known as a FOOT, consists of one stressed syllable (´) and one or more unstressed syllables (˘). The most common meter in English is IAMBIC PENTAMETER—lines with five feet that consist of an unstressed syllable followed by a stressed one, as in the following line from Shelley's "Ozymandias":

˘   ´   ˘   ´ ˘   ˘   ´   ˘   ´ ˘   ´
I met | a trave|ler from | an an|tique land

The charts below show terms that can be combined to indicate the types of feet and the number of feet in a meter. You can practice answering questions about meter as you read the poems by Shelley. Notice not only the type of meter Shelley uses but also instances where he departs from the regular meter of a poem.

TYPE OF FOOT	NUMBER OF FEET
iamb (˘ ´)	monometer—one
trochee (´ ˘)	dimeter—two
anapest (˘ ˘ ´)	trimeter—three
dactyl (´ ˘ ˘)	tetrameter—four
	pentameter—five
	hexameter—six

ADDITIONAL TERMS FOR CRITICAL ANALYSIS

Knowing the following terms can help deepen your understanding of Shelley's poetry:

• A SYMBOL is a person, place, or object that has a concrete meaning in itself and also stands for something beyond itself, such as an idea or feeling.

• An ODE is a complex lyric poem that develops a serious and dignified theme. Many odes celebrate nature, praise people, or commemorate events.

Ozymandias

Percy Bysshe Shelley

BACKGROUND Percy Bysshe Shelley was part of a generation of English poets known as the late romantics. An idealist and a political radical, he passionately opposed all injustice and dreamed of changing the world through poetry. He wrote with the fervent conviction that poetry nourishes the imagination, and that the imagination—by enabling empathy for others—brings about social change.

SECOND READ:
CRITICAL ANALYSIS

MARK & ANALYZE

Read the poems once on your own, marking the text in any way that is helpful to you.

Then read the poems a second time, using the questions in the margins to help you analyze the literature. When you see this pencil ✏, you'll be asked to mark up the text.

I met a traveler from an antique land
Who said: Two vast and trunkless legs[1] of stone
Stand in the desert . . . Near them, on the sand,
Half sunk, a shattered visage[2] lies, whose frown,
5   And wrinkled lip, and sneer of cold command,
Tell that its sculptor well those passions read
Which yet survive, stamped on these lifeless things,
The hand that mocked them, and the heart that fed:[3]
And on the pedestal these words appear:
10   "My name is Ozymandias,[4] king of kings:
Look on my works, ye Mighty, and despair!"
Nothing beside remains. Round the decay
Of that colossal wreck, boundless and bare
The lone and level sands stretch far away. ▶

ANALYZE

"Ozymandias" is written in **iambic pentameter.** Mark the stressed and unstressed syllables in lines 11–14. ✏

Which words does Shelley emphasize by departing from the metrical pattern?

_____

_____

---

1. **trunkless legs:** legs separated from the rest of the body.
2. **visage** (vĭz′ĭj): face.
3. **The hand . . . that fed:** the sculptor's hand that imitated the passions of the king and the heart that fed them.
4. **Ozymandias** (ŏz′ĭ-măn′dē-əs): a Greek name for the Egyptian pharaoh Rameses II, who reigned from 1279 to 1213 B.C.

ODE TO THE
West Wind

Percy Bysshe Shelley

I

O wild West Wind, thou breath of Autumn's being, *a*
Thou, from whose unseen presence the leaves dead *b*
Are driven, like ghosts from an enchanter fleeing, *a*

Yellow, and black, and pale, and hectic[1] red,
5 Pestilence-stricken multitudes: O thou,
Who chariotest to their dark wintry bed

The wingéd seeds, where they lie cold and low,
Each like a corpse within its grave, until
Thine azure sister of the Spring[2] shall blow

10 Her clarion[3] o'er the dreaming earth, and fill
(Driving sweet buds like flocks to feed in air)
With living hues and odors plain and hill:

Wild Spirit, which art moving everywhere;
Destroyer and preserver; hear, oh, hear! ◀

ANALYZE

Identify the interlocking pattern of rhyme in the first four stanzas of section I by writing a letter from *a* to *e* next to each line. The first stanza has been done for you. 🖉

How does the fifth stanza bring the pattern to a close?

---

1. **hectic:** feverish.
2. **sister . . . Spring:** the reviving south wind of spring.
3. **clarion:** a trumpet with a clear, ringing tone.

II

15 Thou on whose stream, mid the steep sky's commotion,
Loose clouds like earth's decaying leaves are shed,
Shook from the tangled bough of Heaven and Ocean,

Angels[4] of rain and lightning: there are spread
On the blue surface of thine aëry[5] surge,
20 Like the bright hair uplifted from the head

Of some fierce Maenad, even from the dim verge
Of the horizon to the zenith's height,[6]
The locks of the approaching storm. Thou dirge[7]

Of the dying year, to which this closing night
25 Will be the dome of a vast sepulcher,[8]
Vaulted with all thy congregated might

Of vapors, from whose solid atmosphere
Black rain, and fire, and hail will burst: oh, hear! ▶

III

Thou who didst waken from his summer dreams
30 The blue Mediterranean, where he lay,
Lulled by the coil of his crystálline[9] streams,

Beside a pumice isle in Baiae's bay,[10]
And saw in sleep old palaces and towers
Quivering within the wave's intenser day,

ANALYZE

Reread lines 27–28, tapping your desk with each stressed syllable to hear the **rhythm**. Then scan the lines again, this time marking the stressed and unstressed syllables. 🖊

How many **feet** are in each line? What type of feet are they? The charts on page 158 can help you answer these questions.

---

4. **angels:** messengers.

5. **aëry:** airy.

6. **Like the bright . . . height:** The clouds lie in streaks from the horizon upward, looking like the streaming hair of a maenad (mē′năd′)—a wildly dancing female worshiper of Dionysus, the Greek god of wine.

7. **dirge:** funeral song.

8. **sepulcher** (sĕp′əl-kər): tomb.

9. **crystálline** (krĭs-tăl′ĭn) **streams:** the different-colored currents of the Mediterranean Sea.

10. **pumice** (pŭm′ĭs): a light volcanic rock; **Baiae's** (bī′ēz′) **bay:** the Bay of Naples, site of the ancient Roman resort of Baiae.

TestSmart

What does the wind symbolize in lines 53–56?

- (A) a heavy weight
- (B) life's troubles and pain
- (C) delivery from suffering
- (D) a wave, a leaf, a cloud

TIP A test question may ask you to identify a **symbol** in specific lines of poetry. To answer questions like this, it is essential that you understand the lines in question. In this case, carefully reread lines 53–56. If necessary, **paraphrase** them by restating them in your own words. Then find the answer choice that matches.

35 All overgrown with azure moss and flowers
  So sweet, the sense faints picturing them! Thou
  For whose path the Atlantic's level powers[11]

  Cleave themselves into chasms, while far below
  The sea-blooms and the oozy woods which wear
40 The sapless foliage of the ocean, know

  Thy voice, and suddenly grow gray with fear,
  And tremble and despoil themselves: oh, hear!

IV

  If I were a dead leaf thou mightest bear;
  If I were a swift cloud to fly with thee;
45 A wave to pant beneath thy power, and share

  The impulse of thy strength, only less free
  Than thou, O uncontrollable! If even
  I were as in my boyhood, and could be

  The comrade of thy wanderings over Heaven,
50 As then, when to outstrip thy skyey speed[12]
  Scarce seemed a vision;[13] I would ne'er have striven

  As thus with thee in prayer in my sore need.
  Oh, lift me as a wave, a leaf, a cloud!
  I fall upon the thorns of life! I bleed!

55 A heavy weight of hours has chained and bowed
  One too like thee: tameless, and swift, and proud. ◄

---

11. **level powers:** surface.
12. **skyey** (skī'ē) **speed:** the swiftness of clouds moving across the sky.
13. **vision:** something impossible to achieve.

V

Make me thy lyre,[14] even as the forest is:
What if my leaves are falling like its own!
The tumult of thy mighty harmonies

60 Will take from both a deep, autumnal tone,
Sweet though in sadness. Be thou, Spirit fierce,
My spirit! Be thou me, impetuous[15] one!

Drive my dead thoughts over the universe
Like withered leaves to quicken a new birth!
65 And, by the incantation[16] of this verse,

Scatter, as from an unextinguished hearth
Ashes and sparks, my words among mankind!
Be through my lips to unawakened earth

The trumpet of a prophecy! O Wind,
70 If Winter comes, can Spring be far behind? ▶

INTERPRET

What qualities of the west wind are glorified in this **ode**?

_____

_____

_____

_____

---

14. **lyre:** a reference to the Aeolian harp, an instrument whose strings make musical
    sounds when the wind blows over them.

15. **impetuous** (ĭm-pĕch′o͞o-əs): violently forceful; impulsive.

16. **incantation:** recitation, as of a magic spell.

TO A
Skylark

Percy Bysshe Shelley

INTERPRET

Reread the boxed text. What does the skylark **symbolize** for the speaker?

_____

_____

_____

_____

Hail to thee, blithe[1] Spirit!
    Bird thou never wert,
That from Heaven, or near it,
    Pourest thy full heart
5 In profuse strains of unpremeditated[2] art.

Higher still and higher
    From the earth thou springest
Like a cloud of fire;
    The blue deep thou wingest,
10 And singing still dost soar, and soaring ever singest.

In the golden lightning
    Of the sunken sun,
O'er which clouds are bright'ning,
    Thou dost float and run;
15 Like an unbodied joy whose race is just begun.

---

1. **blithe** (blīth): carefree.
2. **unpremeditated** (ŭn'prĭ-mĕd'ĭ-tā'tĭd): natural; not planned out ahead of time.

The pale purple even[3]
   Melts around thy flight;
Like a star of Heaven,
   In the broad daylight
20 Thou art unseen, but yet I hear thy shrill delight,

   Keen as are the arrows
      Of that silver sphere,[4]
Whose intense lamp narrows
      In the white dawn clear
25 Until we hardly see—we feel that it is there.

   All the earth and air
      With thy voice is loud,
As, when night is bare,
      From one lonely cloud
30 The moon rains out her beams, and Heaven is overflowed.

   What thou are we know not;
      What is most like thee?
From rainbow clouds there flow not
      Drops so bright to see
35 As from thy presence showers a rain of melody.

   Like a Poet hidden
      In the light of thought,
Singing hymns unbidden,
      Till the world is wrought
40 To sympathy with hopes and fears it heeded not:

   Like a high-born maiden
      In a palace tower
Soothing her love-laden
      Soul in secret hour
45 With music sweet as love, which overflows her bower:[5] ▶

---

3. **even:** evening.
4. **silver sphere:** the planet Venus, called the morning star because it is visible in the east just before daybreak.
5. **bower:** private room; boudoir or bedroom.

ANALYZE

Reread lines 31, 36, and 41. Mark the stressed and unstressed syllables in each line.

What **meter** are these lines written in?

_____

_____

Like a glowworm[6] golden
    In a dell of dew,
Scattering unbeholden
    Its aërial[7] hue
50 Among the flowers and grass, which screen it from the view!

Like a rose embowered
    In its own green leaves,
By warm winds deflowered,[8]
    Till the scent it gives
55 Makes faint with too much sweet those heavy-wingéd thieves:[9] ◄

Sound of vernal[10] showers
    On the twinkling grass,
Rain-awakened flowers,
    All that ever was
60 Joyous, and clear, and fresh, thy music doth surpass:

Teach us, Sprite or Bird,
    What sweet thoughts are thine:
I have never heard
    Praise of love or wine
65 That panted forth a flood of rapture so divine.

Chorus Hymeneal,[11]
    Or triumphal chant,
Matched with thine would be all
    But an empty vaunt,[12]
70 A thing wherein we feel there is some hidden want.

---

6. **glowworm:** wingless female firefly or firefly larva.
7. **aërial** (âr′ē-əl) **hue:** insubstantial glow.
8. **deflowered:** fully opened.
9. **thieves:** the warm winds.
10. **vernal:** spring.
11. **Chorus Hymeneal** (hī′mə-nē′əl): a wedding song.
12. **vaunt:** boast.

What objects are the fountains[13]
 Of thy happy strain?
What fields, or waves, or mountains?
 What shapes of sky or plain?
75 What love of thine own kind? what ignorance of pain?

With thy clear keen joyance
 Languor[14] cannot be:
Shadow of annoyance
 Never came near thee:
80 Thou lovest—but ne'er knew love's sad satiety.[15]

Waking or asleep,
 Thou of death must deem[16]
Things more true and deep
 Than we mortals dream,
85 Or how could thy notes flow in such a crystal stream?

We look before and after,
 And pine for what is not:
Our sincerest laughter
 With some pain is fraught;
90 Our sweetest songs are those that tell of saddest thought.

Yet if[17] we could scorn
 Hate, and pride, and fear;
If we were things born
 Not to shed a tear,
95 I know not how thy joy we ever should come near. ▶

Better than all measures
 Of delightful sound,
Better than all treasures
 That in books are found,
100 Thy skill to poet were, thou scorner of the ground! ▶

---

13. **fountains:** sources.
14. **languor** (lăng′gər): lack of energy; listlessness.
15. **satiety** (sə-tī′ĭ-tē): fulfillment to excess.
16. **deem:** know.
17. **if:** even if.

COMPARE AND CONTRAST

Reread lines 86–95. According to the speaker, in what ways is the skylark better off than human beings?

_____

_____

_____

_____

ANALYZE

How does the **rhythm** change from the fourth line of each stanza to the fifth line? What effect does this difference in rhythm have?

_____

_____

_____

_____

Teach me half the gladness
    That thy brain must know,
Such harmonious madness
    From my lips would flow
105 The world should listen then—as I am listening now.

Big Question

Review the visualization activity you completed on page 157. How do your thoughts about the element of nature you chose differ from Shelley's characterization of that same element? Explain your answer.

_____

_____

_____

_____

_____

Reading Comprehension

DIRECTIONS *Answer these questions about the poems in this lesson by filling in the correct ovals.*

1. In "Ozymandias," what is ironic about the words inscribed on the statue's pedestal?

   (A) The writing has been worn down over time.

   (B) Ozymandias has been dead for so long.

   (C) Ozymandias's "works" are now ruins.

   (D) The sculpture of Ozymandias was poorly made.

2. In "Ozymandias," what does the inscription on the pedestal symbolize?

   (A) arrogant pride

   (B) decay

   (C) a lost treasure

   (D) a leader's power

3. In the last section of "Ode to the West Wind," the speaker prays that the wind will

   (A) carry him back to his childhood

   (B) churn up waves in the ocean

   (C) bring mild winter weather

   (D) spread his thoughts everywhere

4. What qualities of a skylark are glorified in lines 6–10 of the ode "To a Skylark"?

   (A) knowledge of death

   (B) ability to soar and sing gloriously

   (C) ability to provide relief from suffering

   (D) ignorance of pain

5. What is the "unpremeditated art" referred to in line 5 of "To a Skylark"?

   (A) the speaker's verse

   (B) heavenly music

   (C) the skylark's singing

   (D) clouds in the sky

6. In lines 36–40 of "To a Skylark," Shelley suggests that poets are

   (A) better singers than skylarks

   (B) often ignored by the world

   (C) more mysterious than skylarks

   (D) invisible to nature

7. Which of the following does the speaker of "To a Skylark" want to learn?

   (A) how the skylark remains invisible

   (B) why roses give off a sweet scent

   (C) why humans can't be joyful

   (D) what inspires the skylark's singing

8. In which of the following lines is the meter correctly marked?

   (A) The hánd thát mŏcked thĕm, ánd thĕ héart thăt féd:

   (B) Yéllŏw, ănd bláck, ănd pále, ănd héctĭc réd,

   (C) Ĭf Wíntĕr cómes, căn Spríng bĕ fár bĕhínd?

   (D) Háil tŏ thĕe, blíthĕ Spírĭt!

GO ON ➡

For help, use the ***Test-Taker's Toolkit*** *below.*

Responding in Writing

9. Short Response Choose one poem from this lesson, and record and scan three to five of its lines. In a paragraph, identify the meter of the poem, indicating the type of foot and the number of feet per line. Point out two or three examples of how the stressed syllables in the lines emphasize words that are important to the poem's meaning.

TEST-TAKER'S TOOLKIT

- **ACADEMIC VOCABULARY** When you **scan** a line of poetry, you analyze its **rhythm** by marking the stressed (ˊ) and unstressed (˘) syllables. If you are unsure about any of the terms related to rhythmic patterns, review the instruction and the charts on page 158.
- **GRAPHIC ORGANIZER** In the chart below, record the lines you have chosen to analyze. Then scan the lines, marking the stressed and unstressed syllables. Note how many and what kind of feet the lines contain. Then you can start to consider how the rhythm helps convey the lines' meaning.

Poem:	
Lines from the poem:	
Meter:	**How the rhythm helps convey meaning:**

What's the Connection?

The poetry of Percy Bysshe Shelley celebrates nature as a source of beauty and inspiration. The following online article from The United States National Arboretum explains the scientific causes of one of nature's most brilliant displays.

CHART IT The following article describes a year in the life of a deciduous tree. What do you know about the following topic? Annotate the chart below by listing seasonal changes that might affect trees. Consider such factors as precipitation, temperature change, and hours of daylight and darkness.

The Science of Color in Autumn Leaves
ONLINE ARTICLE

Use with Selected Poetry by Percy Bysshe Shelley, p. 156

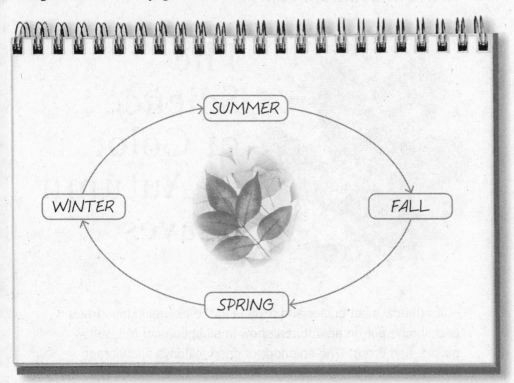

SUMMER

WINTER

FALL

SPRING

LEARN THE SKILL: SUMMARIZE

Summarizing can help you keep track of ideas in a nonfiction text. When you **summarize** an article, you briefly describe its main ideas and most important details. An effective summary should

- describe ideas in the same order in which they appear
- leave out unimportant details

For more on summarizing, see the Nonfiction Skills Handbook beginning on page R2.

SET A PURPOSE

http://www.usna.usda.gov

HOME   **ARTICLES**   EDUCATION   EVENTS   VOLUNTEER

1 | 2 | 3 | 4 ▶

**THE UNITED STATES
NATIONAL ARBORETUM**

The Science of Color in Autumn Leaves

As the days get cooler and frost is in the air, deciduous trees and shrubs put on an autumn show in all shades of red, yellow, purple, and brown. The splendor of crisp fall days and vibrant leaves brings to mind memories for nearly everyone who lives in an area where deciduous forests are the dominant vegetation. In many parts of the country, autumn leaves are an important factor in tourism.

Many think that cool weather or frost causes the leaves to change color. While temperature may dictate the color and its
10 intensity, it is only one of many environmental factors that play a part in painting deciduous woodlands in glorious fall colors.

To understand the whole process, it is important to understand the growth cycle of deciduous trees and shrubs. Most have a relatively short period of annual growth. New stems begin to grow from overwintering buds when the days become long enough and the weather is warm enough to support growth. For most trees, growth is usually completed by late June in the Northern Hemisphere. Next year's leaf buds are set at this time and will

20　not open until they experience the chill and short days of winter followed by the warmth and longer days of spring. Once the leaves are fully expanded and the buds are set, the work of manufacturing and storing carbohydrates to support next year's growth goes full speed ahead. These carbohydrates are stored in the branches, roots, and buds throughout the growing season to support next year's growth. ▶

The process that starts the cascade of events that result in fall color is actually a growth process. In late summer or early autumn, the days begin to get shorter, and nights are longer. Like most plants, deciduous trees and shrubs are rather 30　sensitive to the length of the dark period each day. When nights reach a threshold value and are long enough, the cells near the juncture of the leaf and the stem divide rapidly, but they do not expand. This abscission layer is a corky layer of cells that slowly begins to block transport of materials such as carbohydrates from the leaf to the branch. It also blocks the flow of minerals from the roots into the leaves. Because the starting time of the whole process is dependent on night length, fall colors appear at about the same time each year in a given location, whether temperatures are cooler or warmer than normal.

40　During the growing season, chlorophyll is replaced constantly in the leaves. Chlorophyll breaks down with exposure to light in the same way that colored paper fades in sunlight. The leaves must manufacture new chlorophyll to replace chlorophyll that is lost in this way. In autumn, when the connection between the leaf and the rest of the plant begins to be blocked off, the production of chlorophyll slows and then stops. In a relatively short time period, the chlorophyll disappears completely.

This is when autumn colors are revealed. Chlorophyll normally masks the yellow pigments known as xanthophylls and the 50　orange pigments called carotenoids—both then become visible when the green chlorophyll is gone. These colors are present in the leaf throughout the growing season. Red and purple pigments come from anthocyanins. In the fall anthocyanins are manufactured from the sugars that are trapped in the leaf. In most plants anthocyanins are typically not present during the growing season. ▶

SUMMARIZE

What are the most important things to understand about why trees change color in the fall?

1. environmental factors:

_____

_____

2. growth cycle:

_____

_____

_____

_____

TESTSMART

Which idea from lines 40–56 should *not* be included in a summary of this passage?

Ⓐ Chlorophyll is replaced constantly during the growing season.

Ⓑ In autumn, chlorophyll production slows and then stops.

Ⓒ When the chlorophyll is gone, other pigments are revealed.

Ⓓ Sugar gets trapped in tree leaves in autumn.

TIP A test question may ask you to identify an idea that should not be included in a summary of a passage. To determine the answer, **reread the passage in question** and **look for the most important ideas.** Then read the answer choices and look for one that gives a detail that is not needed in order to understand the overall meaning of the passage.

http://www.usna.usda.gov

SUMMARIZE

Reread the boxed text. Briefly summarize the four factors that influence the quality of fall foliage displays.

1. Temperature:

_____

_____

2. Sunlight:

_____

_____

3. Moisture:

_____

_____

4. Weather:

_____

_____

As autumn progresses, the cells in the abscission layer become more dry and corky. The connections between cells
60 become weakened, and the leaves break off with time. Many trees and shrubs lose their leaves when they are still very colorful. Some plants retain a great deal of their foliage through much of the winter, but the leaves do not retain their color for long. Like chlorophyll, the other pigments eventually break down in light or when they are frozen. The only pigments that remain are tannins, which are brown.

70 Temperature, sunlight, and soil moisture greatly influence the quality of the fall foliage display. Abundant sunlight and low temperatures after the time the abscission layer forms cause the chlorophyll to be destroyed more rapidly. Cool temperatures, particularly at night, combined with abundant sunlight, promote the formation of more anthocyanins. Freezing conditions destroy the machinery responsible for manufacturing
80 anthocyanins, so early frost means an early end to colorful foliage. Drought stress during the growing season can sometimes trigger the early formation of the abscission layer, and leaves may drop before they have a chance to develop fall coloration. A growing season with ample moisture that is followed by a rather dry, cool, sunny autumn that is marked by warm days and cool but frostless nights provides the best weather conditions
90 for development of the brightest fall colors. Lack of wind and rain in the autumn prolongs the display; wind or heavy rain may cause the leaves to be lost before they develop their full color potential. ◄

◀ 1 | 2 | 3 | **4**

The character of autumn color is different in different parts of the world. In New England and the northeast sections of Asia, a few species dominate the deciduous forests. The display there tends to be short but intense because the change is rapid and rather uniform. In the southern Appalachians, the change is often gradual
100 and the fall foliage season may last for more than a month because of the greater diversity of plant species found in the forest there. Mixed forests that have both evergreen conifers, such as spruce, and deciduous trees, such as aspen or larch, are found in the far north or at high elevations. Here, the dominant color is yellow and the change is rapid, with trees often going from green through brilliant yellow to bare over a period of two weeks. Tropical forests often have many deciduous trees that lose their leaves in response to drought; typically the leaves do not change color before they drop. In areas that are often cloudy for much of the autumn, with rather warm
110 temperatures, fall colors are dull at best. This is often the case in much of Europe. ▶

While the whole process of fall color is fairly well understood, the reason for it is less clear. Scientists have long known that xanthophylls and carotenoids play an important part in photosynthesis by helping to capture light energy, but the benefit of anthocyanins is not well understood. It might seem more logical for plants to remove all the carbohydrates they possibly can from the leaf before making it fall off. If this were the case, we wouldn't have the red and purple pigments that we see in sugar maple, black
120 gum, burning bush, or sweet gum. Carbohydrates are needed to manufacture these pigments. Some entomologists believe that the evolutionary reason that plants expend energy to produce fall color is to warn pests. A plant that is healthy is able to produce lots of carbohydrates, and therefore more anthocyanin. This may cause certain insect pests laying eggs in the fall to seek another host plant for their offspring that is weaker and drab by comparison. Some scientists believe that anthocyanins may act as a sunscreen to inhibit the destruction of the chlorophyll, help prevent frost injury to leaf tissues, or limit water loss during dry spells in autumn. As far as
130 the fall foliage watcher is concerned, their purpose is simple—they signal a last hurrah for the growing season and delight the optic nerve. ▶

CONNECT

Which pattern described in lines 95–111 best describes the fall foliage display in the region where you live?

_____

_____

_____

SPECIALIZED Vocabulary

The word *entomologists* in line 121 may be new to you. Write two other words you have seen that contain the ending *–ologist.*

_____

_____

Based on your knowledge of this suffix's meaning and context clues in the text, what do you think an entomologist is? *WORD ANALYSIS*

_____

_____

Reading Comprehension

DIRECTIONS *Answer these questions about the article and the poems in this lesson by filling in the correct ovals.*

1. What factor is the most important in determining when the leaves change color in a region?

   (A) cool temperatures

   (B) night length

   (C) frost

   (D) precipitation

2. What substance do trees produce to nourish leaf buds for the coming year?

   (A) chlorophyll

   (B) carotenoids

   (C) carbohydrates

   (D) tannins

3. What can cause some trees to lose their leaves when the leaves are still very colorful?

   (A) wind and breakdown of the abscission layer

   (B) cool temperatures and abundant sunlight

   (C) frost in early autumn

   (D) ample rain during the growing season

4. Which phrase *best* describes the purpose of the article's last paragraph (lines 112–132)?

   (A) to examine the function of bright pigments

   (B) to discuss purple pigments

   (C) to examine harmful pests

   (D) to explain the cause of fall colors

5. Which ideas should *not* be included in a summary of lines 57–94?

   (A) Coolness and sunlight promote anthocyanins.

   (B) Early frost ends colorful foliage.

   (C) Other pigments break down in sunlight.

   (D) Tannins are brown pigments.

6. Which statement or idea from the article would Shelley most likely agree with?

   (A) Trees "delight the optic nerve."

   (B) "Anthocyanins may act as a sunscreen."

   (C) Autumn colors promote tourism.

   (D) Cool weather causes autumn color.

7. The word *conifers* in line 102 refers to

   (A) the fall foliage season

   (B) trees that don't lose their leaves

   (C) leaves that don't change color

   (D) the diversity of plant species

8. Which word does *not* name a pigment?

   (A) carotenoids

   (B) anthocyanins

   (C) black gum

   (D) tannins

Timed Writing Practice

BUDGET YOUR TIME

You have **45 minutes** to respond. Decide how much time to spend on each step.

Analyze _____

Plan _____

Write _____ 45

Review _____

PROMPT

In his essay "A Defense of Poetry," Shelley writes that poetry "strips the veil of familiarity from the world, and lays bare the naked and sleeping beauty which is the spirit of its forms." Write an analysis of one of Shelley's poems in which you discuss his insight into the beauty or power of nature. In your analysis, refer to specific examples of imagery and figurative language that Shelley uses to convey his idea.

TEST-TAKER'S TOOLKIT

1. ANALYZE THE PROMPT

A. Identify the type of writing you are asked to do.

B. Circle any key words that describe the topic or indicate what you are required to include in your writing. One example has been circled for you.

C. Note that you are asked to focus on one poem. Write the name of the poem you will analyze. _____

2. PLAN YOUR RESPONSE

A. Make notes Create a chart like the one shown to gather specific examples for your essay.

B. Organize your information Use your notes to help structure your essay. Begin with an introduction in which you state your thesis. Then you can write a paragraph for each example of imagery or figurative language that you will analyze. Finish with a conclusion in which you summarize your analysis.

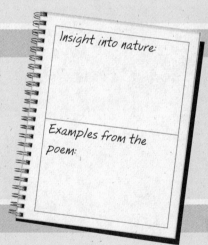

Insight into nature:

Examples from the poem:

3. WRITE AND REVIEW

A. In your introduction, make sure to identify which poem you have chosen and clearly state the insight into nature that you will discuss. Give readers a sense of what is new or exciting about this insight; for example, you might explain how Shelley "strips the veil of familiarity" from the subject of the poem.

B. Write your full response on a separate sheet of paper. Leave time to review your writing.

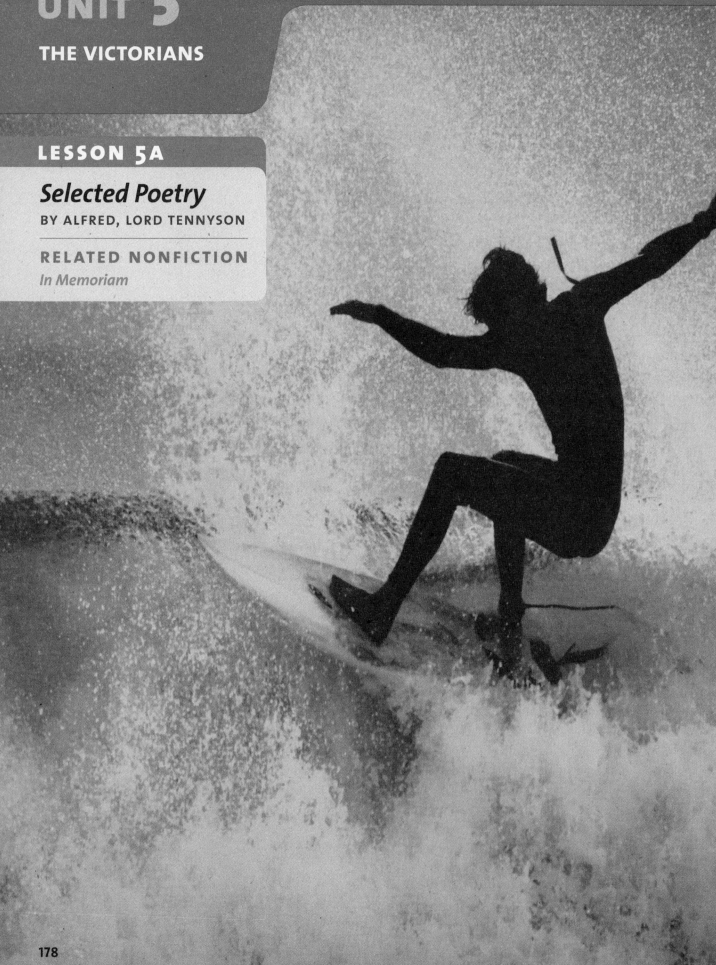

LESSON 5A

Selected Poetry
BY ALFRED, LORD TENNYSON

RELATED NONFICTION
In Memoriam

How do you live LIFE
to the FULLEST?

People who constantly seek out new experiences are said to be "living life to the fullest." Often, this phrase is used to describe adventurers, athletes, connoisseurs, or others who aim for extraordinary goals or seek to enjoy the very best of what life has to offer. In your opinion, what constitutes a full life?

LIST IT List five experiences that you think are essential to living life to the fullest. Discuss your list with a partner or a small group of classmates.

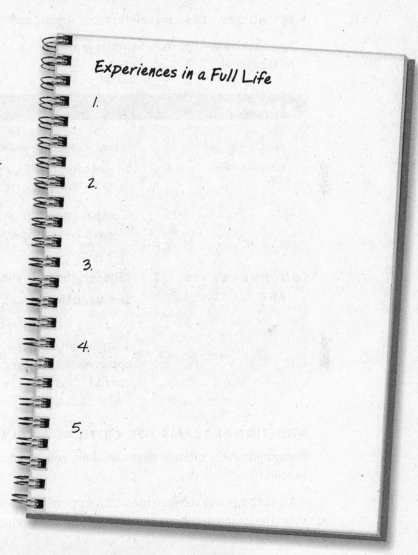

Experiences in a Full Life

1.

2.

3.

4.

5.

ASSESSMENT GOALS

By the end of this lesson, you will be able to . . .

- analyze mood in poetry
- apply critical thinking skills to analyze text
- analyze a literary essay
- analyze a writing prompt and plan a compare-and-contrast essay

Mood

MOOD is the feeling or atmosphere a writer creates for the reader. For example, a poem may be described as mysterious, somber, joyful, or suspenseful. Elements that can help convey the mood of a poem include

- IMAGERY and FIGURATIVE LANGUAGE

- SOUND DEVICES such as alliteration, rhyme, and rhythm

- PARALLELISM—the use of similar grammatical constructions to express related ideas

EXAMPLES

FIGURATIVE LANGUAGE	"How dull it is to pause, to make an end, To rust unburnish'd, not to shine in use!"
	—"Ulysses," lines 22–23
	(Comparing an idle life to a dull, unused sword helps us feel the speaker's dissatisfaction.)
SOUND DEVICES AND PARALLELISM	"She left the web, she left the loom, She made three paces through the room,"
	—"The Lady of Shalott," lines 109–110
	(Parallelism creates a mood of tense apprehension. The regular rhythm and the rhyme intensify this effect.)

ADDITIONAL TERMS FOR CRITICAL ANALYSIS

Knowing these additional terms will help you appreciate the poems you are about to read.

- An ELEGY is an extended meditative poem in which the speaker reflects on death—often in tribute to a person who has died recently—or on an equally serious subject.

- A DRAMATIC MONOLOGUE is a poetic form in which the speaker addresses a silent or absent listener during a moment of high intensity or deep emotion.

THE *Lady* OF SHALOTT

ALFRED, LORD TENNYSON

BACKGROUND Alfred, Lord Tennyson, was the most prominent poet of the Victorian era. His poem "The Lady of Shalott" reflects his fascination with the Arthurian legends. In the excerpts from the long poem *In Memoriam,* that you will read, Tennyson expresses his grief over the loss of his closest friend, Arthur Henry Hallam, who died suddenly at age 22. The two other poems in this selection, "Ulysses" and "Crossing the Bar," both have speakers who face old age with courage and determination.

MARK & ANALYZE

Read the poems once on your own, marking the text in any way that is helpful to you. Then read the poems a second time, using the questions in the margins to help you analyze the literature. When you see this pencil ✏, you'll be asked to mark up the text.

Part I

On either side the river lie
Long fields of barley and of rye,
That clothe the wold¹ and meet the sky;
And through the field the road runs by
5   To many-towered Camelot;
And up and down the people go,
Gazing where the lilies blow²
Round an island there below,
    The island of Shalott.

10 Willows whiten, aspens quiver,
Little breezes dusk and shiver
Through the wave that runs forever
By the island in the river
    Flowing down to Camelot.

---

1. **wold:** rolling plain.
2. **blow:** bloom.

ANALYZE

What **mood** is created by the description of the island in the second stanza?

_____

_____

Underline phrases that contribute to the **mood**.

15 Four gray walls, and four gray towers,
   Overlook a space of flowers,
   And the silent isle imbowers³
       The Lady of Shalott. ◀

   By the margin, willow-veiled,
20 Slide the heavy barges trailed
   By slow horses; and unhailed
   The shallop⁴ flitteth silken-sailed
       Skimming down to Camelot:
   But who hath seen her wave her hand?
25 Or at the casement⁵ seen her stand?
   Or is she known in all the land,
       The Lady of Shalott?

   Only reapers, reaping early
   In among the bearded barley,
30 Hear a song that echoes cheerly
   From the river winding clearly,
       Down to towered Camelot;
   And by the moon the reaper weary,
   Piling sheaves in uplands airy,
35 Listening, whispers "'Tis the fairy
       Lady of Shalott."

Part II
   There she weaves by night and day
   A magic web with colors gay.
   She has heard a whisper say,
40 A curse is on her if she stay
       To look down to Camelot.
   She knows not what the curse may be,
   And so she weaveth steadily,
   And little other care hath she,
45   The Lady of Shalott.

_____

3. **imbowers:** encloses; surrounds.
4. **shallop** (shăl'əp): a small open boat.
5. **casement:** a hinged window that opens outward.

And moving through a mirror clear
That hangs before her all the year,
Shadows of the world appear.[6]
There she sees the highway near
50   Winding down to Camelot;
There the river eddy whirls,
And there the surly village churls,[7]
And the red cloaks of market girls,
     Pass onward from Shalott.

55 Sometimes a troop of damsels[8] glad,
An abbot on an ambling pad,[9]
Sometimes a curly shepherd lad,
Or long-haired page[10] in crimson clad,
     Goes by to towered Camelot;
60 And sometimes through the mirror blue
The knights come riding two and two:
She hath no loyal knight and true,
     The Lady of Shalott.

But in her web she still delights
65 To weave the mirror's magic sights,
For often through the silent nights
A funeral, with plumes and lights
     And music, went to Camelot;
Or when the moon was overhead,
70 Came two young lovers lately wed:
"I am half sick of shadows," said
     The Lady of Shalott. ▶

ANALYZE

How does Tennyson's description in lines 46–72 encourage the reader to sympathize with the Lady of Shalott?

_____

_____

_____

_____

_____

---

6. Weavers often used mirrors while working from the back of a tapestry to view the tapestry's appearance, but this one is used to view the outside world.

7. **surly village churls:** rude members of the lower class in a village.

8. **damsels:** young, unmarried women.

9. **abbot . . . pad:** the head monk in a monastery on a slow-moving horse.

10. **page:** a boy in training to be a knight.

Part III

A bowshot[11] from her bower eaves,[12]
He rode between the barley sheaves,
75 The sun came dazzling through the leaves,
And flamed upon the brazen greaves[13]
    Of bold Sir Lancelot.
A red-cross knight forever kneeled
To a lady in his shield,[14]
80 That sparkled on the yellow field,
    Beside remote Shalott.

The gemmy[15] bridle glittered free,
Like to some branch of stars we see
Hung in the golden Galaxy.
85 The bridle bells rang merrily
    As he rode down to Camelot;
And from his blazoned baldric[16] slung
A mighty silver bugle hung,
And as he rode his armor rung,
90   Beside remote Shalott. ◀

All in the blue unclouded weather
Thick-jeweled shone the saddle leather,
The helmet and the helmet-feather
Burned like one burning flame together,
95   As he rode down to Camelot;
As often through the purple night,
Below the starry clusters bright,
Some bearded meteor, trailing light,
    Moves over still Shalott. ◀

INTERPRET

Reread lines 73–90 and circle the images of light that are associated with Sir Lancelot.

What does this **imagery** suggest about him?

_____

_____

_____

_____

ANALYZE

Reread lines 82–99. What does Tennyson emphasize through repetition in the fifth and ninth lines of each stanza?

_____

_____

_____

---

11. **bowshot:** the distance an arrow can be shot.
12. **bower** (bou′ər) **eaves:** the part of the roof that extends above the lady's private room.
13. **brazen greaves:** metal armor protecting the legs below the knees.
14. **A red-cross . . . shield:** His shield showed a knight wearing a red cross and kneeling to honor a lady. The red cross was a symbol worn by knights who had fought in the Crusades.
15. **gemmy:** studded with gems.
16. **blazoned** (blā′zənd) **baldric:** a decorated leather belt, worn across the chest to support a sword or, as in this case, a bugle.

100 His broad clear brow in sunlight glowed;
    On burnished hooves his war horse trode;
    From underneath his helmet flowed
    His coal-black curls as on he rode,
        As he rode down to Camelot.
105 From the bank and from the river
    He flashed into the crystal mirror,
    "Tirra lirra," by the river
        Sang Sir Lancelot.

    She left the web, she left the loom,
110 She made three paces through the room,
    She saw the water lily bloom,
    She saw the helmet and the plume,
        She looked down to Camelot.
    Out flew the web and floated wide;
115 The mirror cracked from side to side;
    "The curse is come upon me," cried
        The Lady of Shalott. ▶

    Part IV
    In the stormy east wind straining,
    The pale yellow woods were waning,
120 The broad stream in his banks complaining,
    Heavily the low sky raining
        Over towered Camelot;
    Down she came and found a boat
    Beneath a willow left afloat,
125 And round about the prow she wrote
        The Lady of Shalott.

    And down the river's dim expanse
    Like some bold seër[17] in a trance,
    Seeing all his own mischance[18]—
130 With a glassy countenance
        Did she look to Camelot.

---

17. **seër** (sē'ər): someone who can see into the future; a prophet.
18. **mischance:** misfortune; bad luck.

What technique does Tennyson use to create a suspenseful **mood** in the boxed text?

_____

_____

_____

Do you think that this passage is effective? Why or why not?

_____

_____

_____

_____

_____

_____

And at the closing of the day
She loosed the chain, and down she lay;
The broad stream bore her far away,
135   The Lady of Shalott.

Lying, robed in snowy white
That loosely flew to left and right—
The leaves upon her falling light—
Through the noises of the night
140   She floated down to Camelot;
And as the boat-head wound along
The willowy hills and fields among,
They heard her singing her last song,
     The Lady of Shalott.

145 Heard a carol, mournful, holy,
Chanted loudly, chanted lowly,
Till her blood was frozen slowly,
And her eyes were darkened wholly,
     Turned to towered Camelot.
150 For ere[19] she reached upon the tide
The first house by the waterside,
Singing in her song she died,
     The Lady of Shalott.

Under tower and balcony,
155 By garden wall and gallery,
A gleaming shape she floated by,
Dead-pale between the houses high,
     Silent into Camelot.
Out upon the wharfs they came,
160 Knight and burgher,[20] lord and dame,
And round the prow they read her name,
     The Lady of Shalott.

ANALYZE

Reread the boxed text. How do nature **imagery** and **sound devices** help create a tragic **mood**?

_____

_____

_____

_____

TestSmart

Which word *best* describes the mood of the poem in lines 154–162?

- (A) suspenseful
- (B) lonely
- (C) eerie
- (D) calm

TIP If a test question asks you to identify the **mood** of a poem, think about the **images** the poet uses. Images in these lines include a dead woman floating down a river in the dark and a handful of curious onlookers staring at the "dead-pale" body. What feeling do these images evoke?

19. **ere** (âr): before.
20. **burgher:** a middle-class citizen of a town.

Who is this? and what is here?
And in the lighted palace near
165   Died the sound of royal cheer;
And they crossed themselves for fear,
        All the knights at Camelot:
But Lancelot mused a little space;
He said, "She has a lovely face;
170   God in his mercy lend her grace,
        The Lady of Shalott." ▶

MAKE JUDGMENTS

Do you think the Lady of Shalott could have stayed in the tower and been happy? Why or why not?

_____

_____

_____

_____

Ulysses

ALFRED, LORD TENNYSON

COMPARE

Compare the way Ulysses felt about his life when he was younger with the way he feels about it now.

INTERPRET

Reread the boxed text. What does "that untravell'd world" refer to?

It little profits that an idle king,
By this still hearth, among these barren crags,
Match'd with an aged wife, I mete and dole[1]
Unequal laws unto a savage race,
5   That hoard, and sleep, and feed, and know not me.
I cannot rest from travel: I will drink
Life to the lees:[2] all times I have enjoy'd
Greatly, have suffer'd greatly, both with those
That loved me, and alone; on shore, and when
10   Thro' scudding drifts[3] the rainy Hyades[4]
Vext the dim sea: I am become a name;
For always roaming with a hungry heart
Much have I seen and known; cities of men
And manners, climates, councils, governments,
15   Myself not least, but honor'd of them all;
And drunk delight of battle with my peers,
Far on the ringing plains of windy Troy.[5] ◀
I am a part of all that I have met;
Yet all experience is an arch wherethro'
20   Gleams that untravell'd world, whose margin fades
For ever and for ever when I move. ◀
How dull it is to pause, to make an end,
To rust unburnish'd, not to shine in use!
As tho' to breathe were life. Life piled on life
25   Were all too little, and of one to me

---

1. **mete** (mēt) **and dole:** give and distribute.
2. **to the lees:** to the dregs or bottom of the cup; completely.
3. **scudding drifts:** windblown rainclouds.
4. **Hyades:** a constellation whose rising was believed to signify the coming of rain.
5. **Troy:** the ancient city conquered by the Greeks in the Trojan War, in which Ulysses (Odysseus) was among the Greek leaders.

Little remains: but every hour is saved
From that eternal silence, something more,
A bringer of new things; and vile it were
For some three suns[6] to store and hoard myself,
30 And this gray spirit yearning in desire
To follow knowledge like a sinking star,
Beyond the utmost bound of human thought.
This is my son, mine own Telemachus,[7]
To whom I leave the sceptre[8] and the isle—
35 Well-loved of me, discerning to fulfil
This labor, by slow prudence to make mild
A rugged people, and thro' soft degrees
Subdue them to the useful and the good.
Most blameless is he, centred in the sphere
40 Of common duties, decent not to fail
In offices of tenderness, and pay
Meet[9] adoration to my household gods,
When I am gone. He works his work, I mine. ▶
There lies the port; the vessel puffs her sail:
45 There gloom the dark broad seas. My mariners,
Souls that have toil'd, and wrought, and thought with me—
That ever with a frolic[10] welcome took
The thunder and the sunshine, and opposed
Free hearts, free foreheads—you and I are old;
50 Old age hath yet his honor and his toil;
Death closes all: but something ere the end,
Some work of noble note, may yet be done,
Not unbecoming men that strove with Gods.
The lights begin to twinkle from the rocks;
55 The long day wanes; the slow moon climbs; the deep
Moans round with many voices. Come, my friends,
'Tis not too late to seek a newer world.
Push off, and sitting well in order smite
The sounding furrows;[11] for my purpose holds

---

6. **three suns:** three years.

7. **Telemachus** (tə-lĕm′ə-kəs).

8. **sceptre** (sĕp′tər): a staff held by a king or a queen as a symbol of royal authority.

9. **meet:** appropriate.

10. **frolic:** merry.

11. **smite . . . furrows:** strike the waves with the boat's oars.

CONTRAST

How does the **mood** at the end of the poem differ from the mood at the beginning?

_____

_____

_____

_____

60 To sail beyond the sunset, and the baths
   Of all the western stars,[12] until I die.
   It may be that the gulfs will wash us down:
   It may be we shall touch the Happy Isles,
   And see the great Achilles,[13] whom we knew.
65 Tho' much is taken, much abides; and tho'
   We are not now that strength which in old days
   Moved earth and heaven; that which we are, we are;
   One equal temper of heroic hearts,
   Made weak by time and fate, but strong in will
70 To strive, to seek, to find, and not to yield. ◀

---

12. **baths . . . stars:** The ancient Greeks believed the earth was surrounded by an outer ocean or river, into which the stars descended.

13. **Happy Isles . . . Achilles:** the Islands of the Blessed, where the souls of heroes, like Achilles, dwelt after death.

In Memoriam

ALFRED, LORD TENNYSON

27

I envy not in any moods
 The captive void of[1] noble rage,
 The linnet[2] born within the cage,
That never knew the summer woods;

5 I envy not the beast that takes
 His license[3] in the field of time,
 Unfettered[4] by the sense of crime,
To whom a conscience never wakes;

Nor, what may count itself as blest,
10 The heart that never plighted troth
 But stagnates in the weeds of sloth;
Nor any want-begotten rest.[5]

I hold it true, whate'er befall;
 I feel it, when I sorrow most;
15 'Tis better to have loved and lost
Than never to have loved at all. ▶

ANALYZE

In what way do lines 13–16 in part 27 of *In Memorium* reflect the characteristics of an **elegy**?

_____

_____

_____

_____

---

1. **void of:** lacking in.
2. **linnet:** a kind of small songbird.
3. **license:** freedom of action; liberty.
4. **unfettered:** unrestricted.
5. **nor, what . . . rest:** nor do I envy the supposed peace of mind that arises from remaining sunk in inaction, never pledging one's love, or from any deficiency.

54

O, yet we trust that somehow good
 Will be the final goal of ill,
 To pangs of nature,[6] sins of will,
20 Defects of doubt, and taints of blood;[7]

That nothing walks with aimless feet;
 That not one life shall be destroyed,
 Or cast as rubbish to the void,[8]
When God hath made the pile complete;

25 That not a worm is cloven[9] in vain;
 That not a moth with vain desire
 Is shriveled in a fruitless fire,
Or but subserves[10] another's gain.

Behold, we know not anything;
30 I can but trust that good shall fall
 At last—far off—at last, to all,
And every winter change to spring.

So runs my dream; but what am I?
 An infant crying in the night;
35 An infant crying for the light,
And with no language but a cry. ◀

130

Thy voice is on the rolling air;
 I hear thee where the waters run;
 Thou standest in the rising sun,
40 And in the setting thou art fair.

DRAW CONCLUSIONS

How does the tone of lines 33–36 differ from the tone of the previous stanzas in part 54?

_____

_____

_____

_____

Why might Tennyson have chosen to create such a shift in tone?

_____

_____

_____

_____

---

6. **pangs of nature:** physical pain.
7. **taints of blood:** inherited faults.
8. **void:** empty space.
9. **cloven:** split.
10. **subserves:** promotes or assists.

What are thou then? I cannot guess;
    But though I seem in star and flower
    To feel thee some diffusive[11] power,
I do not therefore love thee less.

45 My love involves the love before;
    My love is vaster passion now;
    Though mixed with God and Nature thou,
I seem to love thee more and more.

    Far off thou art, but ever nigh;[12]
50   I have thee still, and I rejoice;
        I prosper, circled with thy voice;
    I shall not lose thee though I die. ▶

11. **diffusive:** scattered about.
12. **nigh:** nearby.

INTERPRET

A paradox is a seemingly contradictory statement that nonetheless suggests an insight or truth. Underline the paradox in the last stanza.

What important insight does the paradox suggest?

_____

_____

_____

CROSSING THE *Bar*

ALFRED, LORD TENNYSON

Sunset and evening star,
    And one clear call for me!
And may there be no moaning of the bar,[1]
    When I put out to sea,

5 But such a tide as moving seems asleep,
    Too full for sound and foam,
When that which drew from out the boundless deep
    Turns again home.

Twilight and evening bell,[2]
10   And after that the dark!
And may there be no sadness of farewell,
    When I embark;

For though from out our bourne of Time and Place[3]
    The flood[4] may bear me far,
15 I hope to see my Pilot face to face
    When I have crossed the bar. ◀

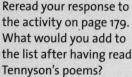

COMPARE

Compare the attitude toward death of the speakers in "Crossing the Bar" and *In Memoriam*.

——————————

——————————

——————————

——————————

Big Question ❔

Reread your response to the activity on page 179. What would you add to the list after having read Tennyson's poems?

——————————

——————————

——————————

---

1. **moaning of the bar:** the sound of the ocean waves pounding against a sandbar at the mouth of a harbor.
2. **evening bell:** a ship's bell rung to announce the changing of the watch.
3. **from out . . . Place:** beyond the boundary of our lifetimes.
4. **flood:** ocean.

Reading Comprehension

DIRECTIONS *Answer these questions about Tennyson's poems by filling in the correct ovals.*

1. In "The Lady of Shalott," what does Camelot symbolize?

   Ⓐ aggression

   Ⓑ experience

   Ⓒ artistry

   Ⓓ seclusion

2. What prompts the Lady of Shalott to risk having a curse fall upon her?

   Ⓐ She finds a boat beneath a willow tree.

   Ⓑ The mirror in her room cracks.

   Ⓒ Sir Lancelot passes by her tower.

   Ⓓ She no longer enjoys weaving.

3. In "Ulysses," what do the "ringing plains of windy Troy" (line 17) represent?

   Ⓐ present sorrows

   Ⓑ present victories

   Ⓒ past loves

   Ⓓ past battles

4. Ulysses wants to convince his mariners to

   Ⓐ accept that old age has made them weak

   Ⓑ sail on another voyage with him

   Ⓒ take back his kingdom from Telemachus

   Ⓓ live peacefully in his kingdom

5. Which words *best* describe the mood in lines 22–32 of "Ulysses"?

   Ⓐ weary and bored

   Ⓑ optimistic and exciting

   Ⓒ mysterious and frightening

   Ⓓ solemn and reverent

6. In part 27 of *In Memoriam,* the speaker suggests that

   Ⓐ we are often deceived by our feelings

   Ⓑ when love goes wrong it is like a cage

   Ⓒ true love never causes suffering

   Ⓓ one should love even if it leads to sorrow

7. In part 130 of *In Memoriam,* the speaker suggests that his loved one has

   Ⓐ become part of nature

   Ⓑ vanished from his life

   Ⓒ undertaken a long journey

   Ⓓ returned to his home

8. The mood in the last stanza of "Crossing the Bar" can *best* be described as

   Ⓐ mysterious

   Ⓑ tragic

   Ⓒ peaceful

   Ⓓ tense

For help, use the **Test-Taker's Toolkit** below.

Responding in Writing

9. Short Response Tennyson is often described as a spokesman for Victorian values. Which of the poems in this lesson seems most relevant to your own generation? What enduring theme does it convey? Use details from the poem to support your answer.

_____

_____

_____

_____

_____

_____

TEST-TAKER'S TOOLKIT

⊗ **GRAPHIC ORGANIZER** Use the chart below to help you plan your response. Reread the poems to help you remember the details.

Poem: _____

Enduring Theme: _____

_____

Details that Make It Relevant Today:

-
-
-

What's the Connection?

The four poems you have read are a small sample of Tennyson's work. For example, you read just three parts of the 131-part poem *In Memoriam*. The literary essay you are about to read explains how Tennyson created this masterpiece over the course of 17 years. It also describes the structure of the individual stanzas and the movement of ideas, emotions, and themes in the poem as a whole.

A ROLLER COASTER RIDE Many people refer to the emotions that result from the death of a loved one as a "roller coaster ride." What emotions do you think accompany the "highs" and "lows" of grieving? Work with a partner to write your ideas below.

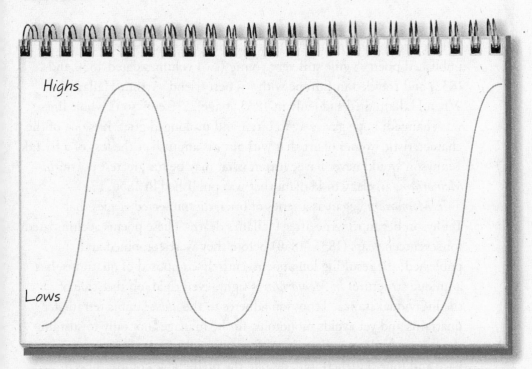

Related Nonfiction

In Memoriam
LITERARY ESSAY

Use with the selected poetry by Alfred, Lord Tennyson, p. 178

LEARN THE SKILL: ANALYZE A LITERARY ESSAY

A **literary essay** seeks to help readers better understand and appreciate a literary work. Typically it does this by providing the following:

- information about the work's historical, biographical, or literary context
- a description of the text itself
- an evaluation of the work that is supported by reasons and evidence

For more on analyzing a literary essay, see the Critical Essays entry in the Nonfiction Skills Handbook beginning on page R2.

SET A PURPOSE

_____

_____

_____

In Memoriam

by Rachel Hadas

Precocious and productive, Alfred, Lord Tennyson wrote and published poetry while still very young (two volumes dated 1830 and 1832) and traveled in Europe with his best friend, Arthur Hallam. When Hallam died suddenly in 1833 at age 22, Tennyson's whole life was changed; hope gave way to bitter and prolonged grief. It is one of the characteristic ironies of art that without his anguish at the loss of a friend, Tennyson would never have written what may be his greatest poem, *In Memoriam*, an elegy to Hallam that was published in 1850. . . .

In Memoriam began as a series of brief, disconnected elegies that
10 Tennyson began to write after Hallam's death. These poems accumulated for seventeen years (1833–1850) before they were combined and published; the resulting long poem, entirely composed of quatrains, has a unique structure. *In Memoriam* is tight, even rigid, on the scale of the individual stanza. Tennyson adheres to the *abba* iambic tetrameter quatrains and yet avoids monotony, for he manages not only to sustain the form—finding endless rhymes, for example—but also to vary its pace and tone. Furthermore, despite the predictable compactness of the individual unit, *In Memoriam* is loose in its overall structure. The poem moves back and forth in time and space as it records the zigzags of
20 emotion and the loopings of memory. In this combination of precision in individual stanzas and a loose overall structure, the poem resembles the translation of the *Rubáiyát*[1] made a few years later by Tennyson's friend Edward FitzGerald; both poems are hypnotic in their formal predictability and yet fluid in their twists and turns. ◀

In Memoriam came entirely from Hallam's death. Its subject matter, grief, is both intensely personal and universal. By giving this intimate and emotional theme so much room to develop, Tennyson created a remarkably honest work of art, one that tells many enduring truths

LITERARY ESSAY

What distinction does the author make in her discussion of the "unique structure" of *In Memoriam*?

_____

_____

_____

---

1. *Rubáiyát* (rōō′bī-yät): a collection of quatrains composed by the 12th-century Persian poet Omar Khayyám.

about the experience of sorrow over time. Reading straight through *In Memoriam* is probably the best way to appreciate the poem's emotional ups and downs, its echoes and revisiting, such as the references to successive Christmases following Hallam's death. *In Memoriam* is also a poem into which readers can profitably dip. Each person will find different places where the poem speaks directly to her or him. Some remarkable passages describe the writer's impatience with banal letters of condolence:

> One writes, that 'Other friends remain,'
> That 'Loss is common to the race'—
> And common is the commonplace,
> And vacant chaff well meant for grain.
>
> That loss is common would not make
> My own less bitter, rather more:
> Too common! Never morning wore
> To evening, but some heart did break.

Tennyson's honest recording of the roller-coaster ups and downs of grief is evident in this passage:

> What words are these have fallen from me?
> Can calm despair and wild unrest
> Be tenants of a single breast,
> Or sorrow such a changeling be? ▶

A precise and beautiful evocation of the motion and effect of Tennyson's chosen verse form is "Short swallow-flights of song, that dip / Their wings in tears, and skim away." Such comments on the poet's own writing give *In Memoriam* a personal, unguarded intimacy that adds to the appealing frankness of the poem as a whole.

Although it is the source of many famous phrases, such as "nature red in tooth and claw" or "'Tis better to have loved and lost / Than never to have loved at all," *In Memoriam* does not lend itself to summary. The poet reaches no hard and fast conclusions about life, death, God, or immortality; as he himself wrote, he touches down only to fly away. In addition, the poem refuses to sentimentalize Hallam; the dead man is evoked chiefly as an absence whose pain grows gradually more bearable. In our own age this remarkable poem, monumental in scale and yet intimate in tone, continues to compel. ▶

LITERARY ESSAY

In your judgment, does the essay provide sufficient **evidence** to support the idea that the poem addresses many aspects of grief? Explain.

_____

_____

_____

_____

TestSmart

Which statement from the last paragraph is an evaluation of the poem?

Ⓐ "The poet reaches no hard and fast conclusions"

Ⓑ "This remarkable poem . . . continues to compel."

Ⓒ "it is the source of many famous phrases"

Ⓓ "the dead man is evoked chiefly as an absence"

TIP A test question may ask you to identify a **judgment.** To answer, look for an answer choice that includes an adjective such as *excellent, mediocre, effective,* or *ineffective.* These words signal that a judgment or opinion is being expressed.

Reading Comprehension

DIRECTIONS *Answer these questions about the essay and the poems in this lesson by filling in the correct ovals.*

1. The thesis of the essay is that Tennyson's masterpiece is

   (A) predictably compact

   (B) varied in pace and tone

   (C) inconclusive about God

   (D) both personal and universal

2. Which statement supports the thesis of the literary essay?

   (A) All readers can benefit from reading the poem.

   (B) Tennyson's grief was crippling at times.

   (C) The poem took 17 years to write.

   (D) Its overall structure is loose.

3. The phrase "one of the characteristic ironies of art" in lines 5–6 suggests that

   (A) *In Memoriam* is a poetic marvel

   (B) suffering often fosters creativity

   (C) anguish can result in elegies

   (D) hope gives way to prolonged grief

4. Parts 27, 54, and 130 of *In Memoriam* are similar to the stanzas that appear in the literary essay in that they express

   (A) the poet's deepest sorrow

   (B) comforting thoughts

   (C) a range of emotions

   (D) conventional wisdom

5. The most likely meaning of the word *banal* in line 35 of the essay is

   (A) boring

   (B) lacking originality

   (C) gratifying

   (D) fresh and original

6. The word *evocation* in line 51 of the essay means

   (A) a suggestion

   (B) an image of

   (C) a reconciliation

   (D) an effort

Timed Writing Practice

PROMPT

Write an essay in which you compare and contrast *In Memoriam* with one of the other poems by Tennyson in this lesson. Discuss how the two poems are similar or different in subject, theme, style, and mood. Include details from the poems to support your ideas.

TEST-TAKER'S TOOLKIT

1. ANALYZE THE PROMPT

A. Underline the type of essay you are being asked to write, and circle key words in the directions. One phrase has been circled for you.

B. Jot down a list of the key elements you need to include in your essay.

2. PLAN YOUR RESPONSE

A. **Make notes** Use a chart like the one shown to note the points your essay will make.

B. **Organize your information** The first paragraph of your essay should state which poems you will compare and explain which elements you will examine. You can then discuss all of the elements of one poem first and then the elements of the other poem. Or you can compare and contrast both poems one point at a time. End your essay with a conclusion in which you sum up your ideas.

In Memoriam	Second poem: _____
Subject:	Subject:
Theme:	Theme:
Style:	Style:
Mood:	Mood:

3. WRITE AND REVIEW

A. In your introduction, include an interesting quote or observation to grab your readers' attention.

B. Be sure to leave time to check your spelling and grammar.

LESSON 5B

Malachi's Cove
BY ANTHONY TROLLOPE

RELATED NONFICTION
Stalking a Killer That Lurks a Few Feet Offshore

How do we learn
_to_ TRUST?

Babies learn to trust instinctively by responding to adults who love them. But as we get older, trust becomes a tricky proposition—especially if experience has taught us to be wary of others. What allows us to overcome suspicion and reach out to others?

LIST IT List five actions or qualities that signal that a person is trustworthy. Then list five actions or qualities that tell you to be wary. Share your response with a group of classmates. How do your lists compare?

You can trust a person who . . .

1. _____
_____

2. _____
_____

3. _____
_____

4. _____
_____

5. _____
_____

You can't trust a person who . . .

1. _____
_____

2. _____
_____

3. _____
_____

4. _____
_____

5. _____
_____

ASSESSMENT GOALS

By the end of this lesson, you will be able to . . .

- analyze realism in a work of fiction
- apply critical thinking skills to analyze text
- analyze information in a graphic aid
- analyze a writing prompt and plan a literary analysis

Realism

REALISM refers to writing that portrays everyday life in accurate detail. It also refers to a literary movement that developed in mid-19th century France and later spread to England. The graphic below shows important characteristics of realism.

You can practice answering questions about realism as you analyze "Malachi's Cove," a short story by one of the masters of realist fiction.

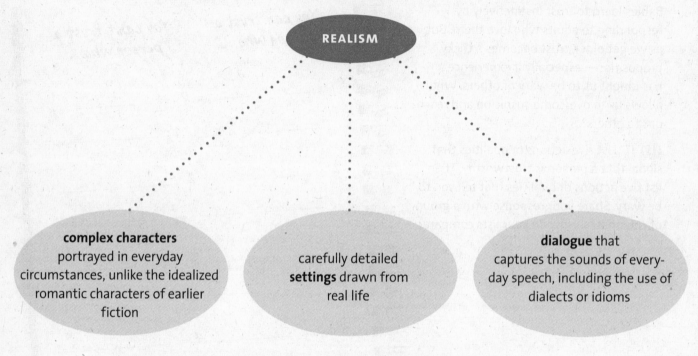

REALISM

complex characters portrayed in everyday circumstances, unlike the idealized romantic characters of earlier fiction

carefully detailed **settings** drawn from real life

dialogue that captures the sounds of every-day speech, including the use of dialects or idioms

ADDITIONAL TERMS FOR CRITICAL ANALYSIS

Knowing these additional terms will help you appreciate the story you are about to read.

- **CHARACTERIZATION** refers to the techniques writers use to develop characters. There are four basic methods of characterization. A writer may reveal a character's traits through physical description; through the character's own speech or thoughts; through the feelings or statements of other characters; or by directly commenting on the character.

- **FORESHADOWING** is a writer's use of hints or clues to indicate events that will occur later in a story. Foreshadowing creates suspense and at the same time prepares the reader for what is to come.

MALACHI'S COVE

Anthony Trollope

BACKGROUND Anthony Trollope (1815–1882) was one of the most prolific writers of the Victorian era. His works are widely respected for their true-to-life characters and astute analysis of class dynamics. Many of his novels are set in England or Ireland. This story takes place on the coast of Cornwall, a rugged, rocky, and remote peninsula in southwestern England. Cornwall is one of Britain's most picturesque regions—and one of its poorest.

MARK & ANALYZE
Read this selection once on your own, marking the text in any way that is helpful to you. Then read the story a second time, using the questions in the margins to help you analyze the literature. When you see this pencil ✐, you'll be asked to mark up the text.

On the northern coast of Cornwall, between Tintagel and Bossiney,[1] down on the very margin of the sea, there lived not long since an old man who got his living by saving seaweed from the waves, and selling it for manure. The cliffs there are bold and fine, and the sea beats in upon them from the north with a grand violence. I doubt whether it be not the finest morsel of cliff scenery in England, though it is beaten by many portions of the west coast of Ireland, and perhaps also by spots in Wales and Scotland. Cliffs should be nearly <u>precipitous</u>, they should be broken in their outlines, and should barely admit here and there of an insecure passage
10 from their summit to the sand at their feet. The sea should come, if not up to them, at least very near to them, and then, above all things, the water below them should be blue, and not of that dead leaden color which is so familiar to us in England. At Tintagel all these requisites are there, except that bright blue color which is so lovely. But the cliffs themselves are bold and well broken, and the margin of sand at high water is very narrow—so narrow that at spring tides there is barely a footing there. ▶

precipitous (prĭ-sĭp′ĭ-təs) *adj.* nearly vertical; very steep

EVALUATE

Underline details that make the **setting** seem **realistic.** ✐

How are these details important later in the story?

_____

_____

_____

_____

---

1. **Cornwall . . . Tintagel** (tĭn-tăj′əl) **and Bossiney** (bôs′ĭ-nē): a remote peninsula on the southwestern tip of England that includes the picturesque village of Tintagel and an adjoining beach area called Bossiney.

Close upon this margin was the cottage or hovel of Malachi Trenglos,[2] the old man of whom I have spoken. But Malachi, or old Glos, as he was commonly called by the people around him, had not built his house 20 absolutely upon the sand. There was a fissure in the rock so great that at the top it formed a narrow ravine, and so complete from the summit to the base that it afforded an opening for a steep and rugged track from the top of the rock to the bottom. This fissure was so wide at the bottom that it had afforded space for Trenglos to fix his habitation on a foundation of rock, and here he had lived for many years. It was told of him that in the early days of his trade he had always carried the weed in a basket on his back to the top, but latterly[3] he had been possessed of a donkey which had been trained to go up and down the steep track with a single pannier[4] over his loins, for the rocks would not admit of panniers hanging by his side; 30 and for this assistant he had built a shed adjoining his own, and almost as large as that in which he himself resided.

But, as years went on, old Glos procured other assistance than that of the donkey, or, as I should rather say, Providence[5] supplied him with other help; and, indeed, had it not been so, the old man must have given up his cabin and his independence and gone into the workhouse at Camelford.[6] For rheumatism[7] had afflicted him, old age had bowed him till he was nearly double, and by degrees he became unable to attend the donkey on its upward passage to the world above, or even to assist in rescuing the coveted weed from the waves.

40 At the time to which our story refers Trenglos had not been up the cliff for twelve months, and for the last six months he had done nothing towards the furtherance of his trade, except to take the money and keep it, if any of it was kept, and occasionally to shake down a bundle of fodder[8] for the donkey. The real work of the business was done altogether by Mahala Trenglos, his granddaughter. ◄

2. **Malachi Trenglos** (măl′ə-kī′ trĕn′glôs): Many Cornish family names begin with *Tre*, which means "dwelling" in Cornish.
3. **latterly:** more recently.
4. **pannier** (păn′yər): one of a pair of baskets usually hung on either side of a pack animal to carry loads.
5. **Providence:** the helpful guidance or aid of God, fate, or nature.
6. **workhouse at Camelford:** the poorhouse at Camelford, a larger town near Tintagel. In Victorian times, poor people whose relatives could not support them were sent to workhouses; healthy residents were put to work.
7. **rheumatism** (rōō′mə-tĭz′əm): painful inflammation and stiffness of the joints and muscles.
8. **fodder:** coarse food for cattle and other farm animals.

Mally Trenglos was known to all the farmers round the coast, and to all the small tradespeople in Camelford. She was a wild-looking, almost unearthly creature, with wild-flowing, black, uncombed hair, small in stature, with small hands and bright black eyes; but people said that she
50 was very strong, and the children around declared that she worked day and night and knew nothing of fatigue. As to her age there were many doubts. Some said she was ten, and others five-and-twenty, but the reader may be allowed to know that at this time she had in truth passed her twentieth birthday. The old people spoke well of Mally, because she was so good to her grandfather; and it was said of her that though she carried to him a little gin and tobacco almost daily, she bought nothing for herself—and as to the gin, no one who looked at her would accuse her of meddling with that. But she had no friends and but few acquaintances among people of her own age. They said that she was fierce and ill-natured, that
60 she had not a good word for anyone, and that she was, complete at all points, a thorough little vixen.[9] The young men did not care for her; for, as regarded dress, all days were alike with her. She never made herself smart on Sundays. She was generally without stockings, and seemed to care not at all to exercise any of those feminine attractions which might have been hers had she studied to attain them. All days were the same to her in regard to dress; and, indeed, till lately, all days had, I fear, been the same to her in other respects. Old Malachi had never been seen inside a place of worship since he had taken to live under the cliff. ▶

But within the last two years Mally had submitted herself to the
70 teaching of the clergyman at Tintagel, and had appeared at church on Sundays, if not absolutely with punctuality, at any rate so often that no one who knew the peculiarity of her residence was disposed to quarrel with her on that subject. But she made no difference in her dress on these occasions. She took her place in a low stone seat just inside the church door, clothed as usual in her thick red serge petticoat[10] and loose brown serge jacket, such being the apparel which she had found to be best adapted for her hard and perilous work among the waters. She had pleaded to the clergyman when he attacked her on the subject of church attendance with vigor that she had got no church-going clothes. He had explained to her
80 that she would be received there without distinction to her clothing. Mally had taken him at his word, and had gone, with a courage which certainly deserved admiration, though I doubt whether there was not mingled with it an obstinacy which was less admirable. ▶

ANALYZE

Reread the boxed text and think about how the author has **characterized** Mally Trenglos. Then underline a trait revealed through physical description; circle a trait revealed through other characters' comments; put a star by a trait directly described by the narrator. ✎

CONTRAST

In what ways is Mally unlike a typical romantic heroine?

_____

_____

_____

_____

For people said that old Glos was rich, and that Mally might have proper clothes if she chose to buy them. Mr. Polwarth, the clergyman, who, as the old man could not come to him, went down the rocks to the old man, did make some hint on the matter in Mally's absence. But old Glos, who had been patient with him on other matters, turned upon him so angrily when he made an allusion to money, that Mr. Polwarth found himself obliged to give that matter up, and Mally continued to sit upon the stone bench in her short serge petticoat, with her long hair streaming down her face. She did so far sacrifice to decency as on such occasions to tie up her black hair with an old shoestring. So tied it would remain through the Monday and Tuesday, but by Wednesday afternoon Mally's hair had generally managed to escape.

As to Mally's **indefatigable** industry there could be no manner of doubt, for the quantity of seaweed which she and the donkey amassed between them was very surprising. Old Glos, it was declared, had never collected half what Mally gathered together; but then the article was becoming cheaper, and it was necessary that the exertion should be greater. So Mally and the donkey toiled and toiled, and the seaweed came up in heaps which surprised those who looked at her little hands and light form. Was there not someone who helped her at nights, some fairy, or demon, or the like? Mally was so snappish in her answers to people that she had no right to be surprised if ill-natured things were said of her. ◀

No one ever heard Mally Trenglos complain of her work, but about this time she was heard to make great and loud complaints of the treatment she received from some of her neighbors. It was known that she went with her plaints to Mr. Polwarth; and when he could not help her, or did not give her such instant help as she needed, she went—ah, so foolishly! to the office of a certain attorney at Camelford, who was not likely to prove himself a better friend than Mr. Polwarth.

Now the nature of her injury was as follows. The place in which she collected her seaweed was a little cove—the people had come to call it Malachi's Cove from the name of the old man who lived there—which was so formed that the margin of the sea therein could only be reached by the passage from the top down to Trenglos's hut. The breadth of the cove when the sea was out might perhaps be two hundred yards, and on each side the rocks ran out in such a way that both from north and south the domain of Trenglos was guarded from intruders. And this locality had been well chosen for its intended purpose.

90

100

110

120

indefatigable
(ĭn′dĭ-făt′ĭ-gə-bəl) *adj.*
tireless

EVALUATE

Reread the underlined text. How does this detail add **realism** to the story?

_____

_____

_____

_____

There was a rush of the sea into the cove, which carried there large, drifting masses of seaweed, leaving them among the rocks when the tide was out. During the equinoctial winds[11] of the spring and autumn the supply would never fail; and even when the sea was calm, the long, soft, salt-bedewed, trailing masses of the weed could be gathered there when they could not be found elsewhere for miles along the coast. The task of getting the weed from the breakers[12] was often difficult and dangerous—so difficult that much of it was left to be carried away by the

130 next incoming tide.

Mally doubtless did not gather half the crop that was there at her feet. What was taken by the returning waves she did not regret; but when <u>interlopers</u> came upon her cove, and gathered her wealth—her grandfather's wealth, beneath her eyes, then her heart was broken. It was this interloping, this intrusion, that drove poor Mally to the Camelford attorney. But, alas, though the Camelford attorney took Mally's money, he could do nothing for her, and her heart was broken! ▶

She had an idea, in which no doubt her grandfather shared, that the path to the cove was, at any rate, their property. When she was told that

140 the cove, and sea running into the cove, were not the freeholds[13] of her grandfather, she understood that the statement might be true. But what then as to the use of the path? Who had made the path what it was? Had she not painfully, wearily, with exceeding toil, carried up bits of rock with her own little hands, that her grandfather's donkey might have footing for his feet? Had she not scraped together crumbs of earth along the face of the cliff that she might make easier to the animal the track of that rugged way? And now, when she saw big farmer's lads coming down with other donkeys—and, indeed, there was one who came with a pony; no boy, but a young man, old enough to know better than rob a poor old man

150 and a young girl—she reviled the whole human race, and swore that the Camelford attorney was a fool.

Any attempt to explain to her that there was still weed enough for her was worse than useless. Was it not all hers and his, or, at any rate, was not the sole way to it his and hers? And was not her trade stopped and <u>impeded</u>? Had she not been forced to back her laden donkey down, twenty yards she said, but it had, in truth, been five, because Farmer Gunliffe's son had been in the way with his thieving pony? Farmer

---

11. **equinoctial** (ē′kwə-nŏk′shəl) **winds:** strong winds around the time of the spring or autumn equinox, when day and night are of equal length.

12. **breakers:** waves that break into foam when they hit the shore.

13. **freeholds:** land that is inherited or held for life.

interloper (ĭn′tər-lō′pər) *n.* intruder

DRAW CONCLUSIONS

Considering what you know about human nature along with details from the story, how do you think the townspeople felt about Mally's visit to the lawyer?

_____

_____

impede (ĭm-pēd′) *v.* to hinder or obstruct

Gunliffe had wanted to buy her weed at his own price, and because she had refused he had set on his thieving son to destroy her in this wicked way.

"I'll hamstring[14] the beast the next time as he's down here!" said Mally to old Glos, while the angry fire literally streamed from her eyes.

Farmer Gunliffe's small homestead—he held about fifty acres of land—was close by the village of Tintagel, and not a mile from the cliff. The sea-wrack, as they call it, was pretty well the only manure within his reach, and no doubt he thought it hard that he should be kept from using it by Mally Trenglos and her obstinacy.

"There's heaps of other coves, Barty," said Mally to Barty Gunliffe, the farmer's son.

"But none so nigh,[15] Mally, nor yet none that fills 'emselves as this place."

Then he explained to her that he would not take the weed that came up close to hand. He was bigger than she was, and stronger, and would get it from the outer rocks, with which she never meddled. Then, with scorn in her eye, she swore that she could get it where he durst[16] not venture, and repeated her threat of hamstringing the pony. Barty laughed at her wrath, jeered her because of her wild hair, and called her a mermaid.

"I'll mermaid you!" she cried. "Mermaid, indeed! I wouldn't be a man to come and rob a poor girl and an old cripple. But you're no man, Barty Gunliffe! You're not half a man."

Nevertheless, Bartholomew Gunliffe was a very fine young fellow as far as the eye went. He was about five feet eight inches high, with strong arms and legs, with light curly brown hair and blue eyes. His father was but in a small way as a farmer, but, nevertheless, Barty Gunliffe was well thought of among the girls around. Everybody liked Barty—excepting only Mally Trenglos, and she hated him like poison. ◀

Barty, when he was asked why so good-natured a lad as he persecuted a poor girl and an old man, threw himself upon the justice of the thing. It wouldn't do at all, according to his view, that any single person should take upon himself to own that which God Almighty sent as the common property of all. He would do Mally no harm, and so he had told her. But Mally was a vixen—a wicked little vixen; and she must be taught to have a civil tongue in her head. When once Mally would speak him civil as he

ANALYZE

Reread the boxed text. What future story event does this description of Barty Gunliffe **foreshadow**?

_____

_____

_____

Underline details that support your answer.

14. **hamstring:** to disable by cutting the hamstring, the large tendon found on the back of the leg in humans or on the hind leg in many quadrupeds.

15. **nigh** (nī): near.

16. **durst:** dare.

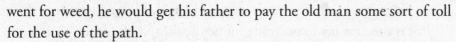

went for weed, he would get his father to pay the old man some sort of toll for the use of the path.

"Speak him civil?" said Mally. "Never; not while I have a tongue in my mouth!" And I fear old Glos encouraged her rather than otherwise in her view of the matter.

But her grandfather did not encourage her to hamstring the pony. Hamstringing a pony would be a serious thing, and old Glos thought it might be very awkward for both of them if Mally were put into prison. He suggested, therefore, that all manner of impediments should be put in the way of the pony's feet, surmising that the well-trained donkey might be able to work in spite of them. And Barty Gunliffe, on his next descent, did find the passage very awkward when he came near to Malachi's hut, but he made his way down, and poor Mally saw the lumps of rock at which she had labored so hard pushed on one side or rolled out of the way with a steady persistency of injury towards herself that almost drove her frantic.

"Well, Barty, you're a nice boy," said old Glos, sitting in the doorway of the hut, as he watched the intruder.

"I ain't a doing no harm to none as doesn't harm me," said Barty. "The sea's free to all, Malachi."

"And the sky's free to all, but I mustn't get up on the top of your big barn to look at it," said Mally, who was standing among the rocks with a long hook in her hand. The long hook was the tool with which she worked in dragging the weed from the waves. "But you ain't got no justice, nor yet no sperrit,[17] or you wouldn't come here to vex an old man like he."

"I didn't want to vex him, nor yet to vex you, Mally. You let me be for a while, and we'll be friends yet."

"Friends!" exclaimed Mally. "Who'd have the likes of you for a friend? What are you moving them stones for? Them stones belongs to grandfather." And in her wrath she made a movement as though she were going to fly at him.

"Let him be, Mally," said the old man; "let him be. He'll get his punishment. He'll come to be drowned some day if he comes down here when the wind is in shore."

"That he may be drowned then!" said Mally, in her anger. "If he was in the big hole there among the rocks, and the sea running in at half tide, I wouldn't lift a hand to help him out."

"Yes, you would, Mally; you'd fish me up with your hook like a big stick of seaweed." ▶

---

17. **sperrit:** dialect for *spirit*, here meaning "courage" or "character."

MAKE INFERENCES

Reread the boxed text. What kind of person is Barty Gunliffe? On the lines below, write three adjectives that describe him.

1. _____

2. _____

3. _____

Next to each adjective, write the line number(s) of the part of the text that reveals that trait.

MAKE INFERENCES

Why do you think Mally considers it a "great injury" that "such a one as Barty Gunliffe" should see her hard at work?

_____

_____

_____

garner (gär′nər) _v._ to gather up and store; to collect

ANALYZE

What details about the **setting** and **characters** add **realism** to the scene described in lines 235–255?

_____

_____

_____

_____

desist (dĭ-sĭst′) _v._ to cease or stop

She turned from him with scorn as he said this, and went into the hut. It was time for her to get ready for her work, and one of the great injuries done her lay in this—that such a one as Barty Gunliffe should come and look at her during her toil among the breakers. ◄

It was an afternoon in April, and the hour was something after four o'clock. There had been a heavy wind from the northwest all the morning, with gusts of rain, and the seagulls had been in and out of the cove all the day, which was a sure sign to Mally that the incoming tide would cover the rocks with weed.

240   The quick waves were now returning with wonderful celerity[18] over the low reefs, and the time had come at which the treasure must be seized, if it was to be **garnered** on that day. By seven o'clock it would be growing dark, at nine it would be high water, and before daylight the crop would be carried out again if not collected. All this Mally understood very well, and some of this Barty was beginning to understand also.

As Mally came down with her bare feet, bearing her long hook in her hand, she saw Barty's pony standing patiently on the sand, and in her heart she longed to attack the brute. Barty at this moment, with a common three-pronged fork in his hand, was standing down on a large

250   rock, gazing forth towards the waters. He had declared that he would gather the weed only at places which were inaccessible to Mally, and he was looking out that he might settle where he would begin.

"Let 'un be, let 'un be," shouted the old man to Mally, as he saw her take a step towards the beast, which she hated almost as much as she hated the man. ◄

Hearing her grandfather's voice through the wind, she **desisted** from her purpose, if any purpose she had had, and went forth to her work. As she passed down the cove, and scrambled in among the rocks, she saw Barty still standing on his perch; out beyond, the white-curling waves were

260   cresting and breaking themselves with violence, and the wind was howling among the caverns and abutments of the cliff.

Every now and then there came a squall[19] of rain, and though there was sufficient light, the heavens were black with clouds. A scene more beautiful might hardly be found by those who love the glories of the coast. The light for such objects was perfect. Nothing could exceed the grandeur of the colors—the blue of the open sea, the white of the breaking waves, the

18. **celerity** (sə-lĕr′ĭ-tē): swiftness of action; speed.
19. **squall** (skwôl): a brief, violent wind storm, usually accompanied by rain or snow.

yellow sands, or the streaks of red and brown which gave such richness to the cliff.

But neither Mally nor Barty were thinking of such things as these. Indeed, they were hardly thinking of their trade after its ordinary forms. Barty was meditating how he might best accomplish his purpose of working beyond the reach of Mally's feminine powers, and Mally was resolving that wherever Barty went she would go farther.

And, in many respects, Mally had the advantage. She knew every rock in the spot, and was sure of those which gave a good foothold, and sure also of those which did not. And then her activity had been made perfect by practice for the purpose to which it was to be devoted. Barty, no doubt, was stronger than she, and quite as active. But Barty could not jump among the waves from one stone to another as she could do, nor was he as yet able to get aid in his work from the very force of the water as she could get it. She had been hunting seaweed in that cove since she had been an urchin of six years old, and she knew every hole and corner and every spot of vantage.[20] The waves were her friends, and she could use them. She could measure their strength, and knew when and where it would cease.

Mally was great down in the salt pools of her own cove—great, and very fearless. As she watched Barty make his way forward from rock to rock, she told herself, gleefully, that he was going astray. The curl of the wind as it blew into the cove would not carry the weed up to the northern buttresses of the cove; and then there was the great hole just there—the great hole of which she had spoken when she wished him evil. ▶

And now she went to work, hooking up the dishevelled hairs of the ocean, and landing many a cargo on the extreme margin of the sand, from whence she would be able in the evening to drag it back before the invading waters would return to reclaim the spoil.[21]

And on his side also Barty made his heap up against the northern buttresses of which I have spoken. Barty's heap became big and still bigger, so that he knew, let the pony work as he might, he could not take it all up that evening. But still it was not as large as Mally's heap. Mally's hook was better than his fork, and Mally's skill was better than his strength. And when he failed in some haul Mally would jeer him with a wild, weird laughter, and shriek to him through the wind that he was not half a man. At first he answered her with laughing words, but before long, as she boasted of her success and pointed to his failure, he became angry, and

ANALYZE

Reread lines 274–290. How does Trollope's description of the cove and Mally's working methods deepen our understanding of her character?

_____

_____

_____

_____

_____

20. **urchin** (ûr′chĭn) . . . **spot of vantage:** a mischievous youngster of six years old, who knew which places would give her the advantage (in her task).

21. **spoil:** treasure seized in battle; plunder or booty.

then he answered her no more. He became angry with himself, in that he missed so much of the plunder before him.

The broken sea was full of the long straggling growth which the waves had torn up from the bottom of the ocean, but the masses were carried past him, away from him—nay, once or twice over him; and then Mally's weird voice would sound in his ear, jeering him. The gloom among the rocks was now becoming thicker and thicker, the tide was beating in with increased strength, and the gusts of wind came with quicker and greater violence. But still he worked on. While Mally worked he would work, and he would work for some time after she was driven in. He would not be beaten by a girl. ◄

The great hole was now full of water, but of water which seemed to be boiling as though in a pot. And the pot was full of floating masses—large treasures of seaweed which were thrown to and fro upon its surface, but lying there so thick that one would seem almost able to rest upon it without sinking.

Mally knew well how useless it was to attempt to rescue aught[22] from the fury of that boiling caldron. The hole went in under the rocks, and the side of it towards the shore lay high, slippery, and steep. The hole, even at low water, was never empty; and Mally believed that there was no bottom to it. Fish thrown in there could escape out to the ocean, miles away—so Mally in her softer moods would tell the visitors to the cove. She knew the hole well. Poulnadioul[23] she was accustomed to call it; which was supposed, when translated, to mean that this was the hole of the Evil One. Never did Mally attempt to make her own of weed which had found its way into that pot.

But Barty Gunliffe knew no better, and she watched him as he endeavoured to steady himself on the treacherously slippery edge of the pool. He fixed himself there and made a haul, with some small success. How he managed it she hardly knew, but she stood still for a while watching him anxiously, and then she saw him slip. He slipped, and recovered himself—slipped again, and again recovered himself. ◄

"Barty, you fool!" she screamed, "if you get yourself pitched in there, you'll never come out no more."

Whether she simply wished to frighten him, or whether her heart relented and she had thought of his danger with dismay, who shall say?

---

22. **aught** (ôt): anything.
23. **Poulnadioul** (pül′nä-jōōl′): Cornish for "pool of the devil."

EVALUATE

Do you think the conflict between Mally and Barty is **realistic?** Why or why not?

_____

_____

_____

_____

TESTSMART

What motivates Barty to try to harvest seaweed from the pool?

(A) a sense of injustice

(B) Mally's taunting

(C) love of adventure

(D) Barty's greed

TIP When a question asks about what **motivates** a character to take a certain action, the answer may not be directly stated in the text. To answer this question, look for clues in Barty's actions, thoughts, and feelings earlier in the scene.

340 She could not have told herself. She hated him as much as ever—but she could hardly have wished to see him drowned before her eyes.

"You go on, and don't mind me," said he, speaking in a hoarse, angry tone.

"Mind you—who minds you?" retorted the girl. And then she again prepared herself for her work.

But as she went down over the rocks with her long hook balanced in her hands, she suddenly heard a splash, and, turning quickly round, saw the body of her enemy tumbling amidst the **eddying** waves in the pool. The tide had now come up so far that every succeeding wave washed into
350 it and over it from the side nearest to the sea, and then ran down again back from the rocks, as the rolling wave receded, with a noise like the fall of a cataract.[24] And then, when the surplus water had retreated for a moment, the surface of the pool would be partly calm, though the fretting bubbles would still boil up and down, and there was ever a simmer on the surface, as though, in truth, the caldron were heated. But this time of comparative rest was but a moment, for the succeeding breaker would come up almost as soon as the foam of the preceding one had gone, and then again the waters would be dashed upon the rocks, and the sides would echo with the roar of the angry wave. ▶

360 Instantly Mally hurried across to the edge of the pool, crouching down upon her hands and knees for security as she did so. As a wave receded, Barty's head and face was carried round near to her, and she could see that his forehead was covered with blood. Whether he were alive or dead she did not know. She had seen nothing but his blood, and the light-colored hair of his head lying amidst the foam. Then his body was drawn along by the suction of the retreating wave; but the mass of water that escaped was not on this occasion large enough to carry the man out with it. ▶

Instantly Mally was at work with her hook, and getting it fixed into his coat, dragged him towards the spot on which she was kneeling. During
370 the half minute of repose she got him so close that she could touch his shoulder. Straining herself down, laying herself over the long bending handle of the hook, she strove to grasp him with her right hand. But she could not do it; she could only touch him.

Then came the next breaker, forcing itself on with a roar, looking to Mally as though it must certainly knock her from her resting place and destroy them both. But she had nothing for it[25] but to kneel, and hold by her hook.

eddying (ĕd′ē-ĭng) adj. moving in a whirlpool; swirling eddy v.

TestSmart

VOCABULARY

Which word below is related to the Latin word *cēdere,* which means "to go"?

Ⓐ cataract

Ⓑ receded

Ⓒ surplus

Ⓓ caldron

TIP Tests sometimes ask you to identify a vocabulary word related to a **Latin word.** Remember that words similar in spelling and structure are often related in meaning. In this case, look for the base of a word that is similar to *cēdere* and that describes a motion.

MAKE JUDGMENTS

Who do you think is more responsible for the accident— Barty or Mally? Why?

_____

_____

_____

_____

---

24. **cataract** (kăt′ə-răkt′): waterfall.
25. **had nothing for it:** had no alternative; could do nothing else.

What prayer passed through her mind at that moment for herself or for him, or for that old man who was sitting unconsciously[26] up at the cabin, who can say? The great wave came and rushed over her as she lay almost prostrate, and when the water was gone from her eyes, and the tumult of the foam, and the violence of the roaring breaker had passed by her, she found herself at her length upon the rock, while his body had been lifted up, free from her hook, and was lying upon the slippery ledge, half in the water and half out of it. As she looked at him, in that instant, she could see that his eyes were open and that he was struggling with his hands.

"Hold by the hook, Barty," she cried, pushing the stick of it before him, while she seized the collar of his coat in her hands.

> Had he been her brother, her lover, her father, she could not have clung to him with more of the energy of despair. He did contrive to hold by the stick which she had given him, and when the succeeding wave had passed by, he was still on the ledge. In the next moment she was seated a yard or two above the hole, in comparative safety, while Barty lay upon the rocks with his still bleeding head resting upon her lap.
>
> What could she do now? She could not carry him; and in fifteen minutes the sea would be up where she was sitting. He was quite insensible and very pale, and the blood was coming slowly—very slowly—from the wound on his forehead. Ever so gently she put her hand upon his hair to move it back from his face; and then she bent over his mouth to see if he breathed, and as she looked at him she knew that he was beautiful. ◀

What would she not give that he might live? Nothing now was so precious to her as his life—as this life which she had so far rescued from the waters. But what could she do? Her grandfather could scarcely get himself down over the rocks, if indeed he could succeed in doing so much as that. Could she drag the wounded man backwards, if it were only a few feet, so that he might lie above the reach of the waves till further assistance could be procured?

She set herself to work and she moved him, almost lifting him. As she did so she wondered at her own strength, but she was very strong at that moment. Slowly, tenderly, falling on the rocks herself so that he might fall on her, she got him back to the margin of the sand, to a spot which the waters would not reach for the next two hours.

Here her grandfather met them, having seen at last what had happened from the door.

"Dada," she said, "he fell into the pool yonder, and was battered against the rocks. See there at his forehead."

26. **unconsciously:** unaware of what was happening to Mally and Barty.

"Mally, I'm thinking that he's dead already," said old Glos, peering down over the body.

"No, dada; he is not dead; but mayhap[27] he's dying. But I'll go at once
420 up to the farm."

"Mally," said the old man, "look at his head. They'll say we murdered him."

"Who'll say so? Who'll lie like that? Didn't I pull him out of the hole?"

"What matters that? His father'll say we killed him."

It was manifest to Mally that whatever anyone might say hereafter, her present course was plain before her. She must run up the path to Gunliffe's farm and get necessary assistance. If the world were as bad as her grandfather said, it would be so bad that she would not care to live longer in it. But be that as it might, there was no doubt as to what she must do
430 now. ▶

So away she went as fast as her naked feet could carry her up the cliff. When at the top she looked round to see if any person might be within ken,[28] but she saw no one. So she ran with all her speed along the headland[29] of the cornfield which led in the direction of old Gunliffe's house, and as she drew near to the homestead she saw that Barty's mother was leaning on the gate. As she approached she attempted to call, but her breath failed her for any purpose of loud speech, so she ran on till she was able to grasp Mrs. Gunliffe by the arm.

"Where's himself?" she said, holding her hand upon her beating heart
440 that she might husband her breath.

"Who is it you mean?" said Mrs. Gunliffe, who participated in the family feud against Trenglos and his granddaughter. "What does the girl clutch me for in that way?"

"He's dying then, that's all."

"Who is dying? Is it old Malachi? If the old man's bad, we'll send some one down."

"It ain't dada; it's Barty! Where's himself? where's the master?" But by this time Mrs. Gunliffe was in an agony of despair, and was calling out for assistance lustily. Happily Gunliffe, the father, was at hand, and with him
450 a man from the neighboring village.

---

27. **mayhap:** perhaps.
28. **within ken:** in view.
29. **headland:** a point of land extending out into a body of water.

"Will you not send for the doctor?" said Mally. "Oh, man, you should send for the doctor!"

Whether any orders were given for the doctor she did not know, but in a very few minutes she was hurrying across the field again towards the path to the cove, and Gunliffe with the other man and his wife were following her.

As Mally went along she recovered her voice, for their step was not so quick as hers, and that which to them was a hurried movement allowed her to get her breath again. And as she went she tried to explain to the father
460 what had happened, saying but little, however, of her own doings in the matter. The wife hung behind listening, exclaiming every now and again that her boy was killed, and then asking wild questions as to his being yet alive. The father, as he went, said little. He was known as a silent, sober man, well spoken of for diligence and general conduct, but supposed to be stern and very hard when angered. ◀

As they drew near to the top of the path the other man whispered something to him, and then he turned round upon Mally and stopped her.

"If he has come by his death between you, your blood shall be taken for his," said he.

470 Then the wife shrieked out that her child had been murdered, and Mally, looking round into the faces of the three, saw that her grandfather's words had come true. They suspected her of having taken the life, in saving which she had nearly lost her own.

She looked round at them with awe in her face, and then, without saying a word, preceded them down the path. What had she to answer when such a charge as that was made against her? If they chose to say that she pushed him into the pool and hit him with her hook as he lay amidst the waters, how could she show that it was not so?

Poor Mally knew little of the law of evidence, and it seemed to her
480 that she was in their hands. But as she went down the steep track with a hurried step—a step so quick that they could not keep up with her—her heart was very full—very full and very high. She had striven for the man's life as though he had been her brother. The blood was yet not dry on her own legs and arms, where she had torn them in his service. At one moment she had felt sure that she would die with him in that pool. And now they said that she had murdered him! It may be that he was not dead, and what would he say if ever he should speak again? Then she thought of that moment when his eyes had opened, and he had seemed to see her. She had no fear for herself, for her heart was very high. But it was full also—
490 full of scorn, disdain, and wrath.

ANALYZE

What methods of **characterization** does the author use to reveal traits of Mrs. Gunliffe and Mr. Gunliffe in the boxed text?

When she had reached the bottom, she stood close to the door of the hut waiting for them, so that they might precede her to the other group, which was there in front of them, at a little distance on the sand.

"He is there, and dada is with him. Go and look at him," said Mally.

The father and mother ran on stumbling over the stones, but Mally remained behind by the door of the hut.

Barty Gunliffe was lying on the sand where Mally had left him, and old Malachi Trenglos was standing over him, resting himself with difficulty upon a stick.

500 "Not a move he's moved since she left him," said he, "not a move. I put his head on the old rug as you see, and I tried 'un with a drop of gin, but he wouldn't take it—he wouldn't take it."

"Oh, my boy! my boy!" said the mother, throwing herself beside her son upon the sand.

"Haud[30] your tongue, woman," said the father, kneeling down slowly by the lad's head, "whimpering that way will do 'un no good."

Then having gazed for a minute or two upon the pale face beneath him, he looked up sternly into that of Malachi Trenglos.

The old man hardly knew how to bear this terrible inquisition.

510 "He would come," said Malachi; "he brought it all upon hisself."

"Who was it struck him?" said the father.

"Sure he struck hisself, as he fell among the breakers."

"Liar!" said the father, looking up at the old man.

"They have murdered him—they have murdered him!" shrieked the mother.

"Haud your peace, woman!" said the husband again. "They shall give us blood for blood." ▶

Mally, leaning against the corner of the hovel, heard it all, but did not stir. They might say what they liked. They might make it out to be 520 murder. They might drag her and her grandfather to Camelford gaol, and then to Bodmin,[31] and the gallows; but they could not take from her the conscious feeling that was her own. She had done her best to save him—her very best. And she had saved him!

She remembered her threat to him before they had gone down on the rocks together, and her evil wish. Those words had been very wicked; but since that she had risked her life to save his. They might say what they pleased of her, and do what they pleased. She knew what she knew.

---

30. **haud:** hold.
31. **to Camelford gaol** (jāl) . . . **Bodmin:** to Camelford jail and then to the county seat of Cornwall at Bodmin (for trial).

ANALYZE

Underline the accusations and the threats the Gunliffes make.

What effect do you think these statements have on the Gunliffes after they learn the truth about Barty's rescue?

orifice (ôr′ə-fĭs) *n.* an opening, especially to a passage within the body

Then the father raised his son's head and shoulders in his arms, and called on the others to assist him in carrying Barty towards the path. They raised him between them carefully and tenderly, and lifted their burden on towards the spot at which Mally was standing. She never moved, but watched them at their work; and the old man followed them, hobbling after them with his crutch.

When they had reached the end of the hut she looked upon Barty's face, and saw that it was very pale. There was no longer blood upon the forehead, but the great gash was to be seen there plainly, with its jagged cut, and the skin livid and blue round the <u>orifice</u>. His light brown hair was hanging back, as she had made it to hang when she had gathered it with her hand after the big wave had passed over them. Ah, how beautiful he was in Mally's eyes with that pale face, and the sad scar upon his brow! She turned her face away, that they might not see her tears; but she did not move, nor did she speak.

But now, when they had passed the end of the hut, shuffling along with their burden, she heard a sound which stirred her. She roused herself quickly from her leaning posture, and stretched forth her head as though to listen; then she moved to follow them. Yes, they had stopped at the bottom of the path, and had again laid the body on the rocks. She heard that sound again, as of a long, long sigh, and then, regardless of any of them, she ran to the wounded man's head.

"He is not dead," she said. "There; he is not dead."

As she spoke Barty's eyes opened, and he looked about him.

"Barty, my boy, speak to me," said the mother.

Barty turned his face upon his mother, smiled, and then stared about him wildly.

"How is it with thee, lad?" said his father. Then Barty turned his face again to the latter voice, and as he did so his eyes fell upon Mally.

"Mally!" he said, "Mally!"

It could have wanted[32] nothing further to any of those present to teach them that, according to Barty's own view of the case, Mally had not been his enemy; and, in truth, Mally herself wanted no further triumph. That word had vindicated her, and she withdrew back to the hut.

"Dada," she said, "Barty is not dead, and I'm thinking they won't say anything more about our hurting him." ◄

Old Glos shook his head. He was glad the lad hadn't met his death there; he didn't want the young man's blood, but he knew what folk would say. The poorer he was the more sure the world would be to trample on

him. Mally said what she could to comfort him, being full of comfort herself.

She would have crept up to the farm if she dared, to ask how Barty was. But her courage failed her when she thought of that, so she went to work again, dragging back the weed she had saved to the spot at which on the morrow she would load the donkey. As she did this she saw Barty's pony still standing patiently under the rock, so she got a lock of fodder and threw it down before the beast.

It had become dark down in the cove, but she was still dragging back the seaweed, when she saw the glimmer of a lantern coming down the pathway. It was a most unusual sight, for lanterns were not common down in Malachi's Cove. Down came the lantern rather slowly—much more slowly than she was in the habit of descending, and then through the gloom she saw the figure of a man standing at the bottom of the path. She went up to him, and saw that it was Mr. Gunliffe, the father.

"Is that Mally?" said Gunliffe.

"Yes, it is Mally; and how is Barty, Mr. Gunliffe?"

"You must come to 'un yourself, now at once," said the farmer. "He won't sleep a wink till he's seed you. You must not say but you'll come."

"Sure I'll come if I'm wanted," said Mally.

Gunliffe waited a moment, thinking that Mally might have to prepare herself, but Mally needed no preparation. She was dripping with salt water from the weed which she had been dragging, and her elfin locks were streaming wildly from her head; but, such as she was, she was ready.

"Dada's in bed," she said, "and I can go now if you please."

Then Gunliffe turned round and followed her up the path, wondering at the life which this girl led so far away from all her sex. It was now dark night, and he had found her working at the very edge of the rolling waves by herself, in the darkness, while the only human being who might seem to be her protector had already gone to his bed.

When they were at the top of the cliff, Gunliffe took her by her hand and led her along. She did not comprehend this, but she made no attempt to take her hand from his. Something he said about falling on the cliffs, but it was muttered so lowly that Mally hardly understood him. But in truth the man knew that she had saved his boy's life, and that he had injured her instead of thanking her. He was now taking her to his heart, and as words were wanting to him, he was showing his love after this silent fashion. He held her by the hand as though she were a child, and Mally tripped along at his side asking him no questions. ▶

CONTRAST

Describe the change in Mr. Gunliffe's feelings toward Mally.

_____

_____

_____

_____

Underline details that support your answer. ✏

What event is foreshadowed by the "future destiny" mentioned in line 612?

Ⓐ old Glos's death

Ⓑ the fate of the cove

Ⓒ Mally's marriage to Barty

Ⓓ Mally's return to the cove

TIP A test question may ask you what a particular event or comment **foreshadows**. Remember that writers use foreshadowing to suggest an upcoming event. To answer this question, think about what Mally's future destiny is in the story. Which answer choice best sums up that destiny?

When they were at the farmyard gate he stopped there for a moment.

"Mally, my girl," he said, "he'll not be content till he sees thee, but thou must not stay long wi' him, lass. Doctor says he's weak like, and wants sleep badly."

610   Mally merely nodded her head, and then they entered the house. Mally had never been within it before, and looked about with wondering eyes at the furniture of the big kitchen. Did any idea of her future destiny flash upon her then, I wonder? But she did not pause here a moment, but was led up to the bedroom above stairs, where Barty was lying on his mother's bed. ◀

"Is it Mally herself?" said the voice of the weak youth.

"It's Mally herself," said the mother, "so now you can say what you please."

"Mally," said he, "Mally, it's along of you[33] that I'm alive this moment."

620   "I'll not forget it on her," said the father, with his eyes turned away from her. "I'll never forget it on her."

"We hadn't a one but only him," said the mother, with her apron up to her face.

"Mally, you'll be friends with me now?" said Barty.

To have been made lady of the manor of the cove for ever, Mally couldn't have spoken a word now. It was not only that the words and presence of the people there cowed her and made her speechless, but the big bed, and the looking-glass, and the unheard-of wonders of the chamber, made her feel her own insignificance. But she crept up to Barty's

630   side, and put her hand upon his.

"I'll come and get the weed, Mally; but it shall all be for you," said Barty.

"Indeed, you won't then, Barty dear," said the mother; "you'll never go near the awesome place again. What would we do if you were took from us?"

"He mustn't go near the hole if he does," said Mally, speaking at last in a solemn voice, and imparting the knowledge which she had kept to herself while Barty was her enemy; "specially not if the wind's any way from the nor'rard."

"She'd better go down now," said the father.

640   Barty kissed the hand which he held, and Mally, looking at him as he did so, thought that he was like an angel.

"You'll come and see us tomorrow, Mally?" said he.

To this she made no answer, but followed Mrs. Gunliffe out of the room. When they were down in the kitchen the mother had tea for her,

---

33. **along of you:** because of you.

and thick milk, and a hot cake—all the delicacies which the farm could afford. I don't know that Mally cared much for the eating and drinking that night, but she began to think that the Gunliffes were good people—very good people. It was better thus, at any rate, than being accused of murder and carried off to Camelford prison.

650   "I'll never forget it on her—never," the father had said.

    Those words stuck to her from that moment, and seemed to sound in her ears all the night. How glad she was that Barty had come down to the cove—oh, yes, how glad! There was no question of his dying now, and as for the blow on his forehead, what harm was that to a lad like him?

    "But father shall go with you," said Mrs. Gunliffe, when Mally prepared to start for the cove by herself. Mally, however, would not hear of this. She could find her way to the cove whether it was light or dark.

    "Mally, thou art my child now, and I shall think of thee so," said the mother, as the girl went off by herself.

660   Mally thought of this, too, as she walked home. How could she become Mrs. Gunliffe's child; ah, how?

    I need not, I think, tell the tale any further. That Mally did become Mrs. Gunliffe's child, and how she became so the reader will understand; and in process of time the big kitchen and all the wonders of the farmhouse were her own. The people said that Barty Gunliffe had married a mermaid out of the sea; but when it was said in Mally's hearing I doubt whether she liked it; and when Barty himself would call her a mermaid she would frown at him, and throw about her black hair, and pretend to cuff him with her little hand. ▶

670   Old Glos was brought up to the top of the cliff, and lived his few remaining days under the roof of Mr. Gunliffe's house; and as for the cove and the right of seaweed, from that time forth all that has been supposed to attach itself to Gunliffe's farm, and I do not know that any of the neighbors are prepared to dispute the right.

SYNTHESIZE

Consider Mally's isolated life with her grandfather. What does being taken into the Gunliffes' home symbolize?

_____

_____

_____

Big Question

Reread your responses in the chart on page 203. After reading "Malachi's Cove," would you change any of your responses? Explain. _EVALUATE_

_____

_____

_____

_____

Reading Comprehension

DIRECTIONS *Answer these questions about the selection by filling in the correct ovals.*

1. What event is foreshadowed by lines 285–290?

   (A) the ferocity of the squall

   (B) Barty's fall into the hole

   (C) Barty's rescue from the hole

   (D) Mally's marriage to Barty

2. What method of characterization does the author use to reveal Mally's character in lines 401–412?

   (A) her thoughts and actions

   (B) the words of others

   (C) direct commentary

   (D) her physical traits

3. Barty didn't know the danger and futility of trying to

   (A) harvest seaweed in the rain

   (B) work in the breakers after dark

   (C) harvest seaweed with an ordinary fork

   (D) retrieve seaweed from "Poulnadioul"

4. In lines 488–489, Mally "had no fear for herself" because she knew that

   (A) she had done the right thing

   (B) evidence was on her side

   (C) Barty would not die

   (D) the Gunliffes were level-headed

5. Which aspect of lines 503–517 adds to the story's realism?

   (A) the seaside setting

   (B) the dialogue of daily life

   (C) fear of death

   (D) a conflict between characters

6. What motivates Gunliffe to take Mally by the hand in lines 597–598?

   (A) fear that she might fall from the cliffs

   (B) gratitude that she saved his son's life

   (C) concern that she might run away from him

   (D) feeling that she cannot take care of herself

7. The word *impediments* in line 201 means

   (A) rocks

   (B) obstacles

   (C) ramps

   (D) tools

8. As it is used in line 396, the word *insensible* means

   (A) imperceptible

   (B) lacking meaning

   (C) indifferent

   (D) unconscious

Responding in Writing

9. Short Response Many of the characters in "Malachi's Cove" change as a result of their experiences. Write a paragraph in which you describe the changes in two of the characters. End your paragraph by identifying the character who, in your opinion, goes through the greatest transformation. Explain why you chose that character.

_____

_____

_____

_____

_____

TEST-TAKER'S TOOLKIT

GRAPHIC ORGANIZER Use the chart below to help you plan your response.

Character	How He or She Changes

Stalking a Killer That Lurks a Few Feet Offshore
NEWS ARTICLE

Use with "Malachi's Cove," p. 202

What's the Connection?

The "devil's hole" in "Malachi's Cove'" was hazardous for anyone who ventured near it. The news article you are about to read explains the hazards of another shoreline phenomenon—a killer that hides just below the water's surface.

DANGER AHEAD What do you know about the hazards that exist on ocean beaches and shorelines? With a group, discuss the different kinds of dangers that beachgoers and swimmers face. Then work independently to create a warning sign in the space below. Write warnings for what you consider to be the three most dangerous hazards. Include a safety tip for avoiding each one.

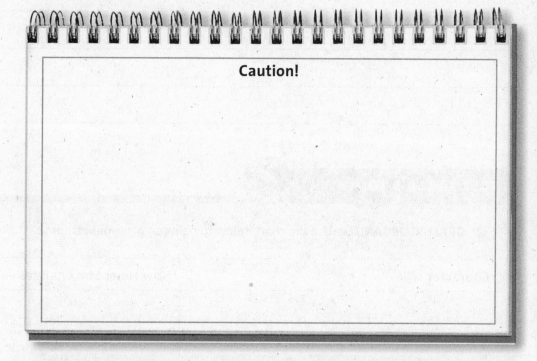

Caution!

LEARN THE SKILL: ANALYZE INFORMATION IN A GRAPHIC AID

A **graphic aid** is a visual resource that gives information in a way that is easy to understand. Graphic aids include **maps, graphs,** and **diagrams.** Nonfiction text often includes graphic aids that support ideas presented in the text. When you encounter a graphic aid, ask yourself:

- What is its purpose?
- How does it support the text?
- What information does it give that the text does not?

For more on analyzing information in graphic aids, see the Nonfiction Skills Handbook beginning on page R2.

from *The New York Times*

Stalking a Killer That Lurks a Few Feet Offshore

by Cornelia Dean

When people think about natural hazards, they usually think about tornadoes or hurricanes or earthquakes. But there is another natural hazard that takes more lives in an average year in the United States than any of those— rip currents.

10 Each year in American waters, rip currents pull about 100 panicked swimmers to their deaths. According to the United States Lifesaving Association, lifeguards pull out at least 70,000 Americans from the surf each year, 80 percent from rip currents.

Because these drownings and near drownings occur one by one, year-round, up and down the 20 coasts, few people recognize rip currents as a major hazard. Only in recent years have meteorologists and coastal geologists begun to measure rip currents precisely in the field and model them in detail in laboratory wave tanks.

The goal is to save lives. The researchers hope to devise ways of predicting when and where rip 30 currents are most likely to occur, so beach managers will know when to add lifeguards or close the beaches.

Rip currents are often erroneously called riptides or undertow, but they are not caused by tidal action. And although waders knocked off their feet by rip currents may end up underwater, the 40 currents themselves pull people along the surface, not down.

Usually rip currents are narrow. But sometimes, according to the National Weather Service, they can be hundreds of yards wide. And although they usually run out of steam just beyond the breakers, they may carry swimmers hundreds of yards offshore. ▶

50 Rip currents form when wind, wave and beach conditions combine to push up water on the beach so that when it flows back out to sea a large volume is squeezed into a relatively narrow passage at a low place in a sandbar, perhaps, or under a pier. A result is a swath of fast-moving water that cuts across the surf zone, where waves 60 are breaking, carrying sand, seaweed and, sometimes, swimmers with it. ▶

SET A PURPOSE

CONNECT

Did you include rip currents in the list of coastal dangers you created on page 226?

☐ yes   ☐ no

What information on this page explains why so few people know about rip currents?

SPECIALIZED *Vocabulary*

The word *sandbar* in line 56 may be unfamiliar to you. Use the word parts and context clues to come up with a definition of the word.

WORD ANALYSIS

SYNTHESIZE

Underline the name of each expert who is quoted up to this point in the article. ✎

What main idea can you synthesize from the statements and information provided by these experts?

_____

_____

_____

_____

Savvy surfers rely on rip currents for free rides beyond the surf zone. But unwary bathers may wade into the water only to find themselves suddenly swept away. If they keep their heads and swim across the current, parallel to shore, they can escape its grip and make their way back to the beach.

But swimmers who try to fight rip currents quickly exhaust themselves and may drown. Would-be rescuers are often among the casualties of rip currents. That was apparently what happened Sunday at Rockaway Beach, Queens, where rip currents are not uncommon. Three 16-year-old boys were swept away—one escaped, one was rescued, but the third is missing, and a man who tried to save him later died of a heart attack.

Rip currents can flow from 1 to 4 miles an hour, or up to 6 feet a second or even faster, scientists say. "You would have to be a good swimmer to swim two miles per hour, and you cannot do that very long," said Dr. Edward Thornton of the Naval Postgraduate School in Monterey, Calif., who studies rip currents.

Dr. Stephen P. Leatherman, director of the Laboratory for Coastal Research at Florida International University in Miami, said some people called rip currents "the drowning machine," because of their almost mechanical ability to exhaust swimmers. . . .

Rip-current drownings and near drownings occur on every state with an ocean coast, most often in California and Florida, which have long coastlines and long beach seasons.

According to Jim Lushine, who retired this year as warning coordinator at the National Weather Service Forecast Office in Miami, 296 people drowned in rip currents in Florida from 1989 to last year, more than the total killed in the state by lightning, tornadoes and hurricanes combined. ◄

Mr. Lushine, who presented this data at a recent conference on beaches at Florida International University, said that nationwide only heat, which on average kills 237 Americans a year, is a more lethal natural hazard than rip currents. Shark attacks, the perennial media favorite, barely rate a mention in Mr. Lushine's roster. On average, 0.6 Americans are killed by sharks each year, he said.

Dr. Leatherman, who organized the conference, said he became fascinated by rip currents when he was director of the Laboratory for Coastal Research at the University of Maryland and he heard of a small boy who was swept out of his father's grasp and drowned in a rip current at Ocean City.

Because outflowing rip currents can dampen incoming waves, they can fool people into thinking that they are calm areas. That was the mistake this father made,

Dr. Leatherman said, and he and his son waded "into the jaws of the current." . . .

Mr. Lushine has developed a scale that combines wind, wave and other factors to rate the risk of rip currents as high, medium or low, and some weather service offices now include the risk for rip currents in their forecasts.

It is not clear how useful these warnings will be, Mr. Lushine conceded in his presentation, because rip currents are highly localized.

Dr. Rob Holman of Oregon State University said it might one day be possible to post camera systems at individual beaches and print out daily maps of where rip currents are flowing.

"The lifeguards are very interested in this," he said, "because a map makes it a little more meaningful."

Meanwhile, though, even scientists who are researching rip currents agree that the most important way to reduce rip-current deaths is to teach people how to swim, and how to swim their way out of a current.

"The biggest thing is not to panic," Dr. Jamie MacMahan said. "The more we can educate, the better."

Rip Currents

High winds or waves cause a larger-than-usual amount of water to collect behind a sandbar.

sandbar

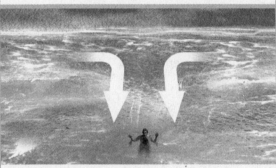

The water breaks through the sandbar and washes rapidly out to sea in a rip current.

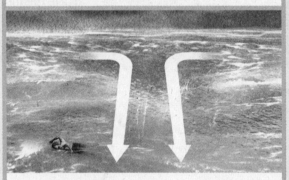

Swimmers can escape a rip current by swimming parallel to shore, out of the narrow current.

Reading Comprehension

DIRECTIONS *Answer these questions about the two selections in this lesson by filling in the correct ovals.*

1. According to the news article, the most life-threatening natural phenomenon in the United States is

   (A) sharks

   (B) heat

   (C) rip currents

   (D) tornadoes

2. What makes rip currents difficult to see?

   (A) The water surrounding currents often seems calm.

   (B) Rip currents move at one to six miles per hour.

   (C) Some rip currents are quite narrow.

   (D) Rip currents run parallel to the shore.

3. Most people who die in rip currents do so because of

   (A) violence of the surf

   (B) frigid water

   (C) the speed of the current

   (D) exhaustion and panic

4. Rip current warnings delivered by weather service reports may not be that useful because rip currents are so

   (A) numerous

   (B) localized

   (C) unpredictable

   (D) unmappable

5. How is the water in Poulnadioul similar to a rip current?

   (A) It bubbles as if it is boiling.

   (B) It can pull someone under.

   (C) It can sweep someone out to sea.

   (D) It is a danger caused by tides.

6. What do the arrows represent in the graphic aid on page 229?

   (A) the direction of waves

   (B) outgoing currents

   (C) water flow

   (D) incoming tide

7. The word *savvy* in line 63 of the news article means

   (A) sophisticated

   (B) knowledgeable

   (C) foolhardy

   (D) reckless

8. In line 125 of the news article, the word *perennial* means

   (A) unnatural

   (B) persistent

   (C) annual

   (D) occasional

Timed Writing Practice

PROMPT

Popular Victorian novelists such as Anthony Trollope created exciting plots to gain wide readership. <u>Write an analysis of the plot of "Malachi's Cove,"</u> examining how Trollope uses external and internal conflicts to move the plot forward and develop his characters. Discuss three conflicts that one or more of the characters experience. Use details and examples from the story to support your ideas.

BUDGET YOUR TIME

You have **45 minutes** to respond. Decide how much time to spend on each step.

Analyze _____

Plan _____

Write _____

Review _____

45

TEST-TAKER'S TOOLKIT

1. ANALYZE THE PROMPT

A. Underline key words and phrases that tell you what you are being asked to do. One phrase has been underlined for you.

B. Jot down a list of elements you need to include in your essay.

2. PLAN YOUR RESPONSE

A. Make notes Use a chart like the one shown to help you examine the story and plan your essay.

B. Organize your information Your chart can help you develop a five-paragraph essay. Your first paragraph should identify the topic of the essay and state your thesis. In each of the following three paragraphs, analyze one of the conflicts in your chart. Then write a conclusion in which you summarize your key points and explain how they deepen your understanding of the story.

3. WRITE AND REVIEW

A. Your introduction should include a thesis statement that explains the significance of the conflicts you will discuss in the essay. To grab readers' attention, you might start off with an interesting quote from the story.

B. Be sure to leave time to check your spelling and grammar.

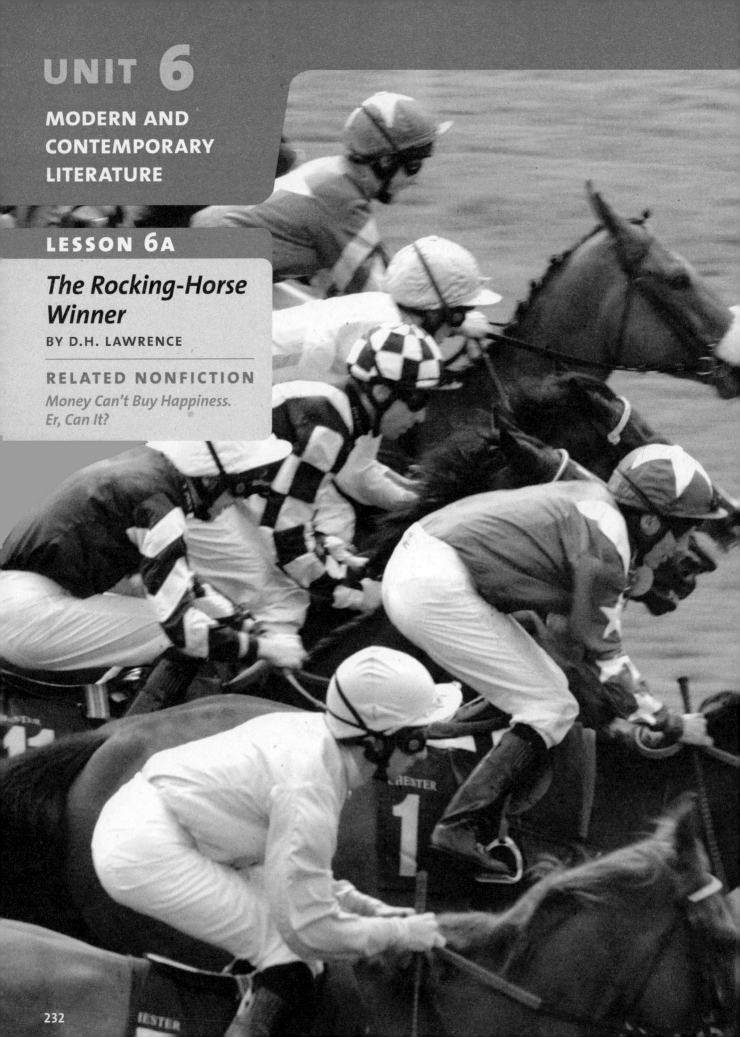

UNIT 6

MODERN AND CONTEMPORARY LITERATURE

LESSON 6A

The Rocking-Horse Winner

BY D.H. LAWRENCE

RELATED NONFICTION
*Money Can't Buy Happiness.
Er, Can It?*

Can money buy
HAPPINESS?

It's easy to imagine that unlimited wealth would lead to almost perfect happiness. With all financial concerns swept away, what else would there be to worry about? The story you're about to read explores the connection between money and happiness.

DISCUSS With a small group, discuss whether money is the key to contentment. Consider the questions in the chart, and use the space provided to jot down other group members' comments and opinions. After the discussion, write your own personal conclusions at the bottom of the chart.

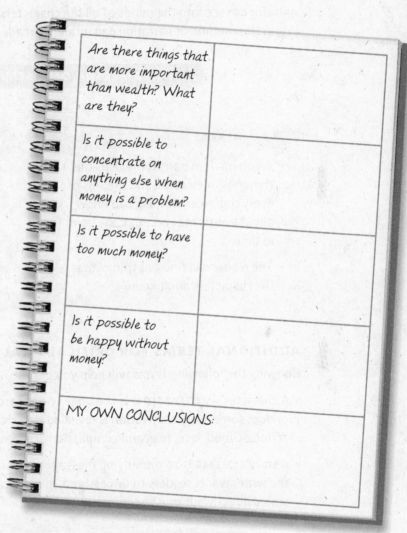

Are there things that are more important than wealth? What are they?	
Is it possible to concentrate on anything else when money is a problem?	
Is it possible to have too much money?	
Is it possible to be happy without money?	
MY OWN CONCLUSIONS:	

Omniscient Point of View

POINT OF VIEW refers to the perspective from which events in a story or novel are told. In the THIRD-PERSON POINT OF VIEW, events are narrated by a voice outside the action, not by one of the characters. A third-person narrator uses pronouns like *he, she,* and *they.* Some third-person narrators are OMNISCIENT, or all-knowing. An omniscient narrator can see into the minds of all the characters. Review the following ways in which this method of narration can influence readers' perception of a story.

THIRD-PERSON OMNISCIENT NARRATOR

ADVANTAGES

- An omniscient narrator reveals the thoughts, memories, and dreams of every character. Readers can know about events that occur at any point in time.

- The reader can find out things that the characters don't know.

DISADVANTAGE

- Because the narrator moves into and out of the thoughts of different characters, readers usually don't become as emotionally involved with any one character as they might be if the narrator were a character in the story or focused on one character.

ADDITIONAL TERMS FOR CRITICAL ANALYSIS

Knowing the following terms will help you get the most out of the story:

- A character's MOTIVATION is the underlying reason why he or she decides or does something. Motivation is revealed by a character's words and actions. Greed, love, fear, and compassion are some examples of motivation.

- A story's THEME is an underlying message about life or human nature that the writer wants readers to understand. In most cases, themes are not stated directly but must be inferred.

The Rocking-Horse Winner

D. H. Lawrence

BACKGROUND Two of the five great annual horseraces in England are the St. Leger Stakes and the Derby. Other notable English races mentioned in this story are the Grand National, the Ascot Gold Cup, and the Lincolnshire. Large sums of money are bet on horseraces. The amount a bettor can win depends on the odds. The odds on each horse are expressed as a ratio—3 to 1, for example—and are determined by what proportion of the total amount bet on the race is bet on that horse. The more money bet on a horse, the lower the odds and the lower the payoff.

MARK & ANALYZE
Read this selection once on your own, marking the text in any way that is helpful to you. Then read the story a second time, using the questions in the margins to help you analyze the literature. When you see this pencil ✎, you'll be asked to mark up the text.

There was a woman who was beautiful, who started with all the advantages, yet she had no luck. She married for love, and the love turned to dust. She had bonny[1] children, yet she felt they had been thrust upon her, and she could not love them. They looked at her coldly, as if they were finding fault with her. And hurriedly she felt she must cover up some fault in herself. Yet what it was that she must cover up she never knew. Nevertheless, when her children were present, she always felt the center of her heart go hard. This troubled her, and in her manner she was all the more gentle and anxious for her children, as if she loved them very

10 much. Only she herself knew that at the center of her heart was a hard little place that could not feel love, no, not for anybody. Everybody else said of her: "She is such a good mother. She adores her children." Only she herself, and her children themselves, knew it was not so. They read it in each other's eyes. ▶

There were a boy and two little girls. They lived in a pleasant house, with a garden, and they had discreet servants, and felt themselves superior to anyone in the neighborhood.

ANALYZE
How does the first paragraph of the story hint at its overall **theme?**

_____

_____

_____

_____

---

1. **bonny:** pretty.

Although they lived in style, they felt always an anxiety in the house.
There was never enough money. The mother had a small income, and the
20 father had a small income, but not nearly enough for the social position
which they had to keep up. The father went into town to some office. But
though he had good prospects, these prospects never **materialized**. There
was always the grinding sense of the shortage of money, though the style
was always kept up.

At last the mother said: "I will see if *I* can't make something." But she
did not know where to begin. She racked her brains, and tried this thing
and the other, but could not find anything successful. The failure made
deep lines come into her face. Her children were growing up, they would
have to go to school. There must be more money, there must be more
30 money. The father, who was always very handsome and expensive in his
tastes, seemed as if he never *would* be able to do anything worth doing.
And the mother, who had a great belief in herself, did not succeed any
better, and her tastes were just as expensive. ◀

And so the house came to be haunted by the unspoken phrase:
There must be more money! There must be more money! The children
could hear it all the time, though nobody said it aloud. They heard it
at Christmas, when the expensive and splendid toys filled the nursery.
Behind the shining modern rocking-horse, behind the smart doll's house,
a voice would start whispering: "There *must* be more money! There *must*
40 be more money!" And the children would stop playing, to listen for a
moment. They would look into each other's eyes, to see if they had all
heard. And each one saw in the eyes of the other two that they too had
heard. "There *must* be more money! There *must* be more money!"

It came whispering from the springs of the still-swaying rocking-horse,
and even the horse, bending his wooden, champing head, heard it. The
big doll, sitting so pink and smirking in her new pram,[2] could hear it quite
plainly, and seemed to be smirking all the more self-consciously because
of it. The foolish puppy, too, that took the place of the teddy bear, he was
looking so extraordinarily foolish for no other reason but that he heard the
50 secret whisper all over the house: "There *must* be more money!"

Yet nobody ever said it aloud. The whisper was everywhere, and
therefore no one spoke it. Just as no one ever says: "We are breathing!" in
spite of the fact that breath is coming and going all the time.

"Mother," said the boy Paul one day, "why don't we keep a car of our
own? Why do we always use uncle's, or else a taxi?"

"Because we're the poor members of the family," said the mother.

---

2. **pram:** baby carriage (a shortened form of *perambulator*).

"But why *are* we, mother?"

"Well—I suppose," she said slowly and bitterly, "it's because your father has no luck."

60   The boy was silent for some time.

"Is luck money, mother?" he asked, rather timidly.

"No, Paul. Not quite. It's what causes you to have money."

"Oh!" said Paul vaguely. "I thought when Uncle Oscar said *filthy lucker,* it meant money."

"*Filthy lucre*[3] does mean money," said the mother. "But it's lucre, not luck."

"Oh!" said the boy. "Then what *is* luck, mother?"

"It's what causes you to have money. If you're lucky you have money. That's why it's better to be born lucky than rich. If you're rich, you may lose
70 your money. But if you're lucky, you will always get more money."

"Oh! Will you? And is father not lucky?"

"Very unlucky, I should say," she said bitterly.

The boy watched her with unsure eyes.

"Why?" he asked.

"I don't know. Nobody ever knows why one person is lucky and another unlucky."

"Don't they? Nobody at all? Does *nobody* know?"

"Perhaps God. But He never tells."

"He ought to, then. And aren't you lucky either, mother?"
80 "I can't be, if I married an unlucky husband."

"But by yourself, aren't you?"

"I used to think I was, before I married. Now I think I am very unlucky indeed."

"Why?"

"Well—never mind! Perhaps I'm not really," she said. ▶

The child looked at her to see if she meant it. But he saw, by the lines of her mouth, that she was only trying to hide something from him.

"Well, anyhow," he said stoutly,[4] "I'm a lucky person."

"Why?" said his mother, with a sudden laugh.
90 He stared at her. He didn't even know why he had said it.

"God told me," he asserted, brazening it out.

"I hope He did, dear!" she said, again with a laugh, but rather bitter.

---

3. *filthy lucre* (lōō′kər): money, especially when obtained through fraud or greed. The term comes from the King James Bible (Titus 1:11) and has passed into familiar usage.

4. **stoutly:** bravely; firmly.

DRAW CONCLUSIONS

What can you conclude about the marriage of Paul's parents based on the conversation in lines 58–85? Explain.

_____

_____

_____

_____

"He did, mother!"

"Excellent!" said the mother, using one of her husband's exclamations.

The boy saw she did not believe him; or rather, that she paid no attention to his assertion. This angered him somewhere, and made him want to compel her attention.

He went off by himself, vaguely, in a childish way, seeking for the clue to "luck." Absorbed, taking no heed of other people, he went about with a sort of stealth, seeking inwardly for luck. He wanted luck, he wanted it, he wanted it. When the two girls were playing dolls in the nursery, he would sit on his big rocking-horse, charging madly into space, with a frenzy that made the little girls peer at him uneasily. Wildly the horse <u>careered</u>, the waving dark hair of the boy tossed, his eyes had a strange glare in them. The little girls dared not speak to him.

When he had ridden to the end of his mad little journey, he climbed down and stood in front of his rocking-horse, staring fixedly into its lowered face. Its red mouth was slightly open, its big eye was wide and glassy-bright.

"Now!" he would silently command the snorting <u>steed</u>. "Now, take me to where there is luck! Now take me!"

And he would slash the horse on the neck with the little whip he had asked Uncle Oscar for. He *knew* the horse could take him to where there was luck, if only he forced it. So he would mount again and start on his furious ride, hoping at last to get there. He knew he could get there. ◀

"You'll break your horse, Paul!" said the nurse.

"He's always riding like that! I wish he'd leave off!" said his elder sister Joan.

But he only glared down on them in silence. Nurse gave him up. She could make nothing of him. Anyhow, he was growing beyond her.

One day his mother and his Uncle Oscar came in when he was on one of his furious rides. He did not speak to them.

"Hallo, you young jockey! Riding a winner?" said his uncle.

"Aren't you growing too big for a rocking-horse? You're not a very little boy any longer, you know," said his mother.

But Paul only gave a blue glare from his big, rather close-set eyes. He would speak to nobody when he was in full tilt.[5] His mother watched him with an anxious expression on her face.

---

5. **in full tilt:** moving at full speed.

career (kə-rîr´) *v.* to move at full speed; to rush wildly

steed (stēd) *n.* a horse, especially a high-spirited riding horse

ANALYZE

Reread the boxed text. What might Paul's frenzied riding of the rocking horse symbolize?

_____

_____

_____

_____

At last he suddenly stopped forcing his horse into the mechanical gallop
130 and slid down.

"Well, I got there!" he announced fiercely, his blue eyes still flaring, and
his sturdy long legs straddling apart.

"Where did you get to?" asked his mother.

"Where I wanted to go," he flared back at her.

"That's right, son!" said Uncle Oscar. "Don't you stop till you get there.
What's the horse's name?"

"He doesn't have a name," said the boy.

"Gets on without all right?" asked the uncle.

"Well, he has different names. He was called Sansovino last week."

140 "Sansovino, eh? Won the Ascot.[6] How did you know his name?"

"He always talks about horse races with Bassett," said Joan.

The uncle was delighted to find that his small nephew was posted with
all the racing news. Bassett, the young gardener, who had been wounded
in the left foot in the war and had got his present job through Oscar
Cresswell, whose batman[7] he had been, was a perfect blade of the "turf."[8]
He lived in the racing events, and the small boy lived with him. ▶

Oscar Cresswell got it all from Bassett.

"Master Paul comes and asks me, so I can't do more than tell him, sir,"
said Bassett, his face terribly serious, as if he were speaking of religious
150 matters.

"And does he ever put anything on a horse he fancies?"

"Well—I don't want to give him away—he's a young sport,[9] a fine sport,
sir. Would you mind asking him himself? He sort of takes a pleasure in it,
and perhaps he'd feel I was giving him away, sir, if you don't mind."

Bassett was serious as a church.

The uncle went back to his nephew and took him off for a ride in the
car.

"Say, Paul, old man, do you ever put anything on a horse?" the uncle
asked.

160 The boy watched the handsome man closely.

"Why, do you think I oughtn't to?" he parried.

"Not a bit of it! I thought perhaps you might give me a tip for the
Lincoln."

CONTRAST

What do lines 135–146 reveal
about Uncle Oscar's character?
In what ways is he different
from Paul's mother?

_____

_____

_____

_____

_____

---

6. **Won the Ascot:** won at the famous horse races held on Ascot Heath, a horsetrack
   southwest of London.

7. **batman:** in Britain, a soldier who acts as an officer's servant.

8. **blade of the "turf":** someone very knowledgeable about horseracing.

9. **sport:** good fellow.

The car sped on into the country, going down to Uncle Oscar's place in Hampshire.

"Honor bright?"[10] said the nephew.

"Honor bright, son!" said the uncle.

"Well, then, Daffodil."

"Daffodil! I doubt it, sonny. What about Mirza?"

170 "I only know the winner," said the boy. "That's Daffodil."

"Daffodil, eh?"

There was a pause. Daffodil was an obscure horse comparatively.

"Uncle!"

"Yes, son?"

"You won't let it go any further, will you? I promised Bassett."

"Bassett be damned, old man! What's he got to do with it?"

"We're partners. We've been partners from the first. Uncle, he lent me my first five shillings,[11] which I lost. I promised him, honor bright, it was only between me and him; only you gave me that ten-shilling note I

180 started winning with, so I thought you were lucky. You won't let it go any further, will you?"

The boy gazed at his uncle from those big, hot, blue eyes, set rather close together. The uncle stirred and laughed uneasily.

"Right you are, son! I'll keep your tip private. Daffodil, eh? How much are you putting on him?"

"All except twenty pounds,"[12] said the boy. "I keep that in reserve."

The uncle thought it a good joke.

"You keep twenty pounds in reserve, do you, you young romancer? What are you betting, then?"

190 "I'm betting three hundred," said the boy gravely. "But it's between you and me, Uncle Oscar! Honor bright?"

The uncle burst into a roar of laughter.

"It's between you and me all right, you young Nat Gould,"[13] he said, laughing. "But where's your three hundred?"

"Bassett keeps it for me. We're partners."

"You are, are you! And what is Bassett putting on Daffodil?"

"He won't go quite as high as I do, I expect. Perhaps he'll go a hundred and fifty."

---

10. **Honor bright:** an expression meaning "on your (or my) honor."
11. **shillings:** former British coins worth 1/20 of a pound.
12. **twenty pounds:** the equivalent of about a thousand dollars in today's money. (In the mid-1920s, a pound was worth about five dollars, and the purchasing power of a dollar was about ten times what it is now.)
13. **Nat Gould:** a well-known British horseracing authority and writer.

"What, pennies?" laughed the uncle.

200 "Pounds," said the child, with a surprised look at his uncle. "Bassett keeps a bigger reserve than I do."

Between wonder and amusement Uncle Oscar was silent. He pursued the matter no further, but he determined to take his nephew with him to the Lincoln races.

"Now, son," he said, "I'm putting twenty on Mirza, and I'll put five on for you on any horse you fancy. What's your pick?"

"Daffodil, uncle."

"No, not the fiver on Daffodil!"

"I should if it was my own fiver," said the child.

210 "Good! Good! Right you are! A fiver for me and a fiver for you on Daffodil."

The child had never been to a race-meeting before, and his eyes were blue fire. He pursed his mouth tight and watched. A Frenchman just in front had put his money on Lancelot. Wild with excitement, he flayed his arms up and down, yelling *Lancelot! Lancelot!* in his French accent.

Daffodil came in first, Lancelot second, Mirza third. The child, flushed and with eyes blazing, was curiously serene. His uncle brought him four five-pound notes, four to one. ▶

"What am I to do with these?" he cried, waving them before the boy's

220 eyes.

"I suppose we'll talk to Bassett," said the boy. "I expect I have fifteen hundred now; and twenty in reserve; and this twenty."

His uncle studied him for some moments.

"Look here, son!" he said. "You're not serious about Bassett and that fifteen hundred, are you?"

"Yes, I am. But it's between you and me, uncle. Honor bright?"

"Honor bright all right, son! But I must talk to Bassett."

"If you'd like to be a partner, uncle, with Bassett and me, we could all be partners. Only, you'd have to promise, honor bright, uncle, not

230 to let it go beyond us three. Bassett and I are lucky, and you must be lucky, because it was your ten shillings I started winning with. . . ."

Uncle Oscar took both Bassett and Paul into Richmond Park for an afternoon, and there they talked.

"It's like this, you see, sir," Bassett said. "Master Paul would get me talking about racing events, spinning yarns, you know, sir. And he was always keen on knowing if I'd made or if I'd lost. It's about a year since,

INTERPRET

Reread the descriptions of Paul's eyes in lines 182–183, 212–213, and 216–217. What does this repeated image suggest about Paul?

now, that I put five shillings on Blush of Dawn for him: and we lost. Then the luck turned, with that ten shillings he had from you: that we put on Singhalese. And since that time, it's been pretty steady, all things considering. What do you say, Master Paul?"

"We're all right when we're sure," said Paul. "It's when we're not quite sure that we go down."

"Oh, but we're careful then," said Bassett.

"But when are you *sure?*" smiled Uncle Oscar.

"It's Master Paul, sir," said Bassett in a secret, religious voice. "It's as if he had it from heaven. Like Daffodil, now, for the Lincoln. That was as sure as eggs."[14]

"Did you put anything on Daffodil?" asked Oscar Cresswell.

"Yes, sir. I made my bit."

"And my nephew?"

Bassett was obstinately silent, looking at Paul.

"I made twelve hundred, didn't I, Bassett? I told uncle I was putting three hundred on Daffodil."

"That's right," said Bassett, nodding. ◀

"But where's the money?" asked the uncle.

"I keep it safe locked up, sir. Master Paul he can have it any minute he likes to ask for it."

"What, fifteen hundred pounds?"

"And twenty! And *forty,* that is, with the twenty he made on the course."

"It's amazing!" said the uncle.

"If Master Paul offers you to be partners, sir, I would, if I were you: if you'll excuse me," said Bassett.

Oscar Cresswell thought about it.

"I'll see the money," he said.

They drove home again, and, sure enough, Bassett came round to the garden-house with fifteen hundred pounds in notes. The twenty pounds reserve was left with Joe Glee, in the Turf Commission deposit.[15]

"You see, it's all right, uncle, when I'm *sure!* Then we go strong, for all we're worth. Don't we, Bassett?"

"We do that, Master Paul."

"And when are you sure?" said the uncle, laughing.

14. **as sure as eggs:** absolutely certain; shortened from the expression "as sure as eggs is eggs."

15. **Turf Commission deposit:** a bank in which bettors keep money for future bets.

"Oh, well, sometimes I'm *absolutely* sure, like about Daffodil," said the boy; "and sometimes I have an idea; and sometimes I haven't even an idea, have I, Bassett? Then we're careful, because we mostly go down."

"You do, do you! And when you're sure, like about Daffodil, what makes you sure, sonny?"

"Oh, well, I don't know," said the boy uneasily. "I'm sure, you know, uncle; that's all."

"It's as if he had it from heaven, sir," Bassett <u>reiterated</u>.

280   "I should say so!" said the uncle.

But he became a partner. And when the Leger was coming on Paul was "sure" about Lively Spark, which was a quite inconsiderable horse. The boy insisted on putting a thousand on the horse, Bassett went for five hundred, and Oscar Cresswell two hundred. Lively Spark came in first, and the betting had been ten to one against him. Paul had made ten thousand.

"You see," he said, "I was absolutely sure of him."

Even Oscar Cresswell had cleared two thousand.

"Look here, son," he said, "this sort of thing makes me nervous."

"It needn't, uncle! Perhaps I shan't be sure again for a long time."

290   "But what are you going to do with your money?" asked the uncle.

"Of course," said the boy, "I started it for mother. She said she had no luck, because father is unlucky, so I thought if I was lucky, it might stop whispering."

"What might stop whispering?"

"Our house. I *hate* our house for whispering."

"What does it whisper?"

"Why—why"—the boy fidgeted—"why, I don't know. But it's always short of money, you know, uncle."

"I know it, son, I know it."

300   "You know people send mother writs,[16] don't you, uncle?"

"I'm afraid I do," said the uncle.

"And then the house whispers, like people laughing at you behind your back. It's awful, that is! I thought if I was lucky—"

"You might stop it," added the uncle. ▶

The boy watched him with big blue eyes, that had an <u>uncanny</u> cold fire in them, and he said never a word.

"Well, then!" said the uncle. "What are we doing?"

"I shouldn't like mother to know I was lucky," said the boy.

"Why not, son?"

310   "She'd stop me."

---

16. **writs:** legal documents, in this case demanding payment of debts.

reiterate (rē-ĭt′ə-rāt′) v. to repeat

TESTSMART

What do you think Paul's motivation is for betting on the races?

(A) His father is unlucky.

(B) He hates the "whispering."

(C) He is greedy.

(D) He loves horseracing.

TIP A test may ask you to identify a character's **motivation**. Motivation is revealed by what a character does and says. Underline the sentence in which Paul directly states his reason for betting on the horseraces. Considering what Paul says and the fact that he hasn't spent any money on himself, what do you think his motivation is?

uncanny (ŭn-kăn′ē) adj. strange or mysterious in a way that causes unease; eerie

"I don't think she would."

"Oh!"—and the boy writhed in an odd way—"I *don't* want her to know, uncle."

"All right, son! We'll manage it without her knowing." ◀

They managed it very easily. Paul, at the other's suggestion, handed over five thousand pounds to his uncle, who deposited it with the family lawyer, who was then to inform Paul's mother that a relative had put five thousand pounds into his hands, which sum was to be paid out a thousand pounds at a time, on the mother's birthday, for the next five years.

320 "So she'll have a birthday present of a thousand pounds for five successive years," said Uncle Oscar. "I hope it won't make it all the harder for her later."

Paul's mother had her birthday in November. The house had been "whispering" worse than ever lately, and, even in spite of his luck, Paul could not bear up against it. He was very anxious to see the effect of the birthday letter, telling his mother about the thousand pounds.

When there were no visitors, Paul now took his meals with his parents, as he was beyond the nursery control. His mother went into town nearly every day. She had discovered that she had an odd knack of 330 sketching furs and dress materials, so she worked secretly in the studio of a friend who was the chief "artist" for the leading drapers.[17] She drew the figures of ladies in furs and ladies in silk and sequins for the newspaper advertisements. This young woman artist earned several thousand pounds a year, but Paul's mother only made several hundreds, and she was again dissatisfied. She so wanted to be first in something, and she did not succeed, even in making sketches for drapery advertisements. ◀

She was down to breakfast on the morning of her birthday. Paul watched her face as she read her letters. He knew the lawyer's letter. As his mother read it, her face hardened and became more expressionless. Then 340 a cold, determined look came on her mouth. She hid the letter under the pile of others, and said not a word about it.

"Didn't you have anything nice in the post for your birthday, mother?" said Paul.

"Quite moderately nice," she said, her voice cold and absent.

She went away to town without saying more.

---

17. **drapers:** British term for a dealer in cloth and dry goods.

MAKE JUDGMENTS

How do Uncle Oscar's actions in lines 288–314 affect your opinion of him? Explain.

_____

_____

_____

_____

MAKE INFERENCES

Reread the boxed text. In what way does this passage reflect the narrator's **omniscient point of view?**

_____

_____

_____

_____

Underline examples that support your answer. ✏

But in the afternoon Uncle Oscar appeared. He said Paul's mother had had a long interview with the lawyer, asking if the whole five thousand could not be advanced at once, as she was in debt. ▶

"What do you think, uncle?" said the boy.

350 "I leave it to you, son."

"Oh, let her have it, then! We can get some more with the other," said the boy.

"A bird in the hand is worth two in the bush, laddie!" said Uncle Oscar.

"But I'm sure to *know* for the Grand National; or the Lincolnshire; or else the Derby.[18] I'm sure to know for *one* of them," said Paul.

So Uncle Oscar signed the agreement, and Paul's mother touched[19] the whole five thousand. Then something very curious happened. The voices in the house suddenly went mad, like a chorus of frogs on a spring evening. There were certain new furnishings, and Paul had a tutor. He was 360 *really* going to Eton, his father's school, in the following autumn. There were flowers in the winter, and a blossoming of the luxury Paul's mother had been used to. And yet the voices in the house, behind the sprays of mimosa and almond-blossom, and from under the piles of <u>iridescent</u> cushions, simply trilled and screamed in a sort of ecstasy: "There *must* be more money! Oh-h-h; there *must* be more money. Oh, now, now-w! Now-w-w—there *must* be more money!—more than ever! More than ever!"

It frightened Paul terribly. He studied away at his Latin and Greek with his tutor. But his intense hours were spent with Bassett. The Grand National had gone by: he had not "known," and had lost a hundred 370 pounds. Summer was at hand. He was in agony for the Lincoln. But even for the Lincoln he didn't "know," and he lost fifty pounds. He became wild-eyed and strange, as if something were going to explode in him.

"Let it alone, son! Don't you bother about it!" urged Uncle Oscar. But it was as if the boy couldn't really hear what his uncle was saying.

"I've got to know for the Derby! I've got to know for the Derby!" the child reiterated, his big blue eyes blazing with a sort of madness.

His mother noticed how <u>overwrought</u> he was.

"You'd better go to the seaside. Wouldn't you like to go now to the seaside, instead of waiting? I think you'd better," she said, looking down at 380 him anxiously, her heart curiously heavy because of him.

But the child lifted his uncanny blue eyes.

18. **Grand National . . . Derby:** three major English horse races held annually. The Derby is England's best-known flat-track race.

19. **touched:** took.

"I couldn't possibly go before the Derby, mother!" he said. "I couldn't possibly!"

"Why not?" she said, her voice becoming heavy when she was opposed. "Why not? You can still go from the seaside to see the Derby with your Uncle Oscar, if that's what you wish. No need for you to wait here. Besides, I think you care too much about these races. It's a bad sign. My family has been a gambling family, and you won't know till you grow up how much damage it has done. But it has done damage. I shall have to send Bassett away, and ask Uncle Oscar not to talk racing to you, unless you promise to be reasonable about it: go away to the seaside and forget it. You're all nerves!"

"I'll do what you like, mother, so long as you don't send me away till after the Derby," the boy said.

"Send you away from where? Just from this house?"

"Yes," he said, gazing at her.

"Why, you curious child, what makes you care about this house so much, suddenly? I never knew you loved it."

He gazed at her without speaking. He had a secret within a secret, something he had not divulged, even to Bassett or to his Uncle Oscar.

But his mother, after standing undecided and a little bit sullen for some moments, said:

"Very well, then! Don't go to the seaside till after the Derby, if you don't wish it. But promise me you won't let your nerves go to pieces. Promise you won't think so much about horse-racing and *events,* as you call them!"

"Oh no," said the boy casually. "I won't think much about them, mother. You needn't worry. I wouldn't worry, mother, if I were you."

"If you were me and I were you," said his mother, "I wonder what we *should* do!"

"But you know you needn't worry, mother, don't you?" the boy repeated.

"I should be awfully glad to know it," she said wearily.

"Oh, well, you *can,* you know. I mean, you *ought* to know you needn't worry," he insisted.

"Ought I? Then I'll see about it," she said.

Paul's secret of secrets was his wooden horse, that which had no name. Since he was emancipated from a nurse and a nursery-governess, he had had his rocking-horse removed to his own bedroom at the top of the house. ◀

"Surely you're too big for a rocking-horse!" his mother had remonstrated.

"Well, you see, mother, till I can have a *real* horse, I like to have *some* sort of animal about," had been his quaint answer.

"Do you feel he keeps you company?" she laughed.

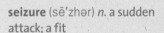

"Oh yes! He's very good, he always keeps me company, when I'm there," said Paul.

So the horse, rather shabby, stood in an arrested prance in the boy's bedroom.

The Derby was drawing near, and the boy grew more and more tense. He hardly heard what was spoken to him, he was very frail, and his eyes were really uncanny. His mother had sudden strange <u>seizures</u> of uneasiness about him. Sometimes, for half an hour, she would feel a
430 sudden anxiety about him that was almost anguish. She wanted to rush to him at once, and know he was safe.

Two nights before the Derby, she was at a big party in town, when one of her rushes of anxiety about her boy, her first-born, gripped her heart till she could hardly speak. She fought with the feeling, might and main,[20] for she believed in common sense. But it was too strong. She had to leave the dance and go downstairs to telephone to the country. The children's nursery-governess was terribly surprised and startled at being rung up in the night.

"Are the children all right, Miss Wilmot?"

440 "Oh yes, they are quite all right."

"Master Paul? Is he all right?"

"He went to bed as right as a trivet.[21] Shall I run up and look at him?"

"No," said Paul's mother reluctantly. "No! Don't trouble. It's all right. Don't sit up. We shall be home fairly soon." She did not want her son's privacy intruded upon.

"Very good," said the governess.

It was about one o'clock when Paul's mother and father drove up to their house. All was still. Paul's mother went to her room and slipped off her white fur cloak. She had told her maid not to wait up for her. She
450 heard her husband downstairs, mixing a whisky and soda.

And then, because of the strange anxiety at her heart, she stole upstairs to her son's room. Noiselessly she went along the upper corridor. Was there a faint noise? What was it? ▶

She stood, with arrested muscles, outside his door, listening. There was a strange, heavy, and yet not loud noise. Her heart stood still. It was a soundless noise, yet rushing and powerful. Something huge, in violent,

seizure (sē′zhər) *n.* a sudden attack; a fit

TESTSMART

Which passage could only have been written in the omniscient point of view?

(A) lines 426–431

(B) lines 439–441

(C) lines 442–445

(D) lines 447–450

TIP A passage written in the **omniscient point of view** presents the thoughts and feelings of more than one character. Reread each set of lines and look for a passage that tells what more than one character thinks and feels.

---

20. **might and main:** with all her strength.

21. **as right as a trivet:** in fine condition.

hushed motion. What was it? What in God's name was it? She ought to know. She felt that she knew the noise. She knew what it was.

Yet she could not place it. She couldn't say what it was. And on and on
460 it went, like a madness.

Softly, frozen with anxiety and fear, she turned the door handle.

The room was dark. Yet in the space near the window, she heard and saw something plunging to and fro. She gazed in fear and amazement.

Then suddenly she switched on the light, and saw her son, in his green pajamas, madly surging on the rocking-horse. The blaze of light suddenly lit him up, as he urged the wooden horse, and lit her up, as she stood, blonde, in her dress of pale green and crystal, in the doorway.

"Paul!" she cried. "Whatever are you doing?"

"It's Malabar!" he screamed in a powerful, strange voice. "It's Malabar!"
470 His eyes blazed at her for one strange and senseless second, as he ceased urging his wooden horse. Then he fell with a crash to the ground, and she, all her tormented motherhood flooding upon her, rushed to gather him up.

But he was unconscious, and unconscious he remained, with some brain-fever. He talked and tossed, and his mother sat stonily by his side.

"Malabar! It's Malabar! Bassett, Bassett, I *know*! It's Malabar!" ◀

So the child cried, trying to get up and urge the rocking-horse that gave him his inspiration.

"What does he mean by Malabar?" asked the heart-frozen mother.

"I don't know," said the father stonily.
480 "What does he mean by Malabar?" she asked her brother Oscar.

"It's one of the horses running for the Derby," was the answer.

And, in spite of himself, Oscar Cresswell spoke to Bassett, and himself put a thousand on Malabar: at fourteen to one.

The third day of the illness was critical: they were waiting for a change. The boy, with his rather long, curly hair, was tossing ceaselessly on the pillow. He neither slept nor regained consciousness, and his eyes were like blue stones. His mother sat, feeling her heart had gone, turned actually into a stone.

In the evening, Oscar Cresswell did not come, but Bassett sent a
490 message, saying could he come up for one moment, just one moment? Paul's mother was very angry at the intrusion, but on second thoughts she agreed. The boy was the same. Perhaps Bassett might bring him to consciousness.

The gardener, a shortish fellow with a little brown mustache and sharp little brown eyes, tiptoed into the room, touched his imaginary cap to Paul's mother, and stole to the bedside, staring with glittering, smallish eyes at the tossing, dying child.

ANALYZE

Reread the boxed text. How does this passage help convey the story's **theme?**

_____

_____

_____

_____

"Master Paul!" he whispered. "Master Paul! Malabar came in first all right, a clean win. I did as you told me. You've made over seventy thousand pounds, you have; you've got over eighty thousand.[22] Malabar came in all right, Master Paul." ▶

"Malabar! Malabar! Did I say Malabar, mother? Did I say Malabar? Do you think I'm lucky, mother? I knew Malabar, didn't I? Over eighty thousand pounds! I call that lucky, don't you, mother? Over eighty thousand pounds! I knew, didn't I know I knew? Malabar came in all right. If I ride my horse till I'm sure, then I tell you, Bassett, you can go as high as you like. Did you go for all you were worth, Bassett?"

"I went a thousand on it, Master Paul."

"I never told you, mother, that if I can ride my horse, and *get there,* then I'm absolutely sure—oh, absolutely! Mother, did I ever tell you? I *am* lucky!"

"No, you never did," said his mother.

But the boy died in the night.

And even as he lay dead, his mother heard her brother's voice saying to her: "My God, Hester, you're eighty-odd thousand to the good, and a poor devil of a son to the bad. But, poor devil, poor devil, he's best gone out of a life where he rides his rocking-horse to find a winner."

DRAW CONCLUSIONS

What **motivation** do you think Bassett has for telling Paul that Malabar won the Derby?

_____

_____

_____

Big Question ?

Reread your conclusion about money and happiness on page 233. How has reading "The Rocking-Horse Winner" affected your views?

_____

_____

---

22. **eighty thousand:** the equivalent of about $4 million in today's dollars.

Reading Comprehension

DIRECTIONS *Answer these questions about "The Rocking-Horse Winner" by filling in the correct ovals.*

1. Paul's parents consider their family to be superior to other families because they have

    (A) wealthy friends and relatives

    (B) pride in their accomplishments

    (C) expensive tastes and fine things

    (D) more money than other families

2. Which sentence best states the theme of this story?

    (A) Obsession with money is destructive.

    (B) Materialism is a superficial value.

    (C) The upper class can be irresponsible.

    (D) Children should not be permitted to have money.

3. When Paul's mother receives a letter informing her of an anonymous birthday gift, her reaction suggests that she feels

    (A) grateful

    (B) curious

    (C) dissatisfied

    (D) happy

4. Which passage could only have been narrated from the omniscient point of view?

    (A) lines 286–293

    (B) lines 315–319

    (C) lines 346–352

    (D) lines 373–380

5. Which of the following is most likely Bassett's motivation for keeping Paul's betting a secret?

    (A) fear

    (B) love

    (C) greed

    (D) loyalty

6. A third-person omniscient narrator is

    (A) an all-knowing character in a story

    (B) an all-knowing outside observer

    (C) a narrator who focuses on one character

    (D) a narrator who misleads the reader

7. The word *assertion* (line 96) means

    (A) polite request

    (B) timid suggestion

    (C) bold statement

    (D) sincere apology

8. The most likely meaning of the word *remonstrated* (line 418) is

    (A) heartily agreed

    (B) suggested politely

    (C) questioned intently

    (D) forcefully objected

For help, use the **Test-Taker's Toolkit** below.

Responding in Writing

9. Short Response Imagine that Paul himself is narrating "The Rocking-Horse Winner." Choose a short scene from the story (other than the last scene) that you would like to retell from Paul's point of view. Rewrite the scene using the first-person point of view, putting Paul in the storyteller's chair.

_____

_____

_____

_____

_____

_____

TEST-TAKER'S TOOLKIT

- ⊗ **ACADEMIC VOCABULARY** Remember that a **first-person** narrator refers to himself or herself as _I_.

- ⊗ **GRAPHIC ORGANIZER** Reread the scene you have selected to help you remember the details. Then use the chart below to help you plan your response.

The scene I have chosen: _____

page: _____   lines: _____

Paul would think: _____

_____

He would feel: _____

_____

He would say: _____

_____

Money Can't Buy Happiness. Er, Can It?
NEWSPAPER ARTICLE

Use with "The Rocking-Horse Winner," p. 232

What's the Connection?

"The Rocking-Horse Winner" is a devastating portrait of a family obsessed with material wealth. In the newspaper article you are about to read, a prominent economist and political columnist looks at the benefits as well as the drawbacks of consumer overspending.

DISCUSS Shopping malls, online stores, luxury boutiques, and superstores have one thing in common—they all reverberate with the constant hum of money changing hands. What effects do you think consumer spending habits have on the economy as a whole, and on individuals? Discuss this question with a partner. Write your ideas in the graphic organizer below.

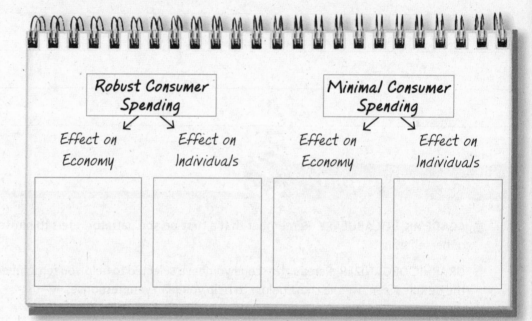

LEARN THE SKILL: IDENTIFY FACTS AND OPINIONS

Nonfiction texts often include a mix of **facts** and **opinions.**

- A **fact** is a statement that can be proven by checking another source. Facts include statistics, dates, and other verifiable data. A factual account is an accurate recording of what people did, said, or believed.

- An **opinion** is a statement of belief or judgment. Opinions cannot be proven. Words such as *better, worse, impressive,* and *shameful* signal that a statement is an opinion.

For more on identifying fact and opinion, see the Evaluate Evidence entry in the Nonfiction Skills Handbook beginning on page R2.

Money Can't Buy Happiness. Er, Can It?

by Paul Krugman
from *The New York Times*

SET A PURPOSE

A few weeks ago my wife and I finally gave in to the pressures of modern life and acquired a cell phone. But it turned out that once we had the thing we had a few questions—questions we couldn't get answered, because customer service was swamped with similar calls from the thousands of other people who had recently signed on.

Meanwhile, my parents started calling contractors about some minor work on their house—only to be told that every carpenter and
10 plumber in the area was booked well into next year.

Talk to almost any middle-class American, and you will hear similar stories—about poor service, excessive traffic, overpriced hous-
ing and so on. In fact, there seems to be a sort of rising chorus of complaints about the annoyances of prosperity—complaints, in effect,
20 that spending lots of money isn't as gratifying as people expected it to be. Most of this is petty stuff, but it is just possible that the chorus of complaints marks the beginning of a broader shift in attitudes—a shift

SYNTHESIZE

What do the two anecdotes the author relates in lines 1–11 have in common?

that will be healthy if it doesn't come too quickly.

Of course, people don't complain about the disappointments of prosperity unless they are prosperous, and in a way all this whining is a symptom of a remarkably successful era in American economic history. Still, you don't have to be an ascetic to wonder if there isn't something a bit manic about the pace of getting and—especially—spending in fin-de-siecle America.

Even the dry statistics suggest that something a little strange is going on. Consider: we are now eight years into an economic expansion. Consumer spending traditionally lags behind the economy as a whole in boom times, because families figure that times will not always be that good and that they should save for a rainy day. ◀

This time, however, consumers are leading the charge: while the economy expanded an impressive 4 percent between the first quarter of 1998 and the first quarter of 1999, consumption grew 5.5 percent, and spending on consumer durables—cell phones, bathroom fixtures, S.U.V.'s and home entertainment systems—surged an incredible 12 percent.

There are at least two reasons to question whether America's consumption boom is really a good thing.

One is that by conventional standards, the typical American family is being a bit, well, imprudent in spending so much—indeed, personal savings, never high in this country, have now disappeared almost completely. True, millions of families have seen their wealth surge because of a soaring stock market, but while more people than ever own stock, most still have no significant personal stake in the market.

You might argue that ordinary families are spending freely, despite sluggish wage growth, because they believe that prosperity is here to stay. But survey evidence suggests that many workers remain nervous about job security, a nervousness that manifests itself in a surprising reluctance to demand wage increases.

So why is spending so high? Much of the surge is driven by those families that do own a lot of stock and have been willing to treat recent capital gains not only as durable but as likely to continue. And at least some of the rest is the result of what Robert Frank calls luxury fever: families with annual incomes of $30,000 try to emulate the consumption of those with $60,000, who try to emulate those with $120,000, and so on. Ultimately we are all trying to keep up with the Gateses,[1] and some of us really can't afford it. ◀

---

1. **Gateses:** a reference to Bill Gates, cofounder of Microsoft and one of the richest men in the world.

FACTS AND OPINIONS

Reread the boxed text. Underline the **opinions** the author gives. ✐

SPECIALIZED Vocabulary

The term *capital gains* (line 92) refers to the profit that results from the sale of an asset, such as shares in a stock. Why might it be unwise to treat capital gains as if they were likely to continue?

And this leads to a deeper concern: there is good reason to think that even those consumers who can afford all this spending will eventually find that they can't get no satisfaction. It is hard to talk about this without sounding either moralistic or supercilious, but it turns out that the folk wisdom is backed by hard statistical evidence: you really can't buy happiness, certainly not for society as a whole.

Partly this is because of congestion effects like the ones my family is experiencing: when few people have cars, the one-car family is king, but when everyone has two, a lot of time is spent in traffic jams.

A more important point, probably, is that human beings are hard-wired to judge themselves not by their absolute standard of living, but in comparison to others. It may be true that in material terms today's borderline poor live as well as the upper-middle class did a few decades back, but that does not stop them from feeling poor. And consumer spending ultimately disappoints because of habituation: once you have become accustomed to a given standard of living, the thrill is gone.

But there is one very powerful argument that can be made on behalf of recent American consumerism: not that it is good for consumers, but that it has been good for producers. You see, spending may not produce happiness, but it does create jobs, and unemployment is very effective at creating misery.

Better to have manic consumers, American style, than the depressive consumers of Japan—a country where the only consumer durables that have sold well the last few years are home safes, the better to hoard cash in.

This attempt to keep up with people richer than ourselves, however ineffectual it may have been on its own terms, has allowed the United States economy to sail through a global financial storm unscathed, and arguably made the difference between a global wobble and a repeat of the 1930's.

There is a strong element of rat race in America's consumer-led boom, but those rats racing in their cages are what have kept the wheels of commerce turning. And while it will be a shame if Americans continue to compete over who can own the most toys, the worst thing of all will be if the competition comes to a sudden stop. ▶

Now there are faint hints in popular culture—though certainly not yet in the spending numbers—that Americans are starting to become disillusioned with high consumption, that in years to come the American consumer will become wiser and more prudent. Let's hope it really happens—but not too fast.

Reading Comprehension

DIRECTIONS *Answer these questions about the two selections in this lesson by filling in the correct ovals.*

1. In "Money Can't Buy Happiness. Er, Can It?," Paul Krugman argues that America's consumption boom is

   A) bad for the economy but good for individuals

   B) good for the economy but bad for individuals

   C) neither good nor bad

   D) not as durable as Japan's spending boom

2. Krugman hopes Americans will not become more prudent spenders all of a sudden because doing so would

   A) help producers in other countries

   B) cause a rise in inflation

   C) lower their standard of living

   D) harm America's economy

3. Which of the following statements is an opinion?

   A) Customer service was swamped with similar calls.

   B) The economy expanded 4 percent in just one year.

   C) This whining is a symptom of a remarkably successful era.

   D) We are now eight years into an economic expansion.

4. Which of the following statements is a fact?

   A) Millions of families have seen their wealth surge.

   B) Consumer spending ultimately disappoints people.

   C) Typical Americans are imprudent spenders.

   D) We are all trying to keep up with the Gateses.

5. Which term used in the article best describes the problem that tears apart the family in "The Rocking-Horse Winner"?

   A) congestion effects (lines 116–117)

   B) luxury fever (line 96)

   C) the annoyances of prosperity (lines 18–19)

   D) habituation (line 134)

6. To which group described in the article would the family in "The Rocking-Horse Winner" belong?

   A) the prosperous

   B) the borderline poor

   C) depressive consumers

   D) manic consumers

7. The word *ascetic* in line 35 of the article can describe someone who is

   A) very frugal

   B) a frequent complainer

   C) an artist

   D) highly prosperous

8. The most likely meaning of *supercilious* in line 111 of the news article is

   A) ethical   C) superstitious

   B) scornful   D) pathetic

Timed Writing Practice

PROMPT

What do you consider to be a healthy attitude toward money?
Write a (persuasive essay) in which you try to convince readers
to make one change in their thinking or behavior that will help
them feel more secure about their financial situation. Provide
at least three reasons and one or two examples to support
each reason. Draw examples from your own experiences and
observations as well as from the two selections you have read.

BUDGET YOUR TIME

You have **45 minutes** to respond.
Decide how much time to spend
on each step.

Analyze _____

Plan _____

Write _____ 45

Review _____

TEST-TAKER'S TOOLKIT

1. ANALYZE THE PROMPT

A. Underline the question in the prompt and circle key words in the sentences
that follow the question. The writing form has been circled for you.

B. Jot down a list of the key elements you need to include in your persuasive essay.

2. PLAN YOUR RESPONSE

A. Make notes In the chart, list three good
reasons for your opinion and examples to
support your reasons.

B. Organize your information In your
introduction, identify the topic of your essay
and present a thesis statement that clearly
identifies the claim you are making. Then
you can write a paragraph for each reason
you noted in the chart. Use your examples
to support each reason. Be sure to include a
conclusion in which you wrap up your ideas.

Reason 1:	Example(s):
Reason 2:	Example(s):
Reason 3:	Example(s):

3. WRITE AND REVIEW

A. You might use a quote to help you craft a memorable ending. Here is an example:

> Author Alexandre Dumas said that money "is a good servant but a bad master."
> Don't let money rule your life!

B. Be sure to leave time to check your spelling and grammar.

UNIT 6

MODERN AND CONTEMPORARY LITERATURE

LESSON 6B

Shooting an Elephant

BY GEORGE ORWELL

RELATED NONFICTION

from *The Trouser People: A Story of Burma*

How important is it to "SAVE FACE"?

George Orwell once said, "An autobiography is only to be trusted when it reveals something disgraceful." Most people have done something that they regret or about which they feel ashamed. Sometimes people make the wrong decision in order to avoid looking foolish. Character flaws are difficult to admit, and people often go to great lengths—even compromising their values—to protect their reputation.

QUICKWRITE Recall a time when you did something you later regretted in order to "save face." Write a short description of the incident on the notebook. Tell what you might do differently if you encountered a similar situation today.

What I did to "save face": _____

_____

_____

_____

_____

_____

What I might do differently today: _____

_____

_____

_____

_____

_____

ASSESSMENT GOALS

By the end of this lesson, you will be able to . . .

- analyze a reflective essay
- use critical thinking skills to analyze text
- identify characteristics of a historical narrative
- analyze a writing prompt and plan a personal narrative

Reflective Essay

In a **REFLECTIVE ESSAY**, the writer makes a connection between a **PERSONAL OBSERVATION** and a **UNIVERSAL IDEA**—such as love, honor, or freedom. Review the characteristics of a reflective essay in the graphic below.

In "Shooting an Elephant," George Orwell reflects on a specific incident from his time as a young police officer in British-ruled Burma during the 1920s. As you read the essay, notice how Orwell uses his personal experience in the British Empire to convey a message about colonialism.

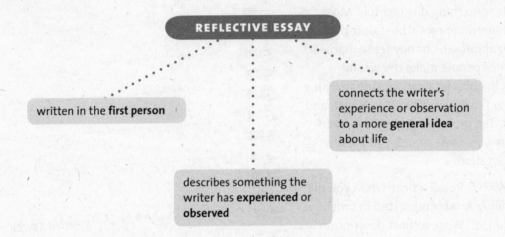

REFLECTIVE ESSAY

written in the **first person**

connects the writer's experience or observation to a more **general idea** about life

describes something the writer has **experienced** or **observed**

ADDITIONAL TERMS FOR CRITICAL ANALYSIS

Knowing these additional terms will help you get the most out of this reflective essay.

- **IRONY** is a contrast between expectation and reality. **SITUATIONAL IRONY** occurs when a character or a reader expects one thing to happen but something else actually happens.

- **DESCRIPTION** is writing that helps readers understand exactly what scenes, characters, and events are like. To create vivid descriptions, writers often use **SENSORY LANGUAGE** that appeals to the five senses and **FIGURATIVE LANGUAGE** that helps readers form a mental picture of what is being described.

Shooting an Elephant

George Orwell

MARK & ANALYZE
Read this selection once on your own, marking the text in any way that is helpful to you. Then read the selection a second time, using the questions in the margins to help you analyze the text. When you see this pencil ✏, you'll be asked to mark up the text.

BACKGROUND Orwell's essay is set in Burma, a Southeast Asian country now known as Myanmar. In a series of wars in the 19th century, the British gained control of Burma and made it a province of British India. The Burmese resented British rule, under which they endured poverty and a lack of political and religious freedom. Like many of his fellow British officers, Orwell was inexperienced in police work when he arrived in Burma at age 19.

In Moulmein, in Lower Burma,[1] I was hated by large numbers of people—the only time in my life that I have been important enough for this to happen to me. I was subdivisional police officer of the town, and in an aimless, petty kind of way anti-European feeling was very bitter. No one had the guts to raise a riot, but if a European woman went through the bazaars alone somebody would probably spit betel juice[2] over her dress. As a police officer I was an obvious target and was baited whenever it seemed safe to do so. When a nimble Burman tripped me up on the football[3] field and the referee (another Burman) looked the other way, the crowd yelled with hideous laughter. This happened more than once. In the end the sneering yellow faces of young men that met me everywhere, the insults hooted after me when I was at a safe distance, got badly on my nerves. The young Buddhist priests were the worst of all. There were

10

---

1. **Moulmein** (mōōl-mān'), **in Lower Burma:** the main city of British-controlled Burma, now the independent Asian nation of Myanmar. Moulmein is now usually called Mawlamyine.

2. **betel** (bēt'l) **juice:** the saliva created when chewing a mixture of betel palm nuts, betel palm leaves, and lime.

3. **football:** soccer.

DRAW CONCLUSIONS

How did Orwell feel about being a police officer in Burma? Underline support for your answer.

_____

_____

imperialism
(ĭm-pîr'ē-ə-lĭz'əm) _n._
the policy of forming and maintaining an empire, especially in the quest for raw materials and more markets

cowed (koud) _adj._ made timid and submissive through fear or awe **cow** _v._

supplant (sə-plănt') _v._ to take the place of

prostrate (prŏs'trāt') _adj._ completely submissive

TestSmart

Orwell's observation of the "dirty work of Empire" suggests that imperialism is

(A) evil

(B) temporary

(C) unclean

(D) necessary

TIP This question asks you to link a specific observation to a more general statement. Reread Orwell's **personal observations** about the British rule of its colonies in lines 16–38. What general point is Orwell making about the British?

despotic (dĭ-spŏt'ĭk) _adj._ ruling absolutely without allowing any dissent; tyrannical

several thousands of them in the town and none of them seemed to have anything to do except stand on street corners and jeer at Europeans.

All this was perplexing and upsetting. For at that time I had already made up my mind that **imperialism** was an evil thing and the sooner I chucked up[4] my job and got out of it the better. Theoretically—and secretly, of course—I was all for the Burmese and all against their
20 oppressors, the British. As for the job I was doing, I hated it more bitterly than I can perhaps make clear. In a job like that you see the dirty work of Empire at close quarters. The wretched prisoners huddling in the stinking cages of the lock-ups, the gray, **cowed** faces of the long-term convicts, the scarred buttocks of the men who had been flogged with bamboos—all these oppressed me with an intolerable sense of guilt. But I could get nothing into perspective. I was young and ill-educated and I had had to think out my problems in the utter silence that is imposed on every Englishman in the East. I did not even know that the British Empire is dying, still less did I know that it is a great deal better than the
30 younger empires that are going to **supplant** it. All I knew was that I was stuck between my hatred of the empire I served and my rage against the evil-spirited little beasts who tried to make my job impossible. With one part of my mind I thought of the British Raj[5] as an unbreakable tyranny, as something clamped down, _in saecula saeculorum,_[6] upon the will of **prostrate** peoples; with another part I thought that the greatest joy in the world would be to drive a bayonet into a Buddhist priest's guts. Feelings like these are the normal by-products of imperialism; ask any Anglo-Indian official, if you can catch him off duty.

One day something happened which in a roundabout way was
40 enlightening. It was a tiny incident in itself, but it gave me a better glimpse than I had had before of the real nature of imperialism—the real motives for which **despotic** governments act. Early one morning the subinspector at a police station the other end of the town rang me up on the phone and said that an elephant was ravaging the bazaar. Would I please come and do something about it? I did not know what I could do, but I wanted to see what was happening and I got on to a pony and started out. I took my rifle, an old .44 Winchester and much too small to kill an elephant, but I thought the noise might be useful _in terrorem._[7]

---

4. **chucked up:** threw off; gave up.

5. **British Raj:** India and adjoining areas (such as Burma) controlled by Britain in the 19th and early 20th centuries. _Raj_ is the word for "kingdom" or "rule" in Hindi, a chief language of India.

6. _**in saecula saeculorum**_ (ĭn sĕk'yə-lə sĕk-yə-lôr'əm) _Latin:_ forever and ever.

7. _**in terrorem**_ (ĭn tĕ-rôr'əm) _Latin:_ for terror.

Various Burmans stopped me on the way and told me about the elephant's
doings. It was not, of course, a wild elephant, but a tame one which had
gone "must."[8] It had been chained up as tame elephants always are when
their attack of "must" is due, but on the previous night it had broken
its chain and escaped. Its mahout,[9] the only person who could manage
it when it was in that state, had set out in pursuit, but had taken the
wrong direction and was now twelve hours' journey away, and in the
morning the elephant had suddenly reappeared in the town. The Burmese
population had no weapons and were quite helpless against it. It had
already destroyed somebody's bamboo hut, killed a cow and raided some
fruit-stalls and devoured the stock; also it had met the municipal rubbish
van, and, when the driver jumped out and took to his heels, had turned
the van over and inflicted violences upon it. ▶

The Burmese subinspector and some Indian constables[10] were waiting
for me in the quarter where the elephant had been seen. It was a very poor
quarter, a <u>labyrinth</u> of squalid bamboo huts, thatched with palm-leaf,
winding all over a steep hillside. I remember that it was a cloudy stuffy
morning at the beginning of the rains. We began questioning the people
as to where the elephant had gone, and, as usual, failed to get any definite
information. That is invariably the case in the East; a story always sounds
clear enough at a distance, but the nearer you get to the scene of events the
vaguer it becomes. Some of the people said that the elephant had gone in
one direction, some said that he had gone in another, some professed not
even to have heard of any elephant. I had almost made up my mind that
the whole story was a pack of lies, when we heard yells a little distance
away. There was a loud, scandalized cry of "Go away, child! Go away this
instant!" and an old woman with a switch in her hand came round the
corner of a hut, violently shooing away a crowd of naked children. Some
more women followed, clicking their tongues and exclaiming; evidently
there was something there that the children ought not to have seen. I
rounded the hut and saw a man's dead body sprawling in the mud. He was
an Indian, a black Dravidian coolie,[11] almost naked, and he could not have
been dead many minutes. The people said that the elephant had come
suddenly upon him round the corner of the hut, caught him with its trunk,
put its foot on his back and ground him into the earth. This was the rainy

ANALYZE

Reread lines 39–61. Find and
underline the sentence that
foreshadows the **universal
truth** Orwell comes to realize
later in the story. 🖉

labyrinth (lăb′ə-rĭnth′) *n.* an
intricate structure of winding
passages; a maze

8. **gone "must":** had an attack of must, a dangerous frenzy that periodically seizes
   male elephants.
9. **mahout** (mə-hout′): an elephant keeper.
10. **constables:** police officers.
11. **Dravidian** (drə-vĭd′ē-ən) **coolie:** a dark-skinned menial laborer from the south of
    India.

season and the ground was soft, and his face had scored a trench a foot deep
and a couple of yards long. He was lying on his belly with arms crucified
and head sharply twisted to one side. His face was coated with mud,
the eyes wide open, the teeth bared and grinning with an expression of
unendurable agony. (Never tell me, by the way, that the dead look peaceful.
Most of the corpses I have seen looked devilish.) The friction of the great
90   beast's foot had stripped the skin from his back as neatly as one skins a
rabbit. As soon as I saw the dead man I sent an orderly[12] to a friend's
house nearby to borrow an elephant rifle. I had already sent back the pony,
not wanting it to go mad with fright and throw me if it smelled the
elephant. ◀

ANALYZE

Underline the details in the
boxed text that help you
picture the dead man. ✎

On the lines below, write one
example of a **sensory detail**
and one example of **figurative
language** contained in this
description.

_____

_____

_____

_____

The orderly came back in a few minutes with a rifle and five cartridges,
and meanwhile some Burmans had arrived and told us that the elephant
was in the paddy fields[13] below, only a few hundred yards away. As I
started forward practically the whole population of the quarter flocked
out of the houses and followed me. They had seen the rifle and were all
100   shouting excitedly that I was going to shoot the elephant. They had not
shown much interest in the elephant when he was merely ravaging their
homes, but it was different now that he was going to be shot. It was a bit
of fun to them, as it would be to an English crowd; besides, they wanted
the meat. It made me vaguely uneasy. I had no intention of shooting the
elephant—I had merely sent for the rifle to defend myself if necessary—
and it is always unnerving to have a crowd following you. I marched down
the hill, looking and feeling a fool, with the rifle over my shoulder and
an ever-growing army of people jostling at my heels. At the bottom, when
you got away from the huts, there was a metalled road and beyond that a
110   miry waste of paddy fields a thousand yards across, not yet ploughed but
soggy from the first rains and dotted with coarse grass. The elephant was
standing eighty yards from the road, his left side towards us. He took not
the slightest notice of the crowd's approach. He was tearing up bunches of
grass, beating them against his knees to clean them and stuffing them into
his mouth. ◀

I had halted on the road. As soon as I saw the elephant I knew with
perfect certainty that I ought not to shoot him. It is a serious matter to
shoot a working elephant—it is comparable to destroying a huge and
costly piece of machinery—and obviously one ought not to do it if it can

INTERPRET

Describe what the elephant is
doing. What is **ironic** about this
situation?

_____

_____

_____

_____

---

12. **orderly:** a military aid.
13. **paddy fields:** rice fields.

120 possibly be avoided. And at that distance, peacefully eating, the elephant looked no more dangerous than a cow. I thought then and I think now that his attack of "must" was already passing off; in which case he would merely wander harmlessly about until the mahout came back and caught him. Moreover, I did not in the least want to shoot him. I decided that I would watch him for a little while to make sure that he did not turn savage again, and then go home.

But at that moment I glanced round at the crowd that had followed me. It was an immense crowd, two thousand at the least and growing every minute. It blocked the road for a long distance on either side. I looked
130 at the sea of yellow faces above the <u>garish</u> clothes—faces all happy and excited over this bit of fun, all certain that the elephant was going to be shot. They were watching me as they would watch a conjurer about to perform a trick. They did not like me, but with the magical rifle in my hands I was momentarily worth watching. And suddenly I realized that I should have to shoot the elephant after all. The people expected it of me and I had got to do it; I could feel their two thousand wills pressing me forward, irresistibly. And it was at this moment, as I stood there with the rifle in my hands, that I first grasped the hollowness, the futility of the white man's dominion in the East. Here was I, the white man with
140 his gun, standing in front of the unarmed native crowd—seemingly the leading actor of the piece; but in reality I was only an absurd puppet pushed to and fro by the will of those yellow faces behind. I perceived in this moment that when the white man turns tyrant it is his own freedom that he destroys. He becomes a sort of hollow, posing dummy, the conventionalized figure of a sahib.[14] For it is the condition of his rule that he shall spend his life in trying to impress the "natives," and so in every crisis he has got to do what the "natives" expect of him. He wears a mask, and his face grows to fit it. I had got to shoot the elephant. I had committed myself to doing it when I sent for the rifle. A sahib has got to
150 act like a sahib; he has got to appear resolute, to know his own mind and do definite things. To come all that way, rifle in hand, with two thousand people marching at my heels, and then to trail feebly away, having done nothing—no, that was impossible. The crowd would laugh at me. And my whole life, every white man's life in the East, was one long struggle not to be laughed at. ▶

---

14. **sahib** (sä´ĭb): a title of respect formerly used by native Indians to address a European gentleman.

garish (gâr´ĭsh) *adj.* too bright or showy; gaudy; glaring

ANALYZE

Reread the boxed text. What connection does Orwell draw between his **personal experience** and British colonialism?

_____

_____

_____

_____

Underline the part of the text that expresses the realization of a larger, more **universal idea.** 🖉

But I did not want to shoot the elephant. I watched him beating his bunch of grass against his knees, with that preoccupied grandmotherly air that elephants have. It seemed to me that it would be murder to shoot him. At that age I was not squeamish about killing animals, but I had never
160 shot an elephant and never wanted to. (Somehow it always seems worse to kill a *large* animal.) Besides, there was the beast's owner to be considered. Alive, the elephant was worth at least a hundred pounds; dead, he would only be worth the value of his tusks—five pounds, possibly. But I had got to act quickly. I turned to some experienced-looking Burmans who had been there when we arrived, and asked them how the elephant had been behaving. They all said the same thing: he took no notice of you if you left him alone, but he might charge if you went too close to him.

It was perfectly clear to me what I ought to do. I ought to walk up to within, say, twenty-five yards of the elephant and test his behavior. If
170 he charged I could shoot, if he took no notice of me it would be safe to leave him until the mahout came back. But also I knew that I was going to do no such thing. I was a poor shot with a rifle and the ground was soft mud into which one would sink at every step. If the elephant charged and I missed him, I should have about as much chance as a toad under a steam-roller. But even then I was not thinking particularly of my own skin, only of the watchful yellow faces behind. For at that moment, with the crowd watching me, I was not afraid in the ordinary sense, as I would have been if I had been alone. A white man mustn't be frightened in front of "natives"; and so, in general, he isn't frightened. The sole thought in
180 my mind was that if anything went wrong those two thousand Burmans would see me pursued, caught, trampled on and reduced to a grinning corpse like that Indian up the hill. And if that happened it was quite probable that some of them would laugh. That would never do. There was only one alternative. I shoved the cartridges into the magazine and lay down on the road to get a better aim. ◀

The crowd grew very still, and a deep, low, happy sigh, as of people who see the theater curtain go up at last, breathed from innumerable throats. They were going to have their bit of fun after all. The rifle was a beautiful German thing with cross-hair sights. I did not then know that
190 in shooting an elephant one should shoot to cut an imaginary bar running from ear-hole to ear-hole. I ought, therefore, as the elephant was sideways on, to have aimed straight at his ear-hole; actually I aimed several inches in front of this, thinking the brain would be further forward.

CONTRAST

Contrast the effect that shooting the elephant will likely have on Orwell's public reputation with the effect it will have on his own self-image.

When I pulled the trigger I did not hear the bang or feel the kick—one never does when a shot goes home—but I heard the devilish roar of glee that went up from the crowd. In that instant, in too short a time, one would have thought, even for the bullet to get there, a mysterious, terrible change had come over the elephant. He neither stirred nor fell, but every line of his body had altered. He looked suddenly stricken, shrunken,
200 immensely old, as though the frightful impact of the bullet had paralyzed him without knocking him down. At last, after what seemed a long time—it might have been five seconds, I dare say—he sagged flabbily to his knees. His mouth slobbered. An enormous **senility** seemed to have settled upon him. One could have imagined him thousands of years old. I fired again into the same spot. At the second shot he did not collapse but climbed with desperate slowness to his feet and stood weakly upright, with legs sagging and head drooping. I fired a third time. That was the shot that did for him. You could see the agony of it jolt his whole body and knock the last remnant of strength from his legs. But in falling he seemed
210 for a moment to rise, for as his hind legs collapsed beneath him he seemed to tower upwards like a huge rock toppling, his trunk reaching skyward like a tree. He trumpeted, for the first and only time. And then down he came, his belly towards me, with a crash that seemed to shake the ground even where I lay.

I got up. The Burmans were already racing past me across the mud. It was obvious that the elephant would never rise again, but he was not dead. He was breathing very rhythmically with long rattling gasps, his great mound of a side painfully rising and falling. His mouth was wide open—I could see far down into caverns of pale pink throat. I waited a
220 long time for him to die, but his breathing did not weaken. Finally I fired my two remaining shots into the spot where I thought his heart must be. The thick blood welled out of him like red velvet, but still he did not die. His body did not even jerk when the shots hit him, the tortured breathing continued without a pause. He was dying, very slowly and in great agony, but in some world remote from me where not even a bullet could damage him further. I felt that I had got to put an end to that dreadful noise. It seemed dreadful to see the great beast lying there, powerless to move and yet powerless to die, and not even to be able to finish him. I sent back for my small rifle and poured shot after shot into his heart and down his
230 throat. They seemed to make no impression. The tortured gasps continued as steadily as the ticking of a clock. ▶

senility (sǐ-nǐl′ǐ-tē) n. the mental deterioration that sometimes comes with old age

TESTSMART

Which line or lines in the boxed text contain a simile that appeals to the sense of hearing?

A lines 217–218

B line 222

C line 226

D lines 230–231

TIP This test question asks you to find one or more lines that contain two types of **description—figurative language** and **sensory language**. To answer, reread each line or set of lines listed above and ask yourself if it contains *both* elements you are looking for.

VOCABULARY

The word *pretext* (line 244) means

(A) permission

(B) prior reason

(C) message

(D) premonition

TIP If a test question asks you to choose the meaning of a word, you can use the **process of elimination** to find the right answer. To answer this question, substitute each answer choice for the word *pretext* in line 244. Eliminate the ones that don't make sense, given the overall story context.

Big Question ?

Does Orwell seem to feel that he made the right choice by shooting the elephant to "save face"? Explain your response. *DRAW CONCLUSIONS*

_____

_____

_____

_____

In the end I could not stand it any longer and went away. I heard later that it took him half an hour to die. Burmans were arriving with dahs[15] and baskets even before I left, and I was told they had stripped his body almost to the bones by the afternoon.

Afterwards, of course, there were endless discussions about the shooting of the elephant. The owner was furious, but he was only an Indian and could do nothing. Besides, legally I had done the right thing, for a mad elephant has to be killed, like a mad dog, if its owner fails to control it.

240 Among the Europeans opinion was divided. The older men said I was right, the younger men said it was a damn shame to shoot an elephant for killing a coolie, because an elephant was worth more than any damn Coringhee[16] coolie. And afterwards I was very glad that the coolie had been killed; it put me legally in the right and it gave me a sufficient pretext for shooting the elephant. I often wondered whether any of the others grasped that I had done it solely to avoid looking a fool. ◄

15. **dahs:** large knives.
16. **Coringhee:** coming from a port in southeastern India.

Reading Comprehension

DIRECTIONS *Answer these questions about "Shooting an Elephant" by filling in the correct ovals.*

1. The incident with the elephant made Orwell realize that he was

   (A) a poor shot with a rifle

   (B) fighting for the wrong side

   (C) capable of violating his conscience

   (D) more powerful than he imagined

2. Orwell's observation of the crowd of Burmese following him (lines 127–155) suggests that oppressed people

   (A) are always unhappy

   (B) develop a cruel streak

   (C) find cruelty humorous

   (D) have power over their oppressors

3. What universal truth is expressed in lines 139–147?

   (A) Those who imprison others imprison themselves.

   (B) Man is a hollow, posing dummy.

   (C) British rule is mostly about impressing native peoples.

   (D) An unarmed native crowd can be menacing.

4. Which lines contain a simile that appeals to the sense of hearing?

   (A) lines 168–169

   (B) lines 174–175

   (C) lines 186–188

   (D) lines 192–193

5. The British think they have control over Burma, but in many ways the Burmese control the British. What is this an example of?

   (A) dramatic tension

   (B) expressive thinking

   (C) descriptive detail

   (D) situational irony

6. Which phrase *best* sums up the attitude of the Burmese toward the British?

   (A) impatient tolerance

   (B) simmering bitterness

   (C) overt and violent hostility

   (D) sorrowful resignation

7. The most likely meaning of the word *conjurer* (line 132) is

   (A) emperor

   (B) magician

   (C) hunter

   (D) marksman

8. Based on context clues in lines 184–185, you can tell that a *magazine* is the

   (A) part of a gun that ejects a bullet

   (B) place where the British store their rifles

   (C) cross-hairs on a German rifle

   (D) compartment from which bullets are fed into the firing chamber

GO ON

For help, use the **Test-Taker's Toolkit** below.

Responding in Writing

9. Short Response Write a paragraph in which you evaluate George Orwell's decision to shoot the elephant. Explain why the decision was so difficult for him, and discuss whether you would have taken the same action.

_____

_____

_____

_____

_____

_____

TEST-TAKER'S TOOLKIT

⊗ **GRAPHIC ORGANIZER** Use the chart below to help you plan your response.

Why the decision was so difficult:
My opinion about Orwell's decision:
Why I feel that way:

What's the Connection?

"Shooting an Elephant" recounts a dramatic incident from the point of view of a British officer in Burma during British rule. This excerpt from the book *The Trouser People* is a historical account of the days and months that followed the British takeover of Burma. It includes the observations of some who witnessed this event firsthand.

PREDICT Imagine that a foreign power has invaded your community. The new rulers declare themselves the owners of the land and everything on it—they also demand complete obedience from everyone who lives there. How do you think people would respond? Discuss this question with a group of classmates. Then fill in the chart below.

from *The Trouser People*
BOOK EXCERPT

Use with "Shooting an Elephant," p. 258

If a foreign power ...	People might ...
threw out old laws and imposed new ones	
sent leaders into exile	
imprisoned people who opposed them	
seized people's wealth and personal property	

LEARN THE SKILL: IDENTIFY CHARACTERISTICS OF A HISTORICAL NARRATIVE

A **narrative** is a story. A **historical narrative** is a nonfiction story about an event in history. The following points will help you to analyze historical narratives:

- Historical narratives are **colorful;** they are not dry, scholarly treatises.
- Historical narratives include **vivid characters,** the unfolding of **dramatic events,** and exciting **pacing.**
- Historical narratives can include such things as **quotes** and **diary entries** from the time period. These can be signaled by **quotation marks, italicized passages,** and **indented text.**

For more on identifying characteristics of a historical narrative, see the Narrative Nonfiction entry in the Nonfiction Skills Handbook beginning on page R2.

SET A PURPOSE

_____

_____

_____

PREVIEW

Look at the photograph. Then underline the title and circle the subtitle on this page. 🖉

1. Who do you think the "Trouser People" might be?

_____

_____

2. Why might the author have chosen this title?

_____

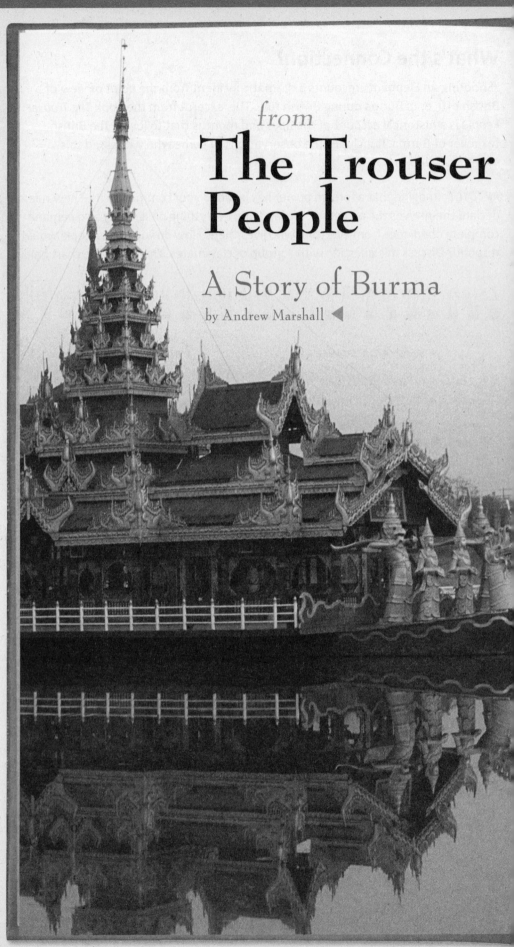

from
The Trouser People

A Story of Burma

by Andrew Marshall ◀

On 20 October 1885 the wife of Lord Dufferin, viceroy of India, made the following entry in her diary: "We breakfasted at eight o'clock. At a quarter past the Viceroy signed the declaration of war with Burmah." And by half past eight the breakfast things were cleared away and all Burma was in British hands. Or so it seemed. Imperial warships steamed up the Irrawaddy, and Mandalay was taken with less than 1,000 troops. Thibaw's last sovereign act was formally to surrender to what a Burmese historian would call "those trousered creatures," the British. The annexation of Upper Burma was announced on 1 January
10 1886, as a New Year's present for Queen Victoria. ▶

King Thibaw left his palace in a covered bullock cart, with Queen Supayalat at his side. Flanked by Welsh Fusiliers, the cart bumped along an unpaved Mandalay street lined with weeping Burmese women. The sun had set by the time this sad procession reached the river bank, and the royals boarded a British steamboat in darkness. Then they were shipped down the Irrawaddy to Rangoon, and from there across the Bay of Bengal to eventual exile in the coastal town of Ratnagiri, south of Bombay. This was the first time the king had ever left the palace; and it was the last time he ever saw Burma. The white elephant died
20 ten days later and, without ceremony, was hauled on to an enormous sledge built by British military carpenters and dragged from the palace for burial. Its death marked the end of the old regime—and, it seemed, an inauspicious start for the new one. ▶

At first the British occupation of Mandalay Palace—now renamed Fort Dufferin—brought little stability to the city. The ease with which Thibaw's puny army had been swept aside left the British unprepared for the fury of the Burmese resistance that came after. The following weeks saw an alarming increase in disorder. Thibaw's scattered troops forged new careers in armed gangs led by princes, patriots or thieves
30 which robbed civilians and attacked British patrols. While walking in the palace grounds one day, Dufferin asked his general how far British power in Burma now extended. The general pointed to a sentry on the ramparts and replied, "Up to that man and no further, sir."

Two months later, in April 1886, George Scott returned to Mandalay—not as a journalist this time, but as a member of a hand-picked cadre of British administrators set up to carry the great imperial gift of civilization into the Burmese wilderness. The city must have seemed scarcely less chaotic than during his first visit, six years before. In the month he arrived, several police officers were hacked to death and a
40 portion of the city was set ablaze by rebels loyal to an exiled son of King Mindon. The climate added to the apocalyptic atmosphere. It was just before the monsoon, the hottest time of the year, recalled

HISTORICAL NARRATIVE

Reread the boxed text. Underline the **diary entry**. 🖉

What is revealed about the attitude of the British toward the Burmese?

_____

_____

_____

_____

INTERPRET

In Burma, white elephants are considered sacred symbols of power and good fortune. Why do you think the author included the story of the white elephant in his **narrative**?

_____

_____

_____

Scott, when scorching winds scoured the dirt streets and "sudden dust-storms made the sky dark at midday."

The British response to the growing chaos in Mandalay was merciless. In the first few weeks alone, dozens of Burmese were summarily tried then publicly executed by firing squad at Fort Dufferin. But it would be years until the city was at peace. News of one insurrection reached Scott as he enjoyed after-dinner coffee and cheroots at the Upper Burma Club, the social focus of colonial life in Mandalay, housed in a sumptuous teak pavilion that had formerly served as Queen Supayalat's private quarters. An old monk claiming to be the reincarnation of a long-dead Burmese prince was marching upon the palace's south gate to reclaim the throne. He was accompanied by a band of devotees, most of them unarmed, who were convinced that the venerable monk possessed the supernatural ability to make them invisible to their enemies. Hadn't he already proved this by walking three times around his monastery and vanishing himself? In the event, Burmese voodoo was no match for Major Dobble of the Indian Army, who opened fire on the approaching band, killing the monk and four of his highly visible followers. Scott, who had abandoned his coffee and dashed to the scene, arrived to find the palace walls splashed with blood. Ten more people were rounded up in the days that followed, tried, then hanged publicly as a warning to anyone else tempted to pit his occult powers against British Maxim guns firing 600 rounds per minute. ◀

As the British imposed order on Mandalay, Scott found that the so-called "City of Gems" was losing its sparkle: "Mandalay is a vastly less interesting place than it used to be," he wrote:

> The pigs have all been eaten up and the pariah dogs poisoned by municipal order; A, B, and C roads testify to the unromantic stolidity of the Military Intelligence Department; electric trams make it easier for the Burman to move to the suburbs and leave the town to the hustling foreigner. There are no agreeable scallywags. The Palace, instead of being tawdrily magnificent, smells horribly of bats. ◀

Fortunately, Scott's work lay in the rugged Shan mountains that rose darkly to the east of the city. "There is in this particular region," he observed, "a collection of races diverse in feature, language and customs, as cannot, perhaps, be paralleled in any other part of the world." Scott would spend a quarter of a century exploring this vast, landlocked nowhereland. Acutely aware of how British influence erased the ancient societies it touched, he would study the tribes he encountered in intimate detail, record their beliefs and rituals, learn their languages, and photograph their way of life.

TestSmart

VOCABULARY

The word *insurrection* (line 48) means

- Ⓐ argument
- Ⓑ squeamish
- Ⓒ revolt
- Ⓓ development

TIP A test question may ask you to figure out the meaning of an unfamiliar word. Sometimes the **context clues** appear in later sentences. To answer this question, reread lines 52–60.

HISTORICAL NARRATIVE

Underline details in the **indented text** (lines 69–74) that describe Burmese life before British occupation. 🖊

What do these details suggest about Scott's feelings toward the two cultures?

_____

_____

_____

_____

_____

Reading Comprehension

DIRECTIONS *Answer these questions about the two selections in this lesson by filling in the correct ovals.*

1. George Scott's observations in the excerpt from *The Trouser People* suggest that the takeover of Burma was

   Ⓐ unfortunate but necessary

   Ⓑ ill advised

   Ⓒ well executed

   Ⓓ chaotic and destructive

2. Which term *best* describes how the British treated the royalty of Burma?

   Ⓐ ceremonially

   Ⓑ disrespectfully

   Ⓒ inhumanely

   Ⓓ carefully

3. When the Burmese revolted in Mandalay, the British responded by

   Ⓐ destroying the "city of gems"

   Ⓑ executing people as a warning

   Ⓒ exiling the royals

   Ⓓ gathering at the Upper Burma Club

4. The last paragraph of *The Trouser People* focuses on George Scott's

   Ⓐ fascination with diverse cultures

   Ⓑ desire to spread British influence

   Ⓒ administrative work in Mandalay

   Ⓓ dislike of imperialistic violence

5. Details in both *The Trouser People* and "Shooting an Elephant" illuminate all of the following *except* the

   Ⓐ contrasts between two cultures

   Ⓑ violence of everyday life

   Ⓒ sacredness of the white elephant

   Ⓓ mixed feelings among the occupiers

6. *The Trouser People* is different from "Shooting an Elephant" because it is

   Ⓐ about a dramatic incident

   Ⓑ not a primary source

   Ⓒ set in Burma

   Ⓓ autobiographical

7. In line 36 of *The Trouser People*, the word *cadre* means a

   Ⓐ place where secret business is conducted

   Ⓑ Military Intelligence Unit

   Ⓒ place where exiled royalty are sent

   Ⓓ core unit of a larger organization

8. What is the meaning of *apocalyptic* in line 41 of *The Trouser People*?

   Ⓐ filled with excitement

   Ⓑ likely to change

   Ⓒ prophetic of ultimate doom

   Ⓓ weakened in strength

GO ON

Timed Writing Practice

BUDGET YOUR TIME

You have **45 minutes** to respond. Decide how much time to spend on each step.

Analyze _____

Plan _____

Write _____   45

Review _____

PROMPT

Think of an incident or event in your life that you can connect to a more universal idea such as love, freedom, or courage. Write a (personal narrative) in which you use your personal experience to discuss one of life's great truths. Remember to use the first-person point of view.

TEST-TAKER'S TOOLKIT

1. ANALYZE THE PROMPT

A. Read the prompt twice. Underline the phrases that tell what your narrative should include.

B. Circle the key elements you will need to include. The writing form has been circled for you.

C. Restate the prompt in your own words.

2. PLAN YOUR RESPONSE

A. Make notes Use the key elements you circled in the prompt to take notes. Organize your notes into a graphic organizer like the one shown.

B. Organize your information Because a narrative is the retelling of a story, the events are usually told in sequence. Knowing this can help you organize your narrative.

> Personal experience I will write about: _____
>
> What happened: _____
>
> When it happened: _____
>
> Why I remember it: _____
>
> How it connects to a universal idea: _____

3. WRITE AND REVIEW

A. Use vivid language and precise descriptions to help give your narrative emotional impact. Here is an example of how careful word choice can improve a sentence:

ORIGINAL:
Once I went to my uncle's farm and watched him kill a pig for food.

REVISED:
Visiting my uncle's farm had always been a treat—until the traumatic day when I watched him slaughter, skin, and prepare a pig for our family dinner.

B. Write your narrative, using your notes to guide you. Be sure to leave enough time to reread your narrative carefully, correct any errors, and make sure you have met all the requirements of the prompt.

Student Handbooks

Nonfiction Skills Handbook

Test-Taking Handbook

Argument

ACADEMIC VOCABULARY

argument: speaking or writing that expresses a position on an issue and supports it with reasons and evidence

claim: the writer's position on an issue or problem in an argument

counterargument: an argument made to oppose another argument

evidence: a fact, example, or quotation that supports a claim

fallacy: an error in reasoning

generalization: a general principle derived from evidence

inductive reasoning: logically reasoning from specific observation to arrive at a general conclusion or principle

logic: system of reasoning. Good logic finds a valid or reasonable connection between two things. Faulty logic creates a mistaken or unreasonable connection between two things.

reasons: declarations that explain or justify an action, decision, or belief

STEP 1 Identify the claim. Ask yourself: What assertion or opinion is expressed in the argument? Write the claim as a complete statement.

STEP 2 Look for reasons and evidence to support the claim. *Reasons* explain or justify an opinion or action. They usually appeal to logic or common sense. *Evidence* is factual support, such as facts, statistics, examples, and quotations from experts.

STEP 3 Check that reasons make sense and are logical. Take note of sound reasons. Question or reject others.

STEP 4 Check that evidence is AAA: accurate, appropriate, adequate. Ask yourself: Is the supporting evidence *accurate*—correct (documented), and not distorted or exaggerated? Is the supporting evidence *appropriate*—relevant to the particular claim? Is it *adequate*—or enough—to prove the claim?

STEP 5 Check that there is no faulty reasoning. Look for errors in judgment or logic. How logical is the argument? Does it make sense or are there errors or fallacies in the reasoning? Is it slanted to gain political power as in propaganda?

STEP 6 Look for counterarguments. Raising opposing viewpoints and countering them firmly but respectfully can strengthen an argument.

STEP 7 Evaluate. Decide if the argument is weak or strong. Is the argument free of loaded language, attacks on people, and emotional appeals that mislead?

Author's Craft

details: examples, anecdotes, facts, and explanations chosen by the writer to develop the ideas and descriptions

diction: a writer's choice of words and way of arranging the words in sentences. Diction can be formal or informal, abstract or concrete, technical or common, and literal or figurative.

figurative language: language that communicates meanings beyond the literal meanings of words. Simile, metaphor, and personification are examples of figurative language.

imagery: descriptive words and phrases that re-create sensory experiences for the reader. Imagery usually appeals to the five senses.

pattern of organization: the structure of a piece of writing. A writer may choose a comparison-and-contrast order or chronological order, for example.

quotations: the exact words of another writer usually enclosed in quotation marks

tone: the attitude a writer takes toward a subject. Tone reflects the feelings of the writer and is communicated through choice of words and details.

word choice: the writer's choice of words is an important signal of the tone. The words may reflect the writer's humorous, sad, playful, or sarcastic tone, for example.

STEP 1 **Examine the choice of details.** What details does the writer include to support his or her ideas? What do these details tell you about the writer's overall purpose?

STEP 2 **Look at the language.** Examine the language the writer uses. Focus on:

- **tone**—what are the writer's feelings toward this subject? Is the tone angry, happy, humorous? What words convey the tone?

- **figurative language**—does the writer include any similes or metaphors? Does the use of figurative language make the writing vivid and interesting?

- **imagery**—does the writer use language that appeals to the senses? What effect does this language have on the writing?

- **quotations**—if the writer has included quotations, how does the language and content of the quotations affect you as a reader?

STEP 3 **Study the pattern of organization.** Has the writer chosen an organizational pattern that supports the ideas? If the writer wants a "you are there" feeling, has he or she written about events in the order they happened? If the writer wants readers to understand the causes of an event, has he or she used a clear cause-and-effect order?

Author's Purpose

> **ACADEMIC VOCABULARY**
>
> **author's purpose:** the reason(s) an author has for writing a particular work
>
> **audience:** the person or persons for whom a text is written
>
> **tone:** the attitude a writer takes toward the subject

STEP 1 **Learn common purposes.** Keep the four common author purposes in mind as you read:

- **to explain or inform**
- **to persuade**
- **to entertain**
- **to express emotion and ideas**

STEP 2 **Identify clues to author's purpose.** As you read a text, look for clues in the work's title, subject, and **tone;** the choice of details and words; the context, or intended **audience;** the effects on you as a reader; and the pattern of organization, or **structure.**

- Tone is an especially helpful clue to the author's purpose. For example, because a political speech is usually meant to persuade, the author may include words and phrases that establish a forceful or inspiring tone.
- There are some common match-ups between text structure and purpose, but be aware that there are no firm rules.

EXAMPLE

Sequence, cause-effect, or **main idea and details** are often used to explain or to inform.

Problem-solution, proposition-support, or **compare-contrast order** may signal that the author's purpose is to persuade.

Chronological order is often used in dramatic histories or storytelling and may signal that the purpose is to entertain.

Order of degree or **spatial order** may be used to express emotion.

STEP 3 **Determine the audience.** Is the text intended for children, for informed adults, for undecided voters, or for some other audience? The intended audience will influence the writer's choice of words, the structure, the explanations, and many other elements of the writing.

STEP 4 **Use purpose to understand and evaluate work.** Use the author's purpose to guide how you read. Take notes on an informational piece, or jot down arguments or opinions about a persuasive piece. Entertainment may come through better if you relax. Evaluate the piece in light of the author's purpose: How well or poorly did the passage achieve the goal? How well were you entertained, informed, persuaded, or instructed?

Author's Perspective

STEP 1 **Identify the author.** Look for the author's name and any additional information about the person. This usually can be found at the beginning or end of a text, sometimes set off as a separate feature. Ask the following questions for clues about the author's experiences, values, and beliefs:

- What does the author's name suggest about the person's sex and possibly nationality?
- What is the author's education? How has that education or lack of it, affected the author's life?
- What do the author's activities, responsibilities, and publications say about his or her reliability?
- What social and cultural values have influenced the author?

STEP 2 **Examine the text for clues to the author's point of view.** Carefully read the text, looking for indications of the author's point of view. Focus on:

- **word choice**—words with strong positive or negative emotional associations, or connotations
- **selective details**—facts and opinions that support a specific point of view
- **biased language**—statements that reveal a one-sided belief
- **direct statements**—clear admissions of point of view, often beginning with the words "I believe" or "In my opinion"

STEP 3 **Identify the author's perspective.** Review the evidence you have discovered and ask yourself, "What does this information tell me about the author's point of view on the topic?" Then write a sentence describing that point of view. Finally, read through the text again, keeping the author's perspective in mind. Write down questions, comments, or counterevidence that occurs to you as you read. Take this information into account as you evaluate the reliability or usefulness of the text.

Cause-and-Effect Order

ACADEMIC VOCABULARY

cause-and-effect order: a method of organizing ideas and information in an essay that shows causal relationships

cause: why something happens

effect: a result; what happened as an outcome of the cause

STEP 1 **Look for effects.** Ask: "What was the outcome?" Check for multiple effects.

EXAMPLE

Because Harry left the cage open, <u>the canary escaped</u> and <u>flew around the room</u>.

STEP 2 **Look for causes.** Ask: "Why did it happen?" Check for multiple causes.

EXAMPLE

<u>Because Harry left the cage open</u> and <u>never noticed</u>, the canary escaped.

STEP 3 **Check for cause-effect chains.** A cause can lead to an effect that then causes another effect, and so on. A series of such linked events is a cause-effect chain.

EXAMPLE

Harry left the <u>cage open</u>, allowing the <u>canary to escape</u>. As a result, <u>Harry chased the bird</u> around the room for an hour.

STEP 4 **Find signal words.** Signal words and phrases for cause and effect include: *because, since, as a result, therefore,* and *due to.*

EXAMPLE

I forgot to study, and <u>as a result</u>, I didn't do very well on the quiz.

STEP 5 **Use a graphic organizer.** Arrange ideas in a cause-and-effect diagram or chain.

EXAMPLE

STEP 6 **Check your logic.** The cause must spark, or set in motion the result. They do not have to be presented in sequence. In many sentences, the effect appears first.

EXAMPLE

Angel missed the bus <u>due to</u> oversleeping.

Charts and Other Graphic Aids

STEP 1 **Read the title.** Ask yourself: What information does the graphic aid display? Does the title include time periods, locations, ages, or other details about the subject?

STEP 2 **Study the data.** Use these tips to analyze various charts and graphs:

- **Line Graph:** Check what's being measured on the vertical axis and the horizontal axis. Study the slant of the line. The steeper the line, the faster the rate of change.
- **Bar Graph:** Check what's being measured on the vertical axis and the horizontal axis. Check the range of numbers: small differences can look big if the range is small.
- **Pie Chart/Circle Graph:** Determine what the "whole" is and what the "parts" are. Then look at the relative size of the slices to understand the percentage of the whole.
- **Chart:** Read down the outside column and across the top. Note the headings. Make sure you understand what data are being shown and any abbreviations or terms. To find specific data, run your finger down the outside column to the correct row. Then move across that row to a specific column. Compare the information in the rows and columns to get an idea of any similarities, differences, or patterns.

STEP 3 **Draw conclusions.** Decide why the information in the graphic aid is useful and how it could be used. Ask yourself:

- What can I conclude from the information in the graphic aid?
- Which data allow me to make that conclusion?
- What further information would be helpful?
- What new questions arise from learning this data?

Chronological Order

ACADEMIC VOCABULARY

chronological order: organization in order of occurrence, forward in time, usually used to tell stories, to report events, or to record histories

sequence order: the order in which events should, may, or usually occur; sequence order is used to give directions or to show steps or events in a process

STEP 1 Look for times, dates, or numbers that show order. Clue words such as *first, second,* and so on indicate sequence of information. Numerals (*1, 2, 3, . . .*) or dates and times may give order of events.

STEP 2 Organize information in a graphic. Based on any time-order clue words, place the events in a graphic organizer. The organizer can be a numbered list. Or you can create a left-to-right series of boxes and arrows to track information.

STEP 3 Look for words and phrases that show duration or sequence. Certain signal words and phrases help structure both chronological and sequential texts: *then, next, before, after, during, finally,* and so on.

STEP 4 Infer the author's purpose. The author may want to explain how to carry out a task or report a story about how events unfolded in time. Ask yourself: Why does the author arrange details in this way? What is he or she trying to achieve?

Classification Order

STEP 1 Look for words and phrases that signal groups. Words and phrases writers use to indicate a subject's class include *group, category, kind, set, type, class, classification, division, divided into,* and *common characteristics.* Notice how many groups there are.

STEP 2 Look for how classes or groups are defined. What do each of these objects, ideas, or facts have in common? What qualities or attributes unite the items in each group?

STEP 3 Look for subgroups. Under each of your major groups or classes, are there other items that share common attributes with each other?

STEP 4 Write categories and subcategories in a graphic organizer. A classification organizer like the one shown can help you keep track of the major groups and subgroups mentioned in the text. Recognizing classification order can help you understand the relationships between ideas and details and help you remember important information.

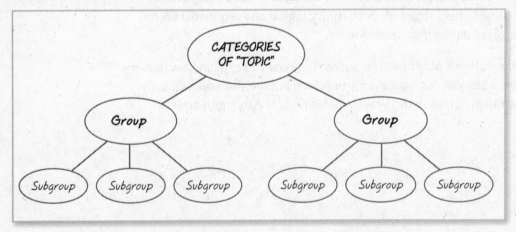

Connect Texts

ACADEMIC VOCABULARY

fiction: writing that contains imaginary elements. Although fiction can be inspired by real events and people, it usually springs from writers' imaginations.

nonfiction: writing that tells about real people, places, and events

theme: the underlying message about life or human nature that a writer wants the reader to understand

treatment: the way a topic is handled, includes the form a writer uses, the writer's purpose, and tone

STEP 1 **Identify the topic or theme you wish to examine.** Choose a topic or theme that is specific and narrow enough to find several texts that examine it.

STEP 2 **Find related texts.** If your topic or theme is clear and specific, you are more likely to find texts that cover it or you may already be studying two texts that have been presented together.

STEP 3 **Examine how the texts treat the subject.** Make a note of the tone of each text. Does one writer seem more serious than the other, for example? Does one writer include more facts and the other include more anecdotes? If the texts are fiction, what are the differences in approach?

STEP 4 **What ideas are covered?** Do the writers share some ideas or are the ideas very different? Note the major ideas of each text.

STEP 5 **Identify contradictory ideas.** Do the two writers contradict each other? If so, you may have to do further reading. What have you learned from connecting these texts that you wouldn't learn from one text alone?

Critical Essays

ACADEMIC VOCABULARY

analysis: separation of a whole into parts for individual study

conclusion: a judgment or decision reached after close study

critical essay: an essay in which a writer interprets and analyzes a topic, such as a literary work

essay: a short work of nonfiction that deals with a single subject

evidence: specific pieces of information that support an idea. Evidence can take the form of facts, quotations, examples, explanations, and personal experiences, among others.

interpretation: an explanation of the meaning of a work such as an essay or literary work

tone: the attitude a writer takes toward a subject. Tone reflects the feeling of the writer and is communicated through choice of words and details.

STEP 1 Identify the writer's tone. What are the writer's feelings toward this subject? Is the tone sarcastic, understanding, measured, or bitter, for example? What words convey the tone?

STEP 2 Identify the conclusions the writer makes. What is the writer saying about this topic? What critical conclusions are expressed? Make sure you understand exactly what the writer is saying about the topic.

STEP 3 Examine the evidence. Now that you are clear about the interpretations the writer is making, what evidence supports those conclusions? Focus on:

- **facts**—does the writer include any facts as support?
- **quotations**—does the writer choose relevant quotations from the work to back up the ideas?
- **examples**—are the examples the writer uses relevant to the ideas?
- **explanations**—does the writer explain the ideas clearly with relevant details?
- **personal experiences**—if the writer includes some personal experiences as support, are the experiences relevant to the ideas?

Evaluate Evidence

ACADEMIC VOCABULARY

evaluate evidence: determine the strength and quality of the facts, statistics, reasons, examples, and sources that support a position or claim

evidence: a reason, fact, statistic, example, or expert opinion that supports a proposition or claim

fact: a statement that can be proved

objective: not influenced by emotions or personal prejudices; factual

opinion: a statement that cannot be proved, such as a personal feeling or belief

proposition or claim: the writer's position on an issue or problem

subjective: personal to a given person; existing only in the mind

STEP 1 **Look for opinions to be sure they are supported.** No one can check whether an opinion is true or false. So a writer must support any claims, positions, or personal opinions with examples, facts, and reasons. For any expert opinions, be sure that sources are clearly identified. Don't accept vague language, such as "experts agree."

STEP 2 **Look for facts—statistics, examples, and expert opinions.** Part of a writer's job is to present enough facts to support each claim. Facts include quotations from experts, anecdotes and examples, and definitions, as well as **statistics** (mathematical data). Decide whether there is enough evidence. Decide if the evidence is up to date. If there are no data to back up the ideas, don't accept the claim.

STEP 3 **Look for ways in which sources are documented.** Writers should name the source of their facts. Look for sources that are **objective** and **credible,** like an encyclopedia, rather than **subjective** and **biased** like a personal blog. Good documentation includes the *who, where,* and *when* of each source, so readers can check it.

STEP 4 **Weigh the evidence.** After evaluating the support, the hard data, and the documentation, a reader can decide whether to accept or agree with the writer's position or not. You can also weigh how reasonable, valuable, or useful the writer's ideas are to you.

Main Ideas and Supporting Details

STEP 1 **Identify the topic.** Ask yourself: What is this passage or paragraph about?

STEP 2 **Think about the main idea.** Ask yourself: What idea does the writer express?

STEP 3 **Look for a topic sentence.** The topic sentence is usually either the first or last sentence in a paragraph, although it can occur anywhere. In some paragraphs, the main idea is not stated directly, but is implied by the supporting details.

STEP 4 **Identify the supporting details.** Writers use different types of details to support different purposes and main ideas. Sensory details describe, examples illustrate, reasons persuade, and facts and statistics explain.

STEP 5 **Use a graphic organizer.** A chart can help you take notes on the main idea and supporting details in a paragraph. List a main idea, then note all the details that support it.

Main Idea	Supporting Details

Narrative Nonfiction

ACADEMIC VOCABULARY

characters: the individuals who participate in the action

conflict: a struggle between opposing forces

feature article: in-depth coverage of human-interest or lifestyle topics found in newspapers or magazines

figurative language: language that communicates meanings beyond the literal meanings of words

historical narrative: a nonfiction story about an event in history

narrative: a story with characters, settings, and events

pacing: the speed at which events in the story unfold. Writers choose a rapid or leisurely pace depending on the purpose the writing serves.

plot events: the actions of the story

setting: the time and place of the action of a story

tone: the attitude the writer takes toward the subject

STEP 1 Identify the author's purpose. Does the writer want to inform, entertain, describe, persuade? What evidence leads you to your conclusion?

STEP 2 Examine the narrative devices. What devices does the writer use to make the narrative appealing? Look for colorful characters, dramatic plot events, figurative language, and strong conflicts.

STEP 3 Evaluate accuracy. Although the events and characters may sound fictional, a nonfiction narrative tells about true people and events. Even though the narrative style reads like a story, the writer must take care to present an accurate picture of what happened. What support does the writer provide to back up his or her version of the events?

Patterns of Organization

ACADEMIC VOCABULARY

cause-and-effect order: shows the relationship between events and their results

chronological order: shows the sequence of events in time

classification: assigns people, places, things, or events to groups based on specific characteristics

comparison-contrast order: presents the similarities and differences between people, places, things, or events

problem-solution: explains a problem and offers a solution

spatial order: presents things or events according to their arrangement in space

STEP 1 Get a general sense of the organization. To form an initial impression of how a text is organized, skim it quickly, asking yourself, "Am I learning about:

- time sequence?"
- relation in space?"
- relative ranking?"
- membership in a category?"
- causes and effects?"
- similarities and differences?"
- the solution to a problem?"

STEP 2 Look for clues to the organization. Each organizational pattern uses a variety of signal words and structural patterns.

Cause-and-Effect Order

- Look for signal words like *because, therefore, since, as a result, the effect of,* and *consequently.*
- Look for answers to the question, "What happens next?"
- Study the text for clues to implied causes and effects.

Chronological Order

- Look for signal words like *first, next, then, afterward,* and *before.*
- Study the text for times, dates, or numbers that show order.

Classification

- Look for words or phrases that signal groups: *group, category, kind, set, type, class, classification, division, divided into, common characteristics.*
- Look for definitions of the groups used in the text. What do each of these objects, ideas, or facts have in common?
- Look for subgroups under the major groups.

Comparison-Contrast Order

- Signal words for this pattern are *similarly, also, both, like, neither, unlike, instead,* and *in contrast.*
- Identify the subjects being compared or contrasted. The subjects usually have similar characteristics.
- Look for the pattern. Does the text compare each subject in turn, or does it compare each subject feature by feature?

Problem-Solution Order

- Look for words like *problem, solution, pros, cons,* and *recommendation.*
- Examine the text for a clear statement of the problem, an analysis of the problem, and a proposed solution.
- Look for a discussion of the causes and effects of the problem.

Spatial Order

- Look for signal words such as *in front of, behind, under, above, left, right, top,* and *bottom.*
- Identify the specific way in which the spatial details are organized. A writer usually arranges spatial details in a certain order such as front to back, near to far, low to high, and so on.

STEP 3 Determine the most important ideas and supporting details. Once you have determined how the text is organized, focus on the main ideas the author is presenting and the support that he/she provides. Making an informal outline like the one below can help you understand how the organizational pattern helps convey an author's message.

> *Organizational pattern* _____
>
> I. Main idea
>   A. Supporting detail
>   B. Supporting detail
> II. Main idea related to first idea by _____
>   A. Supporting detail
>   B. Supporting detail
> III. Main idea related to first and second ideas by _____
>   A. Supporting detail
>   B. Supporting detail

Persuasion

STEP 1 Recognize persuasive messages. Notice the writer's purpose. Is the message addressed to a specific audience? What does the writer want readers to do? These messages often appear in speeches, ads, and editorials.

STEP 2 Look for words that stir positive and negative emotions. Does the writer talk about people who are "foolish dreamers" or about those who are "courageous visionaries"? Look carefully at the writer's word choices throughout.

STEP 3 Identify emotional appeals. In addition to using language with strong positive and negative emotions, writers may appeal to readers' sense of fair play or desire to join a group of other smart people, or other strategies. Be critical of such appeals.

STEP 4 Recognize logical fallacies. Look for reasons and examples that offer only two choices, such as "Either we build a new soccer field or our students will not get adequate exercise." Watch for statements that claim that "all" or "everyone" will "always" do something. These statements signal an overgeneralization. Also, watch for statements with claims such as "All you need to know is . . ." or "It is just a question of . . . ." These are oversimplifications.

Primary Sources

ACADEMIC VOCABULARY

eyewitness account: an account written by someone who was present at the event. An eyewitness could be an observer or a participant. Such an account has the advantage of being on the scene, but it can also be incomplete or influenced by the eyewitness's opinions and background.

observer: someone who is watching an event

participant: someone who is part of the action, such as a soldier in battle

primary source: information supplied by an eyewitness to events. Letters, diaries, autobiographies, speeches, and photographs are examples of primary sources.

secondary source: records of events created by writers who were not directly involved. Encyclopedias, textbooks, biographies, and most newspaper and magazine articles are examples of secondary sources.

STEP 1 **Identify the writer.** Ask yourself questions such as these about the writer.

- What is the writer's age and gender?
- What can you tell about the writer's background? You might try to determine the author's educational background or country of origin, for example.
- Was the writer an observer or a participant in the events?
- How might the writer's background influence what he or she writes?

STEP 2 **Determine the author's purpose.** Read the text carefully to determine why the author is writing this material. Some possible questions to ask:

- Does the writer want to provide a full, factual account of the events?
- Does the writer seem to want to explain his or her own behavior or the behavior of others?
- Is the writer trying to persuade you to believe in his or her own version of the events?

STEP 3 **Examine the details.** Look at the details the author includes. Think about any other information that might have been included but was not. Question the reason for any missing information.

Problem-Solution Order

ACADEMIC VOCABULARY

problem-solution order: presents a problem, explores various solutions, and
   identifies a solution, or outcome

STEP 1   Identify the problems or problems. To signal a **problem,** writers may use
words and phrases like *problem, difficulty, issue, conflict,* and *need for change.*

STEP 2   Look for solutions. Signal words and phrases can help you.

- **solutions**—words like *solution, answer, approach, method, way, option, remedy,*
  alternative
- **outcomes**—words and phrases like *but, however, can lead to, would result in,*
  most likely, might also, on the other hand
- **preferred solution**—words and phrases like *best, most effective, useful,*
  helpful, valuable

STEP 3   Use a graphic organizer. Use a chart like the one shown to keep track of
the problem, solutions, and possible outcomes.

State Problem	
Solution 1	**Pros** • • •
	Cons • • •
Solution 2	**Pros** • • •
	Cons • • •
Decision	

Speeches

ACADEMIC VOCABULARY

audience: the people for whom the speech is intended

message: the idea the speaker wants to convey

purpose: the speaker may want to persuade, to inform, to entertain, or to express emotion or ideas

rhetorical devices: techniques writers and speakers use to enhance their arguments. Common rhetorical devices include repetition, rhetorical questions, and others.

speech: a talk or public address

tone: the attitude the speaker takes toward the subject. The tone reflects the feelings of the speaker such as anger, scorn, or pleading.

STEP 1 Determine the audience. Who is listening? Do the audience members already know the subject, or do they need background information? Is the speaker addressing a friendly audience or one that is opposed to the proposed ideas? Answers to these questions will give you better understanding of the speech.

STEP 2 Identify the purpose. Is the speaker trying to persuade the audience to accept his or her ideas? Or does the speaker have another purpose? What tone does the speaker take? If a speaker is pleading or heaping scorn on another person or idea, the tone will affect the audience in various ways.

STEP 3 What is the message? What idea does the speaker want to convey? Does the speaker give relevant reasons and examples to support his or her message? Examining the evidence the speaker uses will help you decide if you can agree with the ideas.

STEP 4 Examine rhetorical devices. What devices does the speaker use to get you to pay attention and to agree with the ideas? A speaker may use repetition to make his or her point. Dr. Martin Luther King's "I Have a Dream" speech uses repetition with great effect. Another device is to ask a question that the audience must answer for themselves.

Summarize and Paraphrase

ACADEMIC VOCABULARY

main idea: the most important idea in a paragraph or essay

paraphrase: to restate information in simpler language. A paraphrase is about the same length as the original text. It includes all the details of the original but is written in simpler language.

scan: to read quickly to find specific information. Scanning involves letting your eyes sweep across a page looking for key words that may lead you to the information you want.

skim: to read quickly to get the general idea of a text. Skimming involves reading only the title, headings, graphic aids, highlighted words, and the first sentence of each paragraph in addition to the introduction, conclusion, or summary.

summarize: to retell the main ideas of a piece of writing in your own words. A summary is usually shorter than the original text.

topic sentence: the main idea of a paragraph. All details in the paragraph provide supporting details. A topic sentence may be stated or implied.

STEP 1 **Skim the text before summarizing.** Skim to find the main ideas. These ideas will be the focus of your summary. Note the stated or implied topic of each paragraph. Leave out details and information that are not essential for understanding the writer's key ideas.

STEP 2 **Paraphrase difficult passages.** Writing a paraphrase may help you understand any difficult main ideas. Use your own words to restate the author's ideas in simpler language. This process will help you clarify main ideas for a summary.

STEP 3 **Identify key details.** The title may give you a clue to the overall main idea, or you may have identified it in another way. Scan the text to find key words related to that idea. Determine which details the author provides are essential for understanding the main idea and which details simply provide additional information. Note the essential details.

STEP 4 **Prepare a summary.** Restate the main ideas and the essential details you have identified. Writing a summary or a paraphrase is a good way to preview for tests.

Synthesize

> **ACADEMIC VOCABULARY**
>
> **synthesize:** to combine individual ideas, influences, or materials to create a new product or idea
>
> **synthesizing information:** drawing from a variety of research materials, combining new ideas with prior knowledge, and applying the information to some new work or creation

STEP 1 **Determine the message in each source.** Decide what is most memorable or important about each work you are using. Then look for details the writers use to support these main ideas.

STEP 2 **Paraphrase the main ideas.** You will find the main ideas easier to work with after you have rephrased them in your own words. You should also paraphrase difficult concepts and wording in each selection to improve your understanding.

STEP 3 **Compare sources in light of author's purpose and audience.** Determine whether each selection was written to explain, inform, express an opinion, persuade, tell a story, or express emotion. You may interpret information in different ways depending on its purpose and audience.

STEP 4 **Ask questions about your sources.** The right questions will help you view your subject from different perspectives. Ask questions starting with *who, what, when, where, why, how,* and even *what if*. For example:

- How do the sources differ?
- What approach has the author of each work taken?
- Whose perspective is, or is *not*, represented?
- Who is the intended audience?
- Why is the message important to the author? to me?
- When and where is the writing set? When and where was it created?

STEP 5 **Connect to other sources, or your own experiences.** Look for ways that key ideas relate to other works on the same subject, or to your prior knowledge of the subject. Use your imagination to find connections that may not seem obvious at first. Ask yourself:

- How does the information confirm or refute other material?
- How does the information relate to my life or to world affairs?

STEP 6 **Synthesize.** After reviewing your sources as a group, piece the information together to create something new—an essay, story, poem, research paper, map, poster, or other work. Be sure to offer your own original insights about the topic.

Text Features

ACADEMIC VOCABULARY

text features: design elements that highlight the organization and especially important information in a text

boldface type: thicker, darker type, often used for key terms

bulleted list: each listed item is signaled with a dot or "bullet"

caption: written information about an illustration, photograph, or graphic

footnote: a numbered note placed at the bottom of a page that provides additional or source information

graphic aid: a visual tool (a photograph, table, graph, or other illustration)

head *or* heading: title that identifies the topic of the content that follows it

key word: important term, may be italicized, boldfaced, or highlighted

numbered or lettered list: each listed item begins with a numeral or a letter of the alphabet to show a sequence or an order of importance

review questions: help readers focus or assess their understanding

sidebar: additional information set in a box or otherwise apart from the main text

subhead *or* subheading: signals the beginning of a new topic or section under a more general heading

title: the name given to a book, chapter, play, film, or poem

STEP 1 Before you read, identify the text features. Knowing the kinds of features that a text contains can help you find information.

STEP 2 Next, preview the text features carefully. Follow these steps:

- **Read the heads and subheads** to get an overview of the material and to determine which details go with which main ideas.
- **Scan for boldfaced terms,** other key words, and lists for important details.
- **Glance at the graphic aids and corresponding captions** to see what kind of data the text offers besides words.
- **Locate any sidebars.** Familiarize yourself with the kind of material that is covered in the sidebars, but don't read them yet.

STEP 3 Now read the text and organize information. As you read, paragraph by paragraph, work in the graphic aids and sidebars as convenient. Use the text features to help your note taking, outlining, summarizing, and questioning.

Transitions and Other Text Clues

ACADEMIC VOCABULARY

demonstrative pronouns: words like *this, these,* and *those* that refer to people, places, and things and clarify relationships between ideas

synonyms: words with similar meanings that help define and elaborate on ideas

transitions: signal words that indicate how ideas relate to each other, such as *but* and *however* for contrast; *like* and *similarly* for comparison; *first, then,* and *next* for sequence, and *so* and *because* for cause

STEP 1 Scan the text for an overall impression. As you skim the title, subheads, graphics, and first few paragraphs, ask yourself:

- What is this text about?
- What is the author's purpose?
- Who is the intended audience?
- What is the author's tone?

STEP 2 Preview the text clues. Look for words that signal relationships between the ideas and list them in a three-column chart like this one.

Demonstrative Pronouns	Synonyms	Transitions

Then add the following information for each entry:

- **demonstrative pronouns**—the word each refers to
- **synonyms**—the meaning (using a dictionary if necessary)
- **transitions**—the type of relationship each transition word signals—comparison, contrast, sequence, or some other connection

STEP 3 Analyze the flow of ideas. Then read the text carefully, using your chart to help you understand the main ideas and how they relate to each other. Make an informal outline as you read or summarize the information afterward to make sure you understand the author's point.

Treatment, Organization, and Scope of Ideas

> **ACADEMIC VOCABULARY**
>
> **organization:** a particular arrangement, or pattern, of ideas in a text
>
> **scope:** the focus of a text; the depth and breadth of detail included
>
> **tone:** the writer's attitude toward his or her subject
>
> **treatment:** the way a topic is handled; includes the form a writer uses, the writer's purpose, and tone

STEP 1 Identify and compare treatment. Look for differences and similarities in form, purpose, and tone between two works. Ask yourself:

- **What is the form, or genre, of each text?** Examples of forms include news reports, summaries, editorials, interviews, and reviews.
- **What is the writer's purpose?** Is it to inform, persuade, instruct, advise, warn, critique, promote, amuse, or inspire readers?
- **What is the tone of the writing?** Is it serious? comical? angry? fearful?

STEP 2 Identify and compare organization. Some common patterns of organization include:

- **Chronological order** arranges events from earliest to latest in time. Reverse chronological order starts with recent events.
- **Deductive order** begins with a general statement, followed by facts and evidence, building toward a specific conclusion.
- **Main idea and supporting details** begins with the main idea, followed by reasons, facts, and examples that strengthen the reader's understanding of it.
- **Cause-effect organization** shows that a certain event, idea, or trend causes a change. The writing may begin with the cause or begin with the effects.

STEP 3 Identify and compare scope. Two texts about one subject may each have a different focus, such as an overview versus a close-up look. Ask:

- **What is the topic?** This may appear in the title or first sentence.
- **What aspects of the topic are covered?** Scan headings or topic sentences throughout the work to see what the focus is.
- **How much and what sort of details are used?** In articles with wide scope, facts and statistics are given and background is provided. A narrow piece covers personal anecdotes and minor incidents.

TEST-TAKING
HANDBOOK

Successful Test Taking

You can prepare for tests in several ways. First, study and understand the content that will be on the test. Second, learn as many test-taking techniques as you can. These techniques will help you better understand the questions and how to answer them. Following are some general suggestions for preparing for and taking tests. Starting on page R32, you'll find more detailed suggestions and test-taking practice.

Study Content Throughout the Year

1. **Master the content of your language arts class.** The best way to study for tests is to read, understand, and review the content of your language arts class. Read your daily assignments carefully. Study the notes that you have taken in class. Participate in class discussions. Work with classmates in small groups to help one another learn. You might trade writing assignments and comment on your classmates' work.

2. **Use your textbook for practice.** Your textbook includes many different types of questions. Some may ask you to talk about a story you just read. Others may ask you to figure out what's wrong with a sentence or how to make a paragraph sound better. Try answering these questions out loud and in writing. This type of practice can make taking a test much easier.

3. **Learn how to understand the information in charts, maps, and graphic organizers.** One type of test question may ask you to look at a graphic organizer, such as a spider map, and explain something about the information you see there. Another type of question may ask you to look at a map to find a particular place. You'll find charts, maps, and graphic organizers to study in your literature textbook. You'll also find charts, maps, and graphs in your science, mathematics, and social studies textbooks. When you look at these, ask yourself, What information is being presented and why is it important?

4. **Practice taking tests.** Use copies of tests you have taken in the past or in other classes for practice. Every test has a time limit, so set a timer for 15 or 20 minutes and then begin your practice. Try to finish the test in the time you've given yourself.

5. **Talk about test-taking experiences.** After you've taken a classroom test or quiz, talk about it with your teacher and classmates. Which types of questions were the hardest to understand? What made them difficult? Which questions seemed easiest, and why? When you share test-taking techniques with your classmates, everyone can become a successful test taker.

Use Strategies During the Test

1. **Read the directions carefully.** You can't be a successful test taker unless you know exactly what you are expected to do. Look for key words and phrases, such as *circle the best answer, write a paragraph,* or *choose the word that best completes each sentence.*

2. **Learn how to read test questions.** Test questions can sometimes be difficult to figure out. They may include unfamiliar language or be written in an unfamiliar way. Try rephrasing the question in a simpler way using words you understand. Always ask yourself, What type of information does this question want me to provide?

3. **Pay special attention when using a separate answer sheet.** If you accidentally skip a line on an answer sheet, all the rest of your answers may be wrong! Try one or more of the following techniques:

   - Use a ruler on the answer sheet to make sure you are placing your answers on the correct line.

   - After every five answers, check to make sure you're on the right line.

   - Each time you turn a page of the test booklet, check to make sure the number of the question is the same as the number of the answer line on the answer sheet.

   - If the answer sheet has circles, fill them in neatly. A stray pencil mark might cause the scoring machine to count the answer as incorrect.

4. **If you're not sure of the answer, make your best guess.** Unless you've been told that there is a penalty for guessing, choose the answer that you think is likeliest to be correct.

5. **Keep track of the time.** Answering all the questions on a test usually results in a better score. That's why finishing the test is important. Keep track of the time you have left. At the beginning of the test, figure out how many questions you will have to answer by the halfway point in order to finish in the time given.

Understand Types of Test Questions

Most tests include two types of questions: multiple-choice and open-ended. Specific strategies will help you understand and correctly answer each type of question.

A **multiple-choice question** has two parts. The first part is the question itself, called the stem. The second part is a series of possible answers. Usually four possible answers are provided, and only one of them is correct. Your task is to choose the correct answer. Here are some strategies to help you do just that.

1. Read and think about each question carefully before looking at the possible answers.

2. Pay close attention to key words in the question. For example, look for the word *not*, as in "Which of the following is *not* a cause of the conflict in this story?"

3. Read and think about all of the possible answers before making your choice.

4. Reduce the number of choices by eliminating any answers you know are incorrect. Then, think about why some of the remaining choices might also be incorrect.

   • If two of the choices are pretty much the same, both are probably wrong.

   • Answers that contain any of the following words are usually incorrect: *always, never, none, all,* and *only.*

5. If you're still unsure about an answer, see if any of the following applies:

   • When one choice is longer and more detailed than the others, it is often the correct answer.

   • When a choice repeats a word that is in the question, it may be the correct answer.

   • When two choices are direct opposites, one of them is likely the correct answer.

   • When one choice includes one or more of the other choices, it is often the correct answer.

   • When a choice includes the word *some* or *often*, it may be the correct answer.

   • If one of the choices is *All of the above,* make sure that at least two of the other choices seem correct.

   • If one of the choices is *None of the above,* make sure that none of the other choices seems correct.

An **open-ended test item** can take many forms. It might ask you to write a word or phrase to complete a sentence. You might be asked to create a chart, draw a map, or fill in a graphic organizer. Sometimes, you will be asked to write one or more paragraphs in response to a writing prompt. Use the following strategies when reading and answering open-ended items:

1. If the item includes directions, read them carefully. Take note of any steps required.

2. Look for key words and phrases in the item as you plan how you will respond. Does the item ask you to identify a cause-and-effect relationship or to compare and contrast two or more things? Are you supposed to provide a sequence of events or make a generalization? Does the item ask you to write an essay in which you state your point of view and then try to persuade others that your view is correct?

3. If you're going to be writing a paragraph or more, plan your answer. Jot down notes and a brief outline of what you want to say before you begin writing.

4. Focus your answer. Don't include everything you can think of, but be sure to include everything the item asks for.

5. If you're creating a chart or drawing a map, make sure your work is as clear as possible.

Functional Reading Test

DIRECTIONS *Study the warranty statement below. Then answer the questions that follow.*

Littleton Electronics Full Five-Year Warranty

Coverage: For five years from the date of original consumer purchase of this product, we promise, without charge, to repair or replace, at our option, any defects in material or workmanship. Warranty coverage does not include defects due to lack of care (see accompanying instructions for guidance) or any other warranties made by any other person, including authorized distributors of our products.

ALL INCIDENTAL AND CONSEQUENTIAL DAMAGES ARE EXCLUDED FROM WARRANTY COVERAGE. SOME STATES DO NOT ALLOW THE EXCLUSION OR LIMITATION OF INCIDENTAL OR CONSEQUENTIAL DAMAGES, SO THE ABOVE EXCLUSION MAY NOT APPLY TO YOU. THIS WARRANTY GIVES YOU SPECIFIC LEGAL RIGHTS, AND YOU MAY ALSO HAVE OTHER RIGHTS THAT VARY FROM STATE TO STATE.

Warranty Service Procedure: When warranty service is needed, deliver or send the product, insured and properly packaged, freight prepaid, with a description of the apparent defect and the means to ascertain the date of original consumer purchase (such as a copy of your receipt or canceled check) to the factory service center listed below. If at any time you are not satisfied with our warranty service, contact Vice President, Service and Distribution, 7777 Eastgate Rd., Wesley, OR 97777.

1. What promise does this warranty offer buyers of the company's product?
   - (A) to replace the product if the buyer is not satisfied
   - (B) to repair or replace a defective product
   - (C) to repair the product for as long as the buyer owns it
   - (D) to refund the buyer's money if the product is returned within five years

2. This warranty will *not* cover damages
   - (E) due to mishandling or improper use of the product in certain states
   - (F) noticed after the product is purchased in every state
   - (G) due to defects in workmanship in certain states
   - (H) made by persons other than the buyers in every state

3. How will a lifetime extended warranty offered by a store that sells Littleton Electronics products affect this warranty?
   - (A) It will cancel out and replace this warranty.
   - (B) It will take effect after this five-year warranty expires.
   - (C) It will extend this warranty for the lifetime of the product.
   - (D) It will have no effect under the terms of this warranty.

Functional Reading Test

DIRECTIONS *Study the following warning label from a can of insect spray. Circle the information you think is most important. Then answer the multiple-choice questions that follow.*

PRECAUTIONARY STATEMENTS

Hazards to Humans and Domestic Animals

CAUTION: Harmful if swallowed or absorbed through the skin. Avoid breathing spray mist. Avoid contact with skin or clothing. Wash thoroughly with soap and water after using. Provide adequate ventilation of area being treated. Do not apply to humans, plants, or pets, or contaminate feed, foodstuffs, dishes, or utensils. Cover and avoid spraying fish aquariums. Cover or remove exposed food, dishes, utensils, and food-handling equipment. Keep out of reach of children.

Practical Treatment

If swallowed: Do not induce vomiting. Call a physician or Poison Control Center immediately. If in eyes: Flush with plenty of water.

If on skin: Wash promptly with soap and water. Get medical attention if irritation develops.

If inhaled: Remove victim to fresh air. Apply artificial respiration if indicated.

NOTE TO PHYSICIAN: Product contains petroleum distillate (aspiration hazard).

Physical or Chemical Hazards

FLAMMABLE. CONTENTS UNDER PRESSURE. Keep away from heat, sparks, open flame, or pilot lights. Do not puncture or incinerate container. Exposure to temperatures above 130° F may cause bursting.

Questions or comments: Call (888) BUG-SPRAY

---

1. What should you do if you accidentally touch an area that has just been sprayed with this product?
   - (A) Call 911.
   - (B) Call (888) BUG-SPRAY.
   - (C) Get medical attention immediately.
   - (D) Wash your hands with lots of soap and water.

2. Why does the warning label include a note to physicians?
   - (E) so the manufacturer of the spray will not be legally responsible for injuries
   - (F) because physicians use more insect sprays than other groups of people do
   - (G) to give them information that will help them treat victims of inhalation
   - (H) to reassure users that the label has been approved by physicians

3. What might cause the bug spray can to burst?

(A) shaking it too hard

(B) placing it near gardening tools

(C) exposing it to high temperatures

(D) dropping it

4. When using this product in the home, what are you advised to do?

(E) Allow air to move through the area during and after treatment.

(F) Drain fish tanks and then refill with fresh water.

(G) Wash all dishes and utensils thoroughly after spraying.

(H) Throw away all foodstuffs that were purchased before spraying the area.

Revising-and-Editing Test

DIRECTIONS *Read the following paragraph carefully. Then answer the multiple-choice questions that follow. After answering the questions, read the material in the side column to check your answer strategies.*

Watch for common errors. Revising-and-editing test questions often focus on typical errors such as mistakes in punctuation, spelling, and capitalization; incomplete sentences; and missing or misplaced information. Circle or underline these errors.

¹Tashi Wangchuk Tenzing an Austrian travel agent was a tired but happy man in May 1997, when he scaled Mount Everest. ²Much of his familys' history has involved mountain climbing. ³In fact, one of his grandfathers, Tenzing Norgay, have the honor of being among the first climbers to reach the top of Mount Everest. ⁴With this feat, he becomes the third generation of his family to successfully reach the summit. ⁵Statistics in the record books for his climb. ⁶Though many people have applauded this accomplishment, they're is a chance that his mountain-climbing days are over. ⁷He is not among the climbers who are planning to return to the peak. ⁸Does this surprise you? ⁹It should. ¹⁰More than 90 percent of the 700 people who have made it to the top of Everest try to scale the mighty mountain again.

1. Which of the following is the correct way to rewrite the first part of sentence 1?
   - (A) Tashi Wangchuk Tenzing an Austrian travel agent,
   - (B) Tashi Wangchuk Tenzing an Austrian, travel agent,
   - (C) Tashi Wangchuk Tenzing, an Austrian travel agent,
   - (D) Tashi Wangchuk Tenzing, an Austrian, travel agent

ANSWER STRATEGIES

Commas Use commas to set off appositives.

2. What is the correct spelling of *familys'* in sentence 2?
   - (E) families'
   - (F) family's
   - (G) familys
   - (H) families

Possessive Nouns The phrase *familys' history* shows possession. Therefore, the correct spelling must include an apostrophe. Also note that *family* is a singular noun.

3. Which sentence in the paragraph is a fragment?
   - (A) sentence 5
   - (B) sentence 8
   - (C) sentence 9
   - (D) sentence 10

Complete Sentences A sentence must express a complete thought.

4. What is the correct way to rewrite the main verb in sentence 3?
   - (E) has
   - (F) have had
   - (G) will have
   - (H) have been

Subject-Verb Agreement Note that the subject of the sentence is *one*. The verb must agree in person and number with this subject.

Vague Pronoun Reference
In sentence 4, *he* is unclear because of the mention of Tenzing Norgay in sentence 3. To find the answer, reread the preceding sentences. Who is the central figure in this paragraph?

Sentence Fragments A sentence fragment is only part of a sentence. In this case, the sentence lacks a predicate.

Commonly Confused Words
There is often confused with *their* and the contraction *they're.* Choose the word that fits grammatically in the sentence.

Supporting Details Reread the paragraph, paying special attention to the sentences listed in the answer choices. Where would the additional information fit most logically?

5. Which phrase should replace *he* in sentence 4 to clarify its meaning?
   (A) his grandfather
   (B) Tashi Wangchuk Tenzing's grandfather
   (C) Tenzing Norgay
   (D) Tashi Wangchuk Tenzing

6. What is the best way to rewrite sentence 5?
   (E) Statistics for his climb have been entered in the record books.
   (F) Statistics have for his climb been entered in the record books.
   (G) Statistics have been entered for his climb in the record books.
   (H) Statistics have been for his climb entered in the record books.

7. Which of the following changes should be made in sentence 6?
   (A) Change *they're* to *there.*
   (B) Change *they're* to *their.*
   (C) Delete the hyphen in *mountain-climbing.*
   (D) Change *Though* to *However.*

8. Where in the paragraph would you add details about why Tenzing does not plan to climb Everest again?
   (E) between sentences 1 and 2
   (F) between sentences 6 and 7
   (G) between sentences 7 and 8
   (H) between sentences 8 and 9

Revising-and-Editing Test

DIRECTIONS *Read the following paragraph carefully. As you read, circle each error you find and identify the error in the side column—for example, you might write* misspelled word *or* not a complete sentence. *When you have finished, fill in the letter of the correct choice for each question that follows.*

¹ How good is your memory? ² Are you able to recall names, dates, and places effortlessly? ³ If you can, you probably have a memory that is more sharper than average. ⁴ Even so it is probably difficult for you to recall entire pages of text. ⁵ That was not the case for the British author and adventurer T. E. Lawrence he accomplished an extraordinary act of memory. ⁶ Toiling long and hard over his book *Seven Pillars of Wisdom*, an account of his Arabian adventures, he took the manuscript to his trusted adviser. ⁷ Following their discussion, Lawrence put the manuscript in a briefcase and headed home. ⁸ The briefcase had been given to him by his grandfather. ⁹ While changing trains, the briefcase was lost. ¹⁰ Lawrence didn't have no choice but to rewrite the manuscript from memory. ¹¹ Yes, that's exactly what he did!

1. Which sentence in this paragraph should be deleted?

- (A) sentence 1
- (B) sentence 5
- (C) sentence 8
- (D) sentence 11

2. What is the correct form of the comparative adjective in sentence 3?

- (E) sharper
- (F) most sharp
- (G) most sharper
- (H) more sharpest

3. Which sentence in the paragraph is a run-on?

- (A) sentence 3
- (B) sentence 5
- (C) sentence 6
- (D) sentence 10

4. Which change should be made to sentence 4?

- (E) Add a comma after *so*.
- (F) Add a comma after *is*.
- (G) Add commas after *even* and *so*.
- (H) Add commas before and after *probably*.

5. Which transitional word or phrase should be inserted at the beginning of sentence 6?

    (A) As a result of

    (B) Meanwhile,

    (C) After

    (D) On the other hand,

6. Which of the following is the *best* way to rewrite sentence 9?

    (E) While changing trains, Lawrence lost the briefcase.

    (F) The briefcase was lost while changing trains.

    (G) While changing trains, the briefcase was lost by Lawrence.

    (H) While the briefcase was lost, Lawrence changed trains.

7. What change, if any, should be made in sentence 10?

    (A) Change *didn't have* to *had*.

    (B) Change *no* to *some*.

    (C) Change *choice* to *choices*.

    (D) No change is necessary.

8. In sentence 11, what is the antecedent of *that?*

    (E) changing trains

    (F) no choice

    (G) the manuscript

    (H) to rewrite the manuscript from memory

Answers:
1.C; 2.E; 3.B; 4.E; 5.C; 6.E; 7.A; 8.H

ACKNOWLEDGMENTS

Acknowledgments

UNIT 1A

Penguin Group (USA) Inc.: Excerpt from *Beowulf* translated by Burton Raffel. Copyright © 1963, renewed 1991 by Burton Raffel. Used by permission of Dutton Signet, a division of Penguin Group (USA) Inc.

Excerpt from "A Monster Fit for Any Medium"

The Star-Ledger: Excerpt from "A monster fit for any medium" by Willa J. Conrad, from *The Star-Ledger.* Copyright © 2006 by The Star-Ledger. Reprinted with permission of the Star-Ledger.

UNIT 1B

University of Chicago Press: Excerpts from *Sir Gawain and the Green Knight,* translated by John Gardner. Copyright © 1965 by the University of Chicago. Reprinted by permission of the University of Chicago Press.

Random House, Inc.: Excerpt from "The Birth of Chivalry" from *A Natural History of Love* by Diane Ackerman. Copyright © 1994 by Diane Ackerman Used by permission of Random House, Inc.

UNIT 2A

Independent Newspapers: Excerpt from "Spain's 'caravans of love' bring romance, and a future, to a man's world" by Elizabeth Nash, from *The Independent,* August 30, 2007. Copyright © 2007 by The Independent. Reprinted by permission of Independent Newspapers.

UNIT 2B

Weider Publications, LLC: Excerpt from "all you need is love" by Jill Neimark, from *Natural Health,* October, 2003. Copyright © 2003 by Natural Health. Reprinted by permission of Weider Publications, LLC.

UNIT 3A

J. Malcolm Garcia: Excerpt from "Guilty of poverty, youth: 'Street kids' in Honduras locked in shelters as nation fights crime, begging, gangs" by Malcolm Garcia, from *The Denver Post,* November 24, 2003. Copyright © 2003 by Malcolm Garcia. Reprinted by permission of the author.

UNIT 3B

International Creative Management, Inc.: Excerpt from "Everyday Equality" by Anna Quindlen from *Newsweek,* September 25, 2006. Copyright © 2006 by Anna Quindlen. Reprinted by permission of International Creative Management, Inc.

UNIT 4A

Beth Baker: Excerpt from "Happy by Nature: Fondness for Plants and Animals May Be Hard-wired, Healthy" by Beth Baker, from *The Washington Post,* June 4, 2002. Copyright © 2002 by Beth Baker. Reprinted by permission of the author.

UNIT 5A

Gale: Excerpt from *"In Memoriam"* by Rachel Hadas, from *World Poets,* Volumes 1–3, the Scribner Writers Series First Edition, edited by Ron Padgett. Copyright © 2000 by Charles Scribner's Sons. Reprinted with permission of Gale, a division of Thomson Learning: www.thomsonrights.com. Fax 800.730.2215.

UNIT 5B

New York Times: "Stalking a Killer that Lurks a Few Feet Offshore" by Cornelia Dean, from the *New York Times,* June 7, 2005. Copyright © 2005 by the New York Times. All rights reserved. Used by permission and protected by the Copyright Laws of the United States. The printing, copying, redistribution, or retransmission of the material without express written permission is prohibited. Reprinted by permission of the New York Times.

UNIT 6A

Penguin Group (USA) Inc.: "The Rocking-Horse Winner," from Complete Stories of *D. H. Lawrence* by D. H. Lawrence. Copyright © 1933 by the Estate of D. H. Lawrence, renewed 1961 by Angelo Ravagli and C. M. Weekley, Executors of the Estate of Frieda Lawrence Ravagli. Used by permission of Viking Penguin, a division of Penguin Group (USA) Inc.

New York Times: "Money Can't Buy Happiness. Er, Can It?" by Paul Krugman from the *New York Times,* June 1, 1999. Copyright © 1999 by the New York Times. All rights reserved. Used by permission and protected by the Copyright Laws of the United States. The printing, copying, redistribution, or retransmission of the material without express written permission is prohibited. Reprinted by permission of the New York Times.

UNIT 6B

Harcourt, Inc.: "Shooting an Elephant," from *Shooting an Elephant and Other Essays* by George Orwell. Copyright © 1950 by Sonia Brownell Orwell and renewed 1978 by Sonia Pitt-Rivers. Reprinted by permission of Harcourt, Inc.

Curtis Brown Group Ltd, London: Excerpt from *The Trouser People: A Story of Burma—In the Shadow of the Empire* by Andrew Marshall. Copyright © 2003 by Andrew Marshall. Reprinted by permission of Curtis Brown Group Ltd., London, on behalf of Andrew Marshall.

FRONT MATTER

ix *Rainy Embankment* (1929), Fox Photos. © Hulton Archive/Getty Images; **x** *Just Starve Us. Tell Ah! Tell Us, Can Aught be Worse?...Great Overseer,* Isaac Robert Cruikshank. British Library, London. Photo © The Bridgeman Art Library; **xiii** © Jupiterimages Corporation; **xiv–xxi** © Alex Staroseltsev/ShutterStock; **xxiv** *Just Starve Us. Tell Ah! Tell Us, Can Aught be Worse?...Great Overseer,* Isaac Robert Cruikshank. British Library, London. Photo © The Bridgeman Art Library; **xxv** © Elmer Martinez/AFP/Getty Images; **xxvii** Map by GeoNova LLC.

UNIT 1A

2 © Vasile Tiplea/ShutterStock; **5** © Wally Stemberger/ShutterStock; **6–31** © DLW-Designs/ShutterStock; **34** © Vasile Tiplea/ShutterStock; **35** © Photo by Robert Millard/Courtesy Los Angeles Opera.

UNIT 1B

40 © Robert H. Creigh/ShutterStock; **42** © Topal/ShutterStock; **43** © Jo Ann Snover/ShutterStock; **44–56** © Mityukhin Oleg Petrovich/ShutterStock; **59** © Robert H. Creigh/ShutterStock; **60** © John Said/ShutterStock.

UNIT 2A

66 © Kevin Eaves/ShutterStock; **68** *Mousehold Heath,* John Crome. Tate Gallery, London. Photo © Sally Chappell/Tate Gallery, London/The Art Archive; **70–72** © Kevin Eaves/ShutterStock; **75** © Kevin Eaves/ShutterStock; **77** © Valerie de la Dehesa; **79** Map by GeoNova LLC.

UNIT 2B

82 Detail of *Francesca da Rimini* (1837), William Dyce. Oil on canvas, 142 cm × 176 cm. National Gallery of Scotland, Edinburgh. © National Gallery of Scotland, Edinburgh/The Bridgeman Art Library; **85** © Jupiterimages Corporation; **86–88** © Robert O. Brown Photography/ShutterStock; **91** Detail of *Francesca da Rimini* (1837), William Dyce. Oil on canvas, 142 cm × 176 cm. National Gallery of Scotland, Edinburgh. © National Gallery of Scotland, Edinburgh/The Bridgeman Art Library; **92** © Steve Snowden/ShutterStock; **95** © Yakobchuk Vasyl/ShutterStock.

UNIT 3A

98 *Just Starve Us. Tell Ah! Tell Us, Can Aught be Worse?...Great Overseer,* Isaac Robert Cruikshank. British Library, London. Photo © The Bridgeman Art Library; *background* © Alex Staroseltsev/ShutterStock; **101** © Jupiterimages Corporation; **102–109** © Alex Staroseltsev/ShutterStock; **112** *Just Starve Us. Tell Ah! Tell Us, Can Aught be Worse?... Great Overseer,* Isaac Robert Cruikshank. British Library, London. Photo © The Bridgeman Art Library; *background* © Alex Staroseltsev/ShutterStock; **113** © Elmer Martinez/AFP/Getty Images; **115** Map by GeoNova LLC.

UNIT 3B

118 © Christa Stadtler/Photofusion Picture Library/Alamy Ltd.; **121** © Jupiterimages Corporation; **122–127** © Bocos Benedict/ShutterStock; **130** © Christa Stadtler/ Photofusion Picture Library/Alamy Ltd.; **131** Joyce Ravid, HO/AP/Wide World Photos.

UNIT 4A

136 © Stephen Strathdee/ShutterStock; **139** © Jupiterimages Corporation; **140–147** © Graham Prentice/ShutterStock; **150** © Stephen Strathdee/ShutterStock; **151** © iofoto/ShutterStock; **152** © Nikita Tiunov/ShutterStock; **153** © Phil Boorman/ Getty Images.

UNIT 4B

156 © Tracy Siermachesky/Shutterstock; **159** © Bill McKelvie/ShutterStock; **160** © Gabe Palmer/Alamy Ltd.; **160–168** © Don Farrell/Getty Images; **164** © Andrew Darrington/Alamy Ltd.; **171** *right* © Tracy Siermachesky/Shutterstock; **171, 172** © Valkr/ShutterStock; **174** © Alexey Stiop/ShutterStock.

UNIT 5A

178 © Mollypix/ShutterStock; **181** © Dickens House Museum, London/The Bridgeman Art Library; **182–194** © Robert O. Brown Photography/ShutterStock; **197** © Mollypix/ShutterStock; **198** © Stephen Strathdee/ShutterStock.

UNIT 5B

202 © Josef Fankhauser/Getty Images; **205** The Granger Collection, New York; **206–223** © Robynrg/ShutterStock; **226** © Josef Fankhauser/Getty Images; **228** © Ampersand Design Group.

UNIT 6A

232 © Andrew Paterson/Alamy Ltd.; **235** © J. Helgason/ShutterStock; **236–249** © Sylvaine Thomas/ShutterStock; **252** © Andrew Paterson/Alamy Ltd.; **253** © Mia Song/Star Ledger/Corbis.

UNIT 6B

258 © Brian L. Lambert/ShutterStock; **261** The Granger Collection, New York; **262–268** © Alon Othnay/ShutterStock; **271** © Brian L. Lambert/ShutterStock; **272** © Nik Wheeler/Corbis.

Back cover © Getty Images.